About This Book

Just as leaders have blind spots, so does the leadership field—in its practices for assessing and developing leaders. Also, leaders are lopsided: they emphasize one skill or approach at the expense of the opposing good thing to do. So too the leadership field is lopsided, placing more weight, for example, on negative feedback than on positive feedback.

This book goes beyond pointing out the leadership field's oversights. It offers fixes for the omissions. Leaders holding up the mirror offered here will receive a fuller picture of their profiles than current assessment methods deliver—a reading not just on their deficiencies but on the strengths they take too far. The book will also make it clear that improvement depends as much on truly getting one's strengths to sink in as it does on facing up to one's weaknesses. The ideas and techniques described here represent a step toward a practical psychology of leadership and leadership development.

The book is divided into three parts. The first part identifies several oversights in the way most organizations assess and develop leaders. While it is common for leaders to be lopsided—for example, too oriented to the short term and not oriented enough to the long term—virtually no assessment tool in common use assesses for lopsidedness.

The second part elaborates the two oppositions on which many a leader is lopsided. These are forceful and enabling leadership and strategic and operational leadership—the "how" and "what" of leadership, respectively.

The third part presents strategies and tactics for overcoming common performance problems. When leaders overdo it, how to throttle back? When leaders underdo it, how to rev up? In either direction, the work of development is defined as both tackling behavior directly and addressing the thoughts and feelings that threw off the behavior in the first place.

In all, the ideas here add a new dimension to the theory and practice of leadership and leadership development. Today's leaders as well as the development specialists working with them will find fresh ways to expand their repertoire and increase their effectiveness.

About Pfeiffer

Pfeiffer serves the professional development and hands-on resource needs of training and human resource practitioners and gives them products to do their jobs better. We deliver proven ideas and solutions from experts in HR development and HR management, and we offer effective and customizable tools to improve workplace performance. From novice to seasoned professional, Pfeiffer is the source you can trust to make yourself and your organization more successful.

Essential Knowledge Pfeiffer produces insightful, practical, and comprehensive materials on topics that matter the most to training and HR professionals. Our Essential Knowledge resources translate the expertise of seasoned professionals into practical, how-to guidance on critical workplace issues and problems. These resources are supported by case studies, worksheets, and job aids and are frequently supplemented with CD-ROMs, websites, and other means of making the content easier to read, understand, and use.

Essential Tools Pfeiffer's Essential Tools resources save time and expense by offering proven, ready-to-use materials—including exercises, activities, games, instruments, and assessments—for use during a training or team-learning event. These resources are frequently offered in looseleaf or CD-ROM format to facilitate copying and customization of the material.

Pfeiffer also recognizes the remarkable power of new technologies in expanding the reach and effectiveness of training. While e-hype has often created whizbang solutions in search of a problem, we are dedicated to bringing convenience and enhancements to proven training solutions. All our e-tools comply with rigorous functionality standards. The most appropriate technology wrapped around essential content yields the perfect solution for today's on-the-go trainers and human resource professionals.

www.pfeiffer.com

Essential resources for training and HR professionals

"The test of a first-rate intelligence is the ability to hold two opposed ideas in mind at the same time and still retain the ability to function."

—*F. Scott Fitzgerald*

"Excess is false success."

—*Harry Kaplan*

The Versatile Leader

Make the Most of Your Strengths Without Overdoing It

Bob Kaplan

with Rob Kaiser

Kaplan DeVries Inc.

A Wiley Imprint
www.pfeiffer.com

Library of Congress Cataloging-in-Publication Data
Kaplan, Robert E.
  The versatile leader: make the most of your strengths without overdoing it
/ Robert E. Kaplan with Robert B. Kaiser.
         p. cm.
  Includes bibliographical references and index.
  ISBN-13: 978-0-7879-7944-7 (cloth)
  ISBN-10: 0-7879-7944-9 (cloth)
1. Leadership. 2. Executive ability.
I. Kaiser, Robert B. II. Title.
  HD57.7.K36 2006
  658.4'092—dc22

Acquiring Editor: Lisa Shannon   Director of Development: Kathleen Dolan Davies
Developmental Editor: Susan Rachmeler   Production Editor: Dawn Kilgore
Editor: Rebecca Taff   Manufacturing Supervisor: Becky Carreño

Printed in the United States of America
Printing   10 9 8 7 6 5 4 3 2 1

To my children, Joshua, Emily and Andrew Kaplan.
Nothing inspires me more than seeing
each of them grow and evolve.

To my Grannie, Clara June Roberts,
who always goes with the flow.

Contents

Part III: Prescriptions for Development   111

The third part offers ways to correct overdoing it, underdoing it, and the
combination of both, lopsidedness. All three chapters describe the
outer/behavioral work of development and the inner/personal work of
development. The book concludes with an elaboration of an ideal of
versatility, which if not a destination that most leaders will reach can
nevertheless serve as a direction for their development.

Acknowledgments

Although I worked long, hard, and happily on the book and although I was glad for the solitude it afforded, this work is also the outgrowth of innumerable intense and rewarding engagements with managers, colleagues, and editors. These engagements both bore the fruit that prompted me to write the book and helped me immeasurably in the actual writing.

Of course, there would be no book if it were not for the managers I have had the privilege to work and learn with. In particular, I want to acknowledge the several individuals who, with their permission, I wrote about at any length, usually as composite cases. To protect their privacy they shall remain nameless. In addition, I want to thank the forty or so managers who responded right at the end to a slate of possible titles and subtitles. *The Versatile Leader* won by a sizeable margin. A version of "Make the Most of Your Strengths" was the subtitle that got the highest rating. Thank you, Mary Nelson, for running the focus group that produced the winning subtitle.

Rob Kaiser is first and foremost on the list of individuals to whom I am indebted. I am enormously grateful to him for helping me elaborate the ideas in this book. Even if I had never known Rob, I would have written this book, but it wouldn't have been as good. In the most constructive sense, he has been a great intellectual sparring partner. Rob also contributed directly in his capacity as co-author of the Leadership Versatile Index, which is integral to the book, conceptually and statistically. Rob played a major editorial role too. He reviewed practically every draft of every chapter, and he always responded quickly with useful, concrete suggestions for improvement and, in Chapters 7 and 8, with techniques and examples from his own consulting practice. In addition, it was Rob who did the statistical analyses that help to support the conceptual framework and which he reported in the Appendix. And it was Rob who wrote most of the references to the academic literature that appear in the end notes.

I am deeply grateful to my tight circle of fellow consultants at Kaplan DeVries Inc.—David DeVries, Denise Lyons, Connie McArthur, and Amy Webb. It was out of our collective practice beginning in 1992 that many of these ideas emerged. As an observation or insight occurred to me, I inevitably talked it over with one or another colleague in restaurants, taxis, or planes. Truly, this book (as well as the Leadership Versatility Index) is of our collective practice and by our practice. These close colleagues also helped greatly with the writing of the book. They were very generous with their time and considered in their judgments of the state of the work. I turned to David DeVries more often than anyone except Rob Kaiser, and every time David responded promptly with sound advice and several telling examples that fortified me as well as the work. In particular I remember that, after having told me that Chapter 1 just didn't grab the reader, he pronounced the revision successful. Apart from her many specific suggestions, if I had to pick a single thing I most appreciate about Denise Lyons' role it is the moment on a walk along a snow-covered road in Breckenridge when she declared about a long paper that was a forerunner to the book, "It's all come together!" Over and over again Connie McArthur held me, most supportively, to a high standard of clarity and practicality. Also, it was she who suggested dividing the final section in each chapter into "highlights" and "questions for reflection." All along I relied heavily on Amy Webb's keen insight into development. After struggling with the two chapters (7 and 8) on remedies for overdoing it and underdoing it, I knew I was in good shape when Amy pronounced them close to finished.

I also want to thank a close colleague, Rebecca Henson, for her concrete help with Chapters 7, 8, and 9.

I was fortunate to have first-rate editorial assistance from four talented individuals. Hilary Hinzmann played the biggest and longest-running part. Through multiple drafts, he worked with me on organization and expression. At the start of the project, he oriented me to the managerial reader: "Imagine yourself in a room with a group of managers interested in getting the next best thing to a consultation from you. . . . Never take your eye off them." He also suggested quite a few choice ideas, references, and analogies. One of my favorites is the technique of slowing the ball down. My young-adult daughter Emily gave me acute advice on several chapters. In many cases her guidance coincided exactly with Hilary's: "Dad, no more than five summary points at the end of the chapter, and make them brief, declarative, and practical!" Repeatedly, I followed her unerring editorial instincts. Chris Bergonzi was kind enough to react to the architecture of the book in outline form before I began the final draft. If the book can be said to have a "story arc," a progression from beginning to middle to end, Chris' guidance is largely responsible. Late in the project, I was fortunate to have Leslie Stephen enter the scene, at the publisher's request, to sort through the external reviews and suggest changes. I most appreciate the independent judgment she exercised and the select few telling revisions she helped me make.

Several managers gave me a reading on how close the manuscript was to reaching the target audience and in which respects it needed redirecting. I am in debt to the following individuals for taking the trouble to read several chapters and not only to serve as a reality check but to offer numerous practical suggestions: Peter Campanella, Ben Jenkins, Matt Kissner, Angelo LaGrega, Gerry Lopez, Marie McKee, and Gwynne Whitley.

Two fellow professionals, Gene Boccialetti and Randy White, reviewed and reacted to a close-to-final draft with extraordinary care and a touching commitment to the work and to me. The book is the better for their respective efforts.

Two colleagues from the academic world, David Day at Penn State and Bart Craig at North Carolina State, read the entire manuscript with an eye out for flaws in my argument and to suggest ways to bolster the case I was making. Each took his part most ably.

Quite a few other people read portions of the manuscript and gave me just the help I was seeking. They are Rick Bakosh, Rebecca Henson, Harvey Hornstein, John Joyce, Jack Jurras, Wayne Kaiser,

Josh Kaplan, Rick O'Leary, Sam Manoogian, Ohad Shvueli, Murray Smith, Steve Strome, and Wendell Weeks.

My wife, Becky, cheerfully served in a number of capacities. She was a willing ear when I wanted to articulate a nascent insight or work through a snag in my thinking. She also indulged my desire to read all ten chapters to her out loud so that I could get her sense of what worked and what didn't. I am enormously grateful to her for providing, in addition to substance, a loving climate in which I could freely lose myself in this work.

Preface
Oversights and Insights

A thousand accidents of memory, attention,
sensation that cross my mind appear in my finished
work. And yet all of it is certainly part of me, since
my weaknesses, my strengths, my lazy repetitions,
my manias, my darkness and my light, can always
be recognized in everything that falls from my
hands.

—*Paul Valery*

I did not set out to discover what the leadership field overlooked. I stumbled on the several oversights that form the basis of this book in the course of working closely with leaders on their development. From time to time over the past twenty-five years I have had a little revelation, like a curtain lifting on part of the drama of leadership. Most of what I have observed is in plain view for all to see, and yet its significance has been missed. Perhaps that is the way of all discovery. In the 1860 presidential election campaign, Abraham Lincoln opened a speech in New York City by saying:

The facts with which I shall deal this evening are mainly old and familiar; nor is there anything new in the general use I shall make of them. If there shall be any novelty, it will be in the mode of presenting the facts, and the inferences and observations following that presentation.[1]

Serendipity has led me to the simple truths that led to this book, yet it has not been pure happenstance. I have enjoyed exceptional, enviable firsthand exposure to the phenomenon of senior leaders, including CEOs of major corporations, attempting to perform better. First at the Center for Creative Leadership (CCL) and now in our own firm, my colleagues and I have long conducted searching assessments of individual leaders. We collect plenty of data so there is little doubt in the person's mind or ours that the findings are valid and credible. And even as we cast the net widely, we systematically reduce the catch down to its essence. Then we stay involved with the individual as he or she attempts to change so we are able to see firsthand what spells success and what does not. Every consultation doubles as informal research. Personally, I know no greater satisfaction than to learn and improve, and to help others learn and improve.

The field's oversights reported here are important because they represent major missed opportunities for leaders to gain effectiveness. I have not simply noted them or talked casually with my colleagues about them. In each case I have developed the thought and turned it into something practical. In each case I have hit on what I believe is a better way for leaders to get a reading on their performance, one that is truer to the realities of managerial work. This includes a cutting-edge assessment tool that breaks from the dominant tradition. I have also hit on novel ways of using the results of an assessment to spur or free leaders to actually change for the better. Leadership development amounts to moving an individual from point A to point B. Each of the practices described in this book offers the leader added leverage for making that move.

Little Epiphanies

There has usually been a signal instance when the pattern has snapped into focus. I remember the feedback session fifteen years ago when it dawned on me that doing too much of something was as much of a problem as doing too little of it. After going over the assessment report with the executive, whom a coworker had described as "an elemental force in nature," I attempted to sum up by saying, "You're a force, a force to be reckoned with." I went on to characterize his weaknesses in a way I hadn't deliberately done before: "The problem is that at times you're overly forceful." I realized later that not one of the assessment tools currently on the market, not even my own, which was distributed by CCL, was equipped to measure strengths overused.

The idea of strengths overused became an organizing principle for my next coworker-feedback survey, the Leadership Versatility Index. I conceived of the tool and put it into practice. Rob Kaiser and I have since turned it into a finished product and brought it to market. The tool has had the side benefit of allowing us to do statistical research. Our findings, complete with pretty bell curves and striking scatter plots, helped shape the book's conceptual framework.

I remember the time ten years ago when it occurred to me that the value of feedback wasn't just in the criticism. Preparing for a feedback session with Rick Freed, I was startled to see that he was so highly regarded that there was practically nothing wrong with his leadership. It unnerved me. "I've got nothing to work with," I thought. It turned out, though, that I had plenty to work with. His idea of his capability had lagged behind the reality. So the assessment became an opportunity for him to catch up with himself. And to my surprise, it was, without exaggeration, a breakthrough that enabled him to raise his level of play even further.

Thanks to Rick Freed, I realized that gifted leaders are often the last ones to know about their gifts. For years I had taken it for granted that, if they didn't already know they were strong in a given area, they simply welcomed the good news like a refreshing drink on a hot day. Wiser now, I hit on another type of leverage for development: much of the work of development is getting the strengths to sink in. Half of leadership development is on the strengths side of the ledger.

Rick Freed is a pseudonym. His story, told at greater length in Chapter 8, is taken largely from one leader's experience, but not entirely. All the cases in the book that are graced with a name are composites, individuals with roughly similar profiles whose managerial appendages, torso, and head have been stitched together into one pseudonymic example. As much as I would like to write about individual leaders and use their real names, the last thing I want to do is invade their privacy or, through the exposure, hurt them in any way.

Disparate realizations like the two mentioned here eventually led, down a baroquely looping path, to this book. From talking up a new idea with anyone who would listen, testing it out informally in my work with managers, studying it systematically, formulating it carefully for presentations, putting it to work in leadership development programs, and writing it up in articles, ideas gradually took shape and then built on each other to form the basis for this book.

For the last several years Rob Kaiser has been my collaborator on the project that led to the publication of both this book and the Leadership Versatility Index. Although I developed the prototype, he and I together have since strengthened the tool's conceptual framework, rewritten questionnaire items, and revamped the feedback report, and he did the statistical analysis that underpins the instrument (see the Appendix). Rob also has helped me flesh out the book's model of leadership and leadership development. Yet since the book's major ideas are mine, the voice you hear on these pages, for better or worse, is my own.

Capstone Concept

The book's capstone concept is versatility. Several characteristics distinguish this notion from the usual sense of versatility.

First, versatility is usually understood as a wide repertoire, along with the capacity to call appropriately on one aptitude or another. I assign versatility a more restrictive definition that describes better what is required of leaders and where they go wrong.

In this conception a wide repertoire comprises *pairs* of aptitudes that complement each other. The reason for structuring aptitudes in complementary pairs is that, in the case of every complementarity known to humans, leaders have a strong tendency to favor one side over the other, to be lopsided, and a pair-wise arrangement throws that tendency into relief (see Figure P.1). Leaving aside for the moment which pairs we have found to be most important to effectiveness, I have used as placeholders matched sets of "yin and yang" dimensions.

Second, versatility is defined as covering all of the two-sided bases that are deemed important. This book is predicated on two major pairs, identified below.

Third, being versatile in this sense departs in another way from the usual meaning of the word. It is not just *having enough* of both sides of every major pair but it is also *not having,* or more precisely not employing, *too much* of either side. Getting it right depends,

Figure P.1. A Model of Versatility

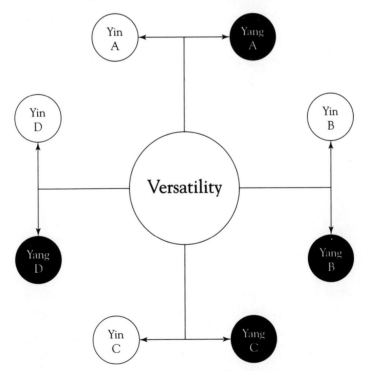

however, on something that is not a foregone conclusion for leaders—having an accurate reading on how much they are deploying, neither too little nor too much.

Fourth, to employ pair-wise capabilities adeptly, two conditions have to be met. The individual must be evenhanded with each pair, when the tendency is to place too high a value on one side and to disparage the other. The second condition is that the leader be self-aware both about the way he or she behaves with respect to each pair and how he or she regards each pair.

From this notion of versatility fall, directly or indirectly, the several implications for the practice of leadership assessment and leadership development covered in this book. Three of the major implications are

1. *Overusing your strengths is no less of a problem than being deficient.* The answer is to modulate your strengths so that you avoid doing too much of a good thing. To accomplish this you must start by finding out what you overdo. However, virtually all standard leadership-assessment tools are geared to capturing deficiencies but not strengths taken too far.

2. *Know your own strength as well as the effect it has.* A chief reason why leaders overuse their strengths is that they underestimate them. Often their gauge is off: they think they're only going 55 miles per hour when in fact they're breaking the speed limit. It helps greatly if the individual can take in the full extent of his or her strengths, but that is more difficult to do than it sounds.

3. *When you overdo a strength, there's typically a complementary skill or quality that gets crowded out.* The trick is to keep two opposing ideas in your head at the same time. It's capitalizing on the power of both sides. It helps to know in what ways your leadership is lopsided, yet, surprisingly, there are hardly any assessment tools designed to identify lopsidedness in leaders.

The book is in three parts. The first part, largely descriptive, lays out the book's foundation.

Chapter 1: Think Volume Control: Don't Overuse Your Strengths

Chapter 2: "Mirror, Mirror . . .": Look for Excess Too

Chapter 3: Know Your Own Strength

Chapter 4: The Impact of Mind-Set: Learning the Inner Game of Leadership

The second part describes the two dualities, major pairs of dimensions, that we found to be critical to a leader's effectiveness.

Chapter 5: Forceful and Enabling Leadership: The Power of Both

Chapter 6: Strategic and Operational Leadership: The Power of Both

The third part offers ways and means to correct overdoing it, underdoing it, and a combination of both, lopsidedness. All three chapters describe the outer, behavioral work and the inner, personal work of development.

Chapter 7: Throttling Back

Chapter 8: Revving Up

Chapter 9: Adjusting Both Sides

The book concludes with an elaboration of the ideal of "multi-versatility," a direction in which leaders can and should attempt to move.

Chapter 10: The Multi-Versatile Leader

You can think of the book as the next best thing to getting a leadership consultation from me or one of my colleagues. It is a chance to try on for size the innovative models and techniques that we have been using and refining for years. In addition to your self-improvement, you can expect the book to inform your efforts to help others develop and improve. In either case, the intent is to provide you with serious developmental leverage.

The book offers developmental leverage on both a behavioral level and a personal level. This is an approach to development that traces back from the leader's behavior to the "crooked thinking" and "trigger points" that threw off that behavior in the first place. This isn't therapy. It's meant to be a step toward a practical psychology of leadership.

The book is also meant to be a resource for leadership specialists of all kinds. I am thinking of trainers who design and run leadership development programs and anyone, either a leadership coach or an HR professional, who consults to individual managers on their development. I am also thinking of specialists who deal with leaders one step removed— HR professionals responsible for talent-management and performance-management systems, test and measurement professionals who design leadership-assessment tools, and leadership researchers.

I intend for this book to be useful not just to the corporate managers I have typically worked with, but to anyone in a leadership position in any walk of organizational life—a manager in a non-profit human-service organization, an elected official, a minister tending a congregation, the head of a non-governmental organization (NGO), a college dean.

Part One

A Perspective on
Leadership Assessment

There is a disconnect between what is generally known about leadership and the way leaders are assessed in most organizations. The first part of the book identifies these oversights and recommends ways of correcting for them.

The first part, largely descriptive, lays out the book's foundation.

Chapter One

Think Volume Control

Don't Overuse Your Strengths

"A man must . . . stand in some terror of his talents.
A transcendent talent draws so largely on his forces
as to lame him."

—*Ralph Waldo Emerson*

"What comes over a man, is it soul or mind,
That no limits and bounds can he stay confined?"

—*Robert Frost*

We have all seen leaders go to counterproductive extremes: when
devotion to consensus-seeking slows decision making to a
crawl, when a leader's fertile mind results in repeated changes in
direction, when a dedication to high-quality work turns a supervisor into a stickler for detail, when keen consideration for others
degenerates into ineffectual niceness, when a willingness to go the
extra mile leads to burnout. Yet somehow the fact of strengths
overused does not have the same grip on leaders and assessment-
and-development specialists that deficiencies have.

Consider the widely used phrase, "strengths and weaknesses."
Since a weakness is a lack of strength, where in that construction is
there a place for the overuse of strengths? Its hazy place in our language is matched by its tenuous position in leadership development.
In most modern organizations, leaders have a much better chance of
being assessed for, and getting help with, their deficiencies than their
excesses.[1] Let's start by making room in the conception of an individual's positives and negatives for strengths overused (Figure 1.1).

Figure 1.1. "Strengths and Weaknesses" Redefined

Consider the case of a gifted senior manager I know well (actually, he's several individuals rolled into one here).

Rich Spire, Exemplary in So Many Ways

Rich Spire has "leader" written all over him. He embodies everything that the word has come to mean in the business world. Leader, as opposed to manager. Someone who spearheads large-scale strategic change. As president of a sector of a large, fast-growing technology company, Rich possesses a stunning set of interlocking strengths.

One, he has an excellent strategic brain. He's extremely intelligent and quite adept at identifying where in the coming few years the big opportunities are likely to emerge. He also has a firm grounding in the business and the industry. A peer commented: "What's unique about Rich is that he understands so well how the business works, how the pieces fit together. And he has a very good ability to see the business from a much more strategic level, based on a very good sense of where the overall industry is going. So he knows how to position the organization."

> Unsolicited praise came from someone on Rich Spire's team: "Clearly his strengths are intelligence, strategic thinking, hard work, dedication to the success of the company, his ability to communicate, his desire to be the lead guy."

Two, he has no problem making big bold moves. No one would accuse him of being risk-averse or slow to make high-stakes decisions. Not rashly: his major decisions are carefully thought out.

Three, he has a gift for exciting people with his vision, his forward-looking, innovative ideas of strengthening the organization's hand in the marketplace. The people around him fairly gushed about what the CEO called "an uncanny ability to communicate—he is enormously articulate." Rich is especially good in front of an audience. The CEO credited him with being "a commanding presence in front of a group of people." Someone two levels down from him had this praise for his presentation skills: "He's excellent on his feet—a great speaker." Another facet of his visionary leadership is that he describes what he sees not just in broad terms but, as someone on his staff said, "with enough color and granularity that people can grasp onto their portion of the vision."

Four, he is a natural leader. Part of it is that he has an animal energy that is palpable to the people around him. "His eyes dance," someone said. Blessed with abundant leadership presence, there's an electric quality to him even when he isn't saying anything. A long-time lieutenant said about him: "He has a big presence, carries a lot of power, and people respond to power." Rich naturally takes the lead. When the game is on the line, he wants the ball in his hands. And he is "a great persuader," his lieutenant went on to say. "He can sell you anything. Not just goods and services but his viewpoints and ideas. He's an extremely persuasive fellow."

One of Rich Spire's direct reports said: "Every once in a while you run across a leader—and I've had only a couple—who is really able to inspire you and make you really work at your best. He can get you to make that extra effort and feel like it is good to do."

Five, he is an impact player who doesn't just strategize; he sees to it that strategy is turned into action. A peer running another sector had to hand it to him: "Despite the fact that we've had disagreements and differences of approach, he is a force for change for the better in the company. In short order he's totally revamped his division's go-to-market strategy and reoriented research and development to be tied much more closely to the commercial side." Everyone who had input to his assessment credited him with a bias for implementation. A lieutenant said: "He's a driver, he makes things happen, he makes people follow him, and he doesn't know failure and therefore he doesn't fail."

Other people, talented in their own right, are given to making glowing statements about him overall. Someone on his staff said: "In the twenty-five years I've been bumping into executives, he is one of the best I've ever run into." And another: "He has more potential than anyone I know. Huge talent—intelligence, instincts, experience, strategic insight. He grasps the problem perfectly. He can deal with people. And it's all wrapped up in a charismatic package."

How could there be anything wrong with this impressive picture?

Rich Spire's Blind Spots

Rich had only two liabilities, and both resulted from taking a considerable strength too far. One, as is often the case with natural leaders, he suffers the downsides of exercising power so readily. Second, his penchant for bold strategic action exceeds his organization's capacity to keep up.

Just as power comes naturally to Rich Spire, so too he uses it too freely. The good news is that he is a strong leader, and that is the bad news too. In meetings he is too quick to state his position. He hasn't learned to let other people offer their views first. "His default mode is to take the lead unless you wrest it away from him," said a member of his staff.

As you might expect, his overly forceful ways have a dampening effect on his team and his organization. One subordinate voiced the concern that "his autocratic style kept him from getting the full story because he assumes he already knows the answer." Yes, some of the people on his team have accommodated to his "style." They have learned to stand up to him. They have learned that if you come back with facts you can change his mind. When he is hypercritical, they manage not to take it personally. But not everyone is so fortunate. Someone two levels down from him reported, "If you don't have the personality to deal with his strong personality or you don't know him well, then there's a tendency to be quiet and go sit in the corner." In one-on-one's with Rich, one dazzlingly astute, articulate man on his team literally became tongue-tied.

Remarkably, this was a blind spot. Rich was oblivious to his own power and impact. Hard to believe that someone who fairly bristles with personal power could be oblivious to that. Even when someone made the occasional remark, though, he couldn't relate to it. For reasons of his upbringing, he actually had the opposite concern: he worried about not being powerful enough.

As to bold moves, Rich has always wanted to make a big splash, has always wanted to make the larger-than-life contribution. As a baseball player in Little League and right through college, he had swung for the fences. Home runs thrilled him. He loved trotting around the bases to sustained applause. A singles hitter he was not. A sacrifice bunt to move a teammate on first base into scoring position was completely absent from his repertoire. He admits he struck out a lot and could have hit for a higher average. But that was a price he was willing to pay.

In his forties, the same raw competitive instinct animates his leadership. He is not content to inch up his organization's position in the marketplace. He wants to gain ground quickly. He wants to score big, impressive wins. The CFO observed: "Rich wants to make the aggressive move and capture territory. It's useful to have vision, but he needs to implement it in a more measured way." The historian Paul Kennedy calls this overstretch, a major reason for the decline of empires.[2] The CFO put it this way: "His vision outstripped our internal capacity. His strategic reach was too great to be executed with the bench strength we had."

This was a blind spot too. Although he respected the CFO, whom he had selected, Rich had trouble taking his concerns about his strategic ambitions seriously. He couldn't see how there could be anything wrong with being an aggressive expansionist in a growth industry.

This is where his two blind spots came together to put the organization at risk. By being far too bullish, for example, he made a major forecasting error, over the CFO's objections, in this case never fully voiced. Facing into the headwind of Rich's forceful personality and his voracious appetite to have an outsized impact, some people on his team gave up trying to influence him. Not that it was impossible to do. It just wasn't worth it. "It takes too much emotional energy to keep confronting this guy," they'd say, throwing up their hands, "and he isn't going to listen anyway."

The Many Faces of Overkill

Whether public figures or middle managers toiling far from the public eye, people in leadership positions are notorious for overdoing it.

Take a historical figure like Napoleon, a brilliant field general, who conquered most of Europe. Driven by a conviction that "a great reputation is a great noise and the more that is made, the farther off it is heard," he didn't know when to stop. In the end, the people of France cried out, "Assez de Napoleon!" [Enough of Napoleon!].[3]

In literature Ahab in *Moby Dick* offers a blatant instance of overkill. Early in the novel, Stubb, the third mate, respectfully asks Ahab, the ship captain, to be considerate of those sleeping below because as Ahab paces the deck, his ivory peg leg makes an incessant tapping noise. Ahab dismisses this reasonable request and to boot hurls an insult: "Down, dog, and kennel!"

Stunned, Stubb gamely tries to stand his ground: "I am not used to be spoken to that way, sir. I do but less than half like it, sir."

Ahab, while showering abuse, now lunges at him so violently that Stubb involuntarily retreats.

As he goes below deck, Stubb struggles to recover his dignity: "What the devil's the matter with me? I don't stand right on my legs? Coming afoul of that old man has sort of turned me wrong side out."

This is the first of three explosive encounters that get touched off when a mate persists in trying to influence Ahab on an important point. Each time Ahab does far too good a job of sticking to his position and guarding his prerogatives. In the second and third episodes, as the stakes climb higher and higher, it is the first mate, Starbuck, who strives mightily to keep Ahab from going overboard.

In business, scandalous instances of the worst excesses are not uncommon. The former CEO of Tyco International, Dennis Koslowski, repeatedly crossed lines, ethical and legal.

At the time of this writing, he and Mark Swartz, the former CFO, were each found guilty of twenty-two counts of grand larceny and other charges for, among other things, awarding themselves $143 million in compensation that was not authorized by the board of directors. They took the normal motivation to make money to a grossly distorted extreme.

> The root of the word "evil," which to my taste is used too loosely, derives from an ancient Teutonic word, *ubiloz*, that means "up" or "over," in the sense of overstepping one's bounds.

Leadership Effectiveness—Skirting Deficiency and Excess

Even though overkill is big as life, it is somehow the forgotten child of leadership performance. A simple, practical way of thinking about performance makes a place for it. In this view, performing well is adjusting a given leadership skill to the right level for the situation, neither too low nor too high. Some individuals perpetually talk too loudly on cell phones or in conversations on an airplane or in a restaurant. Other people are chronically soft-spoken in a meeting with a large group of people or against a car's background noise. You have to strain to hear them. Effective speakers know how to modulate their voices so the volume is neither too high nor too low for fellow participants or for bystanders.

> In the words of one manager: "It is useful for me to think that a strength overused can be as ineffective as a strength underused. In other words, overusing a strength is underperformance."

The idea of getting the volume right applies to practically any dimension of leadership—being detail-oriented, focusing on the big picture, being directive, being open to influence—you name it. The concept of adjusting the volume goes all the way back to Aristotle, who postulated that what is good, virtuous, and effective in thought and action is the mid-point between deficiency and excess.[4] His notion of what it means to be good in a moral sense or to be good at something was anything but static. As he stated in his *Ethics*, the mid-point or right amount varies with the circumstances. It is a moving target. In the practice of leadership you must continually adjust the setting of any attribute to the level that fits the circumstances immediately at hand. You must continually navigate the straits of leadership, steering clear of the shoals of deficiency on one side and the rocks of excess on the other.

Aristotle's precept has mistakenly been taken to mean moderation in all things. Popularized as the "golden mean," it is a serious misreading of his thinking, a bastardization of it. What he called for was a response *proportionate* to the situation. In other words, turning the volume way up is the right amount when the situation calls for that. A mother who yells at the top of her lungs when her small child is about to chase a ball into a street where cars are passing has followed Aristotle's advice perfectly.

Going all out is frequently the only way to go. Rich Spire's boss applauded him for "taking over completely in a business crisis." Even great sacrifice is laudable when that's what the situation requires. Necessary losses may be brutally high. Machiavelli, who advised a prince to use force if that is what it took to lift a city state out of chaos, believed in committing only necessary harm. The trouble comes when, in whatever respect, you go too far, even for an extreme situation. The trouble comes when the losses are not necessary, when the price paid is much higher than it needs to be. It behooves all of us, even *in extremis*, to stay on the right side of the line, however far out it extends.

Parents who constantly yell at their kids over nothing are going too far. Likewise, Rich Spire confessed that, in meetings, "I jump in with both hands and both feet because I only have one speed." The idea is to avoid having your behavior stuck at one setting. Just as a parent's challenge is to raise his or her voice only when it is neces-

> Nothing is enough for the person for whom enough is too little.

sary, your challenge as a leader is to avoid habitually falling short of the mark on key leadership dimensions and likewise to avoid regularly overshooting the mark.

Assessing and Addressing Overused Strengths: Rich Spire's Blind Spots Live On

You might think that leaders who have a "development physical" could count on getting checked out for overkill. Is it not fair to expect a leadership assessment to indicate whether the reading on any important index is dangerously elevated? After all, like high blood pressure, going too far is a silent killer. But, in what makes for a curious disconnect between common knowledge and formal measures of leadership, standard assessment tools don't capture excess.[5]

How has a basic truth about leadership eluded formal systems used to select leaders, evaluate their performance on the job or identify their areas for improvement?[7] The

> A manager who read the recent article Rob Kaiser and I published in *Sloan Management Review*[6] surprised me by saying: "When I first read your article it was unsettling. It was the overdoing aspect. We managers spend so much of our time on development but we spend little time on strengths overused. It was chilling. I really mean that. I said to myself, I have work to do."

explanation for this omission is, in part, purely mechanical. The rating scales most often used in assessment tools aren't designed to identify overuse.[8] Take the most common rating scheme, the frequency scale (how often. . . ?; to what extent. . . ?).

On a 360-degree survey that used a frequency scale, Rich Spire received a very high rating on "Comfortable with the power of the managerial role." That told him what? That he does it a lot. It did not, however, indicate that he does it too much. Likewise, his score on "Grows the business" hit the top end of the rating scale and could only leave the impression that he performed that function well. Rich Spire was in the dark with respect to using power and setting strategic goals, and the assessment tool left him in the dark.

That's the limitation of this type of scale. The highest rating, a 5, doesn't distinguish between doing a heck of a lot and doing too much. Exhibit 1.1 at the end of this chapter goes into detail on this rating scale and another frequently used one, the evaluation scale.[9]

If you have received feedback on a questionnaire that employs a frequency rating scale, take another look at those items on which you received ratings of 5 or close to it and ask yourself whether in any of those cases "a lot" could also mean "too much." For some managers this is a mind-bending exercise. They hadn't thought that way about high scores. Somehow, even though in the backs of their minds they know better, they have slipped into a point of view that says a 5 is an A. Why not: when 2s or 3s are bad scores, it is only logical that high numbers are good scores. One individual who got a perfect 5 on "Drives hard to meet organizational commitments" cried out, "I'd be happy if I got a 10 on this! I don't see how a high score could be a problem." The people who work for her might see it differently. Has she made impossible demands on them? Has she left bodies in her wake?

It is interesting that managers as well as specialists in leadership assessment and development (for a good long time myself included) unwittingly go along with the tacit assumption that on this ubiquitous rating scale higher scores are better.

This little-noticed failure to detect excess is indicative. It is further evidence that the idea of strengths overused hasn't taken root in formal models of leadership or in formal methods for assessing and developing managers.

Lopsidedness, Excess in Another Form

For every excess in your repertoire, there may well be a corresponding deficiency. You may not see the connection, but look behind you: in doing too much of one thing, seesaw-like, you might just be doing too little of the opposing, complementary thing. This is lopsidedness, with excess nested within it (see Figure 1.2).

This is lopsidedness, excess in another form.

The root of "complement" is "to fill." The complementary function fills out the other. Together they make a whole. The problem with excess on one side is that it so often comes at the expense of the other side.

> Lopsided was originally a nautical term. To "lop" is to lean. Years ago when boats were made by hand, all eyes were on a new boat as it was launched. It would not do for it to lean to one side. Likewise, you know a leader is in trouble if, metaphorically speaking, walking or standing he or she is not upright.

Figure 1.2. Lopsidedness

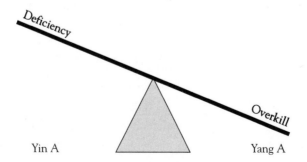

Deficiency

Overkill

Yin A   Yang A

Rich Spire isn't just too aggressive strategically. He also neglects the operational counterpart of strategic leadership, which is to make sure that the organization has the capacity to absorb the rapid growth. Earlier I quoted his CFO as saying that Rich's instinct is to grab strategic ground. The CFO went on to say, "It's useful to have an expansive vision but let's make sure we execute in a measured way so it won't just be a flash of light and burn out." Rich was so caught up in his strategic aspirations that he lost sight of the execution issues, the capacity issues. It is more accurate to say that the one was writ large in his mind and the other appeared in small letters in the back of his mind. (See Table 1.1.)

Rich was also lopsided on the forceful-enabling opposition. Just as he went too far in his use of power, he did not make it easy for other people to influence him. The intellectual firepower, the charisma, the personal power that emanated from him all came together to make it an uphill struggle for many people attempting to hold their own in a conversation with him. A member of his team put it this way: "I think he stakes out his positions too early. Because what happens is that people then want to be in agreement with him, as opposed to bringing their best thinking. So it would be better if he disguised his opinions, especially for people who don't know him well. But beyond that, he needs to get much better at asking questions—elicit what you're thinking versus tell you what he's thinking: 'Tell me how that's going; tell me what's on your mind; tell me what our approach should be,' so the approach becomes, 'Let's figure it out' versus 'Here's what I think you should do.'" But guarding the potency of others was not at the top his mind, nor was enabling others to bring their "A game." And it didn't help that he had no idea how powerful he was.

Table 1.1. Lopsidedness in Rich Spire

Excess	Corresponding Deficiency
Overly expansive strategically	Inattentive to the limits on his organization's capacity to grow
Too big on pushing	Difficult to influence

Rich Spire's lopsidedness pales by comparison to that of the cast of wildly overreaching executives at Enron in the 1990s. Of course, their excesses and accompanying deficiencies were abetted by the company's lack of checks and balances and by the failure of top management to install or enforce control mechanisms.[10] For example:

- Jeffrey Skilling, first the head of the trading operation and later the president of Enron, was a visionary risk-taker to a fault. He came up with business schemes that transformed Enron as well as the oil and gas industry, but his ability to implement was lacking and, when his brilliant theories collided with practical reality, theory won out.

- Rebecca Mark, a gifted, glamorous, and extraordinarily hard-working senior manager, brought an over-the-top can-do attitude to the job of heading Enron International, which struck deals to build pipelines and power plants in developing countries. Her optimism knew no bounds and, as time went on, her decisions on big deals in unstable locales came to be based less on facts and analysis than on her gut feel.

Enron might have survived the lopsidedness of hyperdriven senior leaders like Skilling and Mark if the CEO, Ken Lay, had reined them in. But increasingly Lay, lopsided in his own right, was an absentee landlord caught up in celebrity-seeking. And he favored doling out grossly lavish pay packages over enduring the unpleasantness of telling anyone no. So Skilling was allowed to introduce an accounting method that allowed the trading business to put a long-term contract's revenue on the books at the time the contract was signed. And Mark was allowed to use a compensation structure that paid her and her team a not-small percentage of the project's expected income as soon as the deal was done. No wonder Enron International rushed from deal to deal and did a spotty job of following through on projects.[11]

The chief operating officer, Rich Kinder, disciplined, focused on implementation, hardnosed to a fault, himself lopsided, filled in

Lay's gaps and acted as a hedge against the overheated ambitions of the folks around him. But Kinder left the company when Lay decided not to make him CEO.

Cases of lopsided leaders like those at Enron and like Rich Spire abound. In addition, our research has found statistical evidence, reported in Chapters 5 and 6, of the high incidence of lopsidedness in the managerial population.

Despite the prevalence of lopsidedness, leaders aren't assessed for it for the same reason that they are not assessed for overkill. Standard assessment tools are not designed to pick it up. There is also a second reason, coming up in Chapter 2.

Versatility, the Virtuous Flip Side of Lopsidedness

What is also not measured by standard assessment methods is lopsidedness' virtuous counterpart, *versatility*, the ability to turn, as needed, from side to side on a pair of opposing leadership virtues. To do so means recognizing that both dimensions are good, desirable, and necessary. Work life *and* personal life: they're both important. Making decisions on the basis of full information and careful analysis *and* making decisions in a timely manner: they're both important. Being a thought leader *and* creating conditions for other people to exercise thought leadership: both are highly desirable. To be versatile is to draw on each side to the right degree for the situation.

What distinguishes versatile leaders is that they experience no contradiction between the opposing sides of a pair of leadership virtues. They see them as yin and yang. They can, and do, draw freely on either side as the occasion warrants.

> Leadership is like basketball. The best players can go to the basket with either hand.

To be multi-versatile is to function effectively on both ends of multiple oppositions in leadership. For the purposes of this book there are two: (1) strategic and operational leadership and (2) forceful and enabling leadership. As the "table model" in Figure 1.3 suggests, when your leadership behavior does justice to both sides of both pairs, it's because that capability rests on a firm personal base. When the base is wobbly, the table's surface tips to one side or another.

To paraphrase F. Scott Fitzgerald, the sign of a first-rate leader is the ability to hold two opposing ideas in your head at the same time and still be able to function. As a practical matter, being intelligent in this dialectical way comes down to not placing excessive weight on one of the two ideas, not overusing your strength on that side. And to accomplish that requires that you resist the temptation of a more-is-better mentality.

As it stands, leaders like Rich Spire are implicitly encouraged in the notion that more is better. The best that standard assessment tools can do for him is identify his deficiencies. He would have to look elsewhere to learn how his gifts turn into too much of a good thing.

Figure 1.3. A Table Model of Leadership

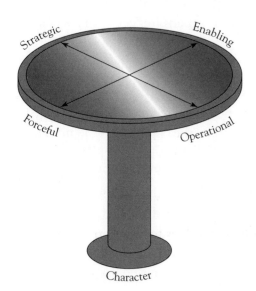

Developing Yourself, Coaching Others

Highlights

1. Overdoing strengths is many a leader's undoing. Over-used strengths pose no less a performance problem than weaknesses.

2. Overuse is overlooked, as is lopsidedness, which is overuse in another form. Most assessment tools don't have a way of detecting strengths overused or lopsidedness.

3. Your organization may be inadvertently breeding a more-is-better mentality in leaders. By not building into its performance evaluation system a means of assessing for overuse, a check against excess, the organization inadvertently colludes with leaders who go overboard.

4. Think volume control. The idea is to get the "volume" right, for example, neither pushing too hard nor not hard enough.

5. Aspire to versatility in the two-sided sense. More than having a wide repertoire, versatility is being good at both sides of a given yin-and-yang of leadership, for example, direct and sensitive to people's feelings. It's good to be good at both, but not too good at either.

Questions for Reflection

1. Do you over-rely on any of your tried-and-true methods to the point where they don't fit the situation?

2. Take another look at the high scores on your 360-degree feedback. Could any of the high scores mask the fact that you go overboard in that area?

3. Have you noticed yourself assuming, as you fill out a leadership survey with a "how much" or "how often" rating scale, that since a low score isn't good that a high score must be best?

4. Do you try as hard not to be excessive as you do not to be deficient?

5. Are you an equal-opportunity supervisor? Do you give each staff member's excesses the attention they deserve?

Exhibit 1.1. Rating Scales and Evaluation Scales

Let's see how well standard assessment tools pick up Rich Spire's blatant overdoing.

An assessment tool's ability to identify overdoing hinges on its rating scale. One of the most common, a frequency scale, typically ranges from "1" to "5," as shown below:

1	2	3	4	5
Not at all	Once in a while	Sometimes	Fairly often	Frequently, if not always

Let's use this scale to assess Rich Spire on the questionnaire item, "Takes stands," a most basic managerial function. It probably goes without saying that most of his coworkers would give him a high score, probably a 5. The question is: What does a "5" tell us (or him for that matter)? Only that he takes stands a great deal of the time but *not* that he does too many of them. A top score of 5 on this scale is misleading. If only the scale kept going! It falls down by making the implicit, if inadvertent, assumption that more is better.

Let's try the also widely used evaluation scale, an example of which appears below:

1	2	3	4	5
Ineffective	Somewhat effective	Effective	Very effective	Outstanding

On this scale Rich would probably receive a rating on "taking stands" toward the low end of the scale—let's say a "2." Again the question is: What does the score indicate? Only that he doesn't do it very well, but *not* that the reason for that is that he takes it to an extreme. The low score is ambiguous: it could mean he doesn't do enough of it or that he does too much of it.

Neither of these standard scales, then, picks up overdoing. Remarkably, this is true of the leadership field in general. The questionnaire-style nets that are cast in search of an individual's managerial strengths and weaknesses don't do a good job of capturing this type of fish. Leadership assessment has ways of working around the limitations of rating scales. Negatively worded items, for example, "Abrasive" or "Overly focused on short-term results," get at overkill, but that's catch-as-catch-can. Verbal descriptions will pick it up too, but again not in a disciplined way.

Chapter Two

"Mirror, Mirror . . ."

Look For Excess Too

"Whoever takes huge strides cannot walk properly."
—*François Jullien*

Just twenty years ago, except for the annual performance appraisal, leaders lacked a systematic way to see themselves as others see them.[1] Now, thanks to 360-degree feedback, so called because input comes from coworkers all around the focal individual, managers in many organizations have gone from being deprived of feedback to being deluged with it—by performance management systems, leadership development programs, and professional coaching. The question now is how complete and accurate the input they are getting is. As the practice of leadership assessment and development has grown, it has taken shape around a standard way of conceptualizing skills (so-called competency models) and a standard way of getting a reading in terms of the competency model. This pattern has since worked itself into a rut that makes it hard for the field to see out of, and has resulted in two omissions:

1. Leaders overdo it all the time, but conventional assessment tools cannot identify overkill, no matter how blatant.

2. On one or another pair of leadership functions, leaders habitually overdo one side and underdo the other, and yet are not assessed for lopsidedness. In addition to being blind to overkill, the reigning tools measure competencies just one dimension at a time and therefore fail to capture the complementary capabilities that are essential for leadership.

Ella Solo's Feedback Report

Ella Solo wasn't in trouble. That wasn't the reason she wanted a second opinion. Her track record in her current job and the two before it extending over the last several years in the same organization was very good. Her boss said, "Obviously, she's done a lot of things well to achieve that level of success in her function and that level of respect in the organization."

> "My father's cardinal lesson was, 'Use the right tool for the job.' If you have ever tried to hammer a nail with a can of WD-40, you know what he means."
> —David Michaelis

She had spent her entire career in sales, although two years earlier she had moved to a different business from the one she had grown up in, and she was also promoted. The new business had long enjoyed a dominant market position that was now being threatened by new entrants. As a result, there was a lot of pressure on her to keep margins from eroding. A highly focused and intense individual, she welcomed the challenge, and her team and senior management had confidence in her ability to meet it. And as an extraverted person, her instinct was to band together with her team to get it done.

To the extent that her effectiveness suffered, it was from the unevenness of her approach to leading. Caught in a classic transition from one level of responsibility to the next, her approach to leading was out of shape the way an adolescent's features haven't yet settled into the proper proportion for his or her face. Ella knew something was off but wanted to get a better grasp of what that was.

Just a year earlier, a few months into the new role, Ella had received feedback on her company's in-house 360-degree survey, developed by an outside consulting firm. The instrument used a typical frequency scale, ranging from 1 to 5. As managers receiving feedback on instruments using this rating scale have come to realize, the problem is that most of the item ratings fall between 3.25 and 4.25.[2] In Ella's case, fully 96 of 110 ratings, or 87 percent, lay

Figure 2.1. Ella Solo's Competency Profile

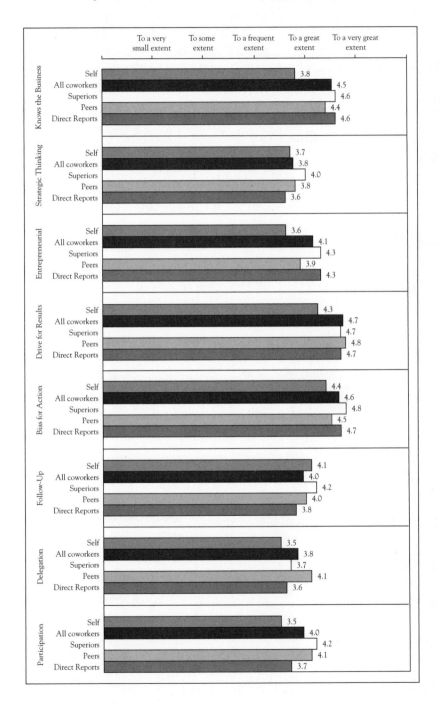

inside that range. Her lowest coworker ratings across eight major sets of skills was 3.6, and the highest was 4.7. As you can see in Figure 2.1, not much stood out in her profile except, on the higher end, her scores on "Drives for results" and "Bias for action" and, on the lower end, her middling score on delegation. Ella felt that the survey didn't give her much to go on.

One Way to Detect Excess

If you want to be more versatile, the first step is to hold up a mirror to your leadership, and that mirror must be designed to reflect excess and not just deficiency. Of the possible ways of designing such an assessment tool, Rob Kaiser and I adopted a rating scale with a provision for indicating too much of a good thing.[3] The scale operates on the Goldilocks principle: this bowl of porridge is too cool, this bowl is too hot, and this one is just right. (See Figure 2.2.)

Figure 2.2. A Rating Scale That Can Detect Excess

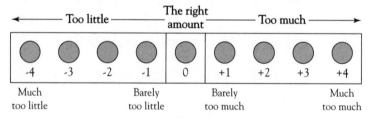

To see how this scale works, take a look at a distribution of ratings of one hundred or so managers in Figure 2.3 on the item "Lets people know clearly where he/she stands."[4]

> "Why do I overrev? Because I don't think I'm revving fast enough."
> —a senior manager

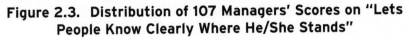

Figure 2.3. Distribution of 107 Managers' Scores on "Lets People Know Clearly Where He/She Stands"

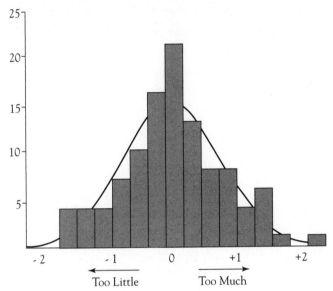

As you can see, the device identifies managers who, on this dimension, do too much, as well as those who do too little and those who do approximately the right amount. It is fair to say then that the scale works.

A modification like this is all it takes to pick up strengths overused.[5] But if the mirror is to assess for lopsidededness, it needs a second feature.

What It Takes to Detect Lopsidedness

To capture lopsidedness in leaders, an assessment tool must array skills in pairs. That is, the underlying concept of leadership must be two-sided. Talk and listen. Lead from the front and lead from the back. Be a forceful leader and an enabling leader. Apply strategic skills and operational skills. And yet when it comes to conceptualizing leadership, a list mentality seems to dominate the managerial mind.

When I ask a group of managers, "What are your truths about effective leadership?," the answers immediately fly out like popcorn popping. In every case the answers look something like this: "Create a vision." "Results-oriented." "Communicate." "Take stands." "Translate strategy into action." "Follow up." "Hold people accountable." "Listen." "Get out of people's way." "Fact-based." "Care about people." "Stamina." "Question assumptions." "Think out of the box." This is a perfectly good list. Note, though, that not one of the items on the list is stated as a pair.

The lists composed spontaneously in a classroom and those carefully assembled for assessment tools are linear, unidimensional, with single dimensions listed one after another. A typical set of "competencies" might consist of: Vision, Business Knowledge, Financial Acumen, Communication Skills, Interpersonal Skills, Developing People, and Results Orientation. I have no argument with the categories on such a list. The difficulty is structural. Lists like this don't respect the reality that for practically every truth about leadership there is an equal and opposing truth. Lists of competencies typically miss what managers calling out their classroom lists miss. They fail to grasp that a leader who has a favored competency but lacks a capacity from its essential complement is like a person with only one leg.

Watson and Crick would never have discovered the structure of DNA if they continued to assume a single helix. After years of investigative struggle, their breakthrough came when they tried out a model with two strands, a double helix. Likewise, leaders will never be assessed for lopsidedness, or versatility in the two-sided sense, unless the model of leadership is

Balance, a word that managers use all the time, originally referred to a weighing scale with *two* pans. But because of its static quality I chose not to use "balance" in the book and opted instead for the more dynamic "versatility."

organized according to the Noah's Ark principle—everything in twos.

To meet both requirements for assessing lopsidedness, Rob Kaiser and I developed the Leadership Versatility Index (LVI), which we and our colleagues have been using in our consulting practice and in leadership development programs since 1994. It arrays leadership dimensions in opposing pairs and it measures overkill.[6] My intent in describing Ella Solo's experience with it is to provide a concrete example of how a device like this works.

Another way to get a feel for the tool is to fill it out on yourself.

A word of caution: No matter how good a diagnostic tool is, questionnaire ratings cannot stand alone. That quantitative data must have verbal flesh on its bones—actual comments from the same coworkers who did the ratings. Also, to benefit from an assessment, you need more than just the content of the report. It is important to have another person—your boss, an HR professional, a development specialist of some kind—go over the data with you and distill it down to something significant and actionable.

You are welcome to fill out the Leadership Versatility Index on yourself on the following website: www.versatileleader.com/. *Note:* This sample survey includes only a subset of the items in the published version and, different from that version, which includes coworkers' ratings, it will tap only your view of your leadership.

The Excesses and Lopsidedness of Ella Solo

Highly motivated to improve and to make the adjustment to an executive role, Ella approached me about getting feedback on the Leadership Versatility Index. All told, two superiors, five peers, and eight direct reports filled it out on her. To supplement the ratings, the survey also solicited their written comments on five open-ended

Table 2.1. Ella Solo's Results on Forceful and Enabling Leadership: Coworkers Indicating "Too Little" and "Too Much"

		Forceful				Enabling	
		Too Little	Too Much			Too Little	Too Much
1f.	Takes charge	0	10	1e.	Empowers—able to let go	15	0
2f.	Steps in	0	12	2e.	Trusts people to handle problems	13	0
3f.	Sets stretch goals	5	2	3e.	Makes herself available	1	1
4f.	Holds people accountable	7	2	4e.	Understanding when people don't deliver	6	3

Note: Respondents rated Nora's leadership on each item one at a time. The results for complementary items (like 1f, "Takes charge" and 1e, "Empowers") are juxtaposed in the feedback report. Also, the item text is abbreviated in this display. The full item text appears in Chapter 3. Also as in Chapter 3, Nora's results are presented in a way that shows the extent of her underdoing and overdoing, as well as those things she does "the right amount," that is, her strengths.

questions. What follows is a much-abbreviated version of what the quantitative and qualitative data turned up.[7]

Ella's Excesses

Just a glance at Table 2.1 shows that Ella overdoes it on the first two forceful dimensions. Of the 15 coworkers who rated her, 10 gave her a too-much rating on "Takes charge," and 12 gave her a too-much rating on "Steps in." Not a single person chose a rating on the too-little side in response to either survey item. *Note:* the scores in the table are frequencies, the number of times that her coworkers rated her as doing too little or too much on each survey item.

Ella's Lopsidedness on Forceful and Enabling Leadership

On the classic distinction between taking charge and empowering others, Ella Solo represents one of the clearest cases of lopsidedness you will ever find. Just as the majority of raters indicated too much on "Takes charge," all 15 rated her too little on "Empowers—able to let go" (see the top pair of items in Table 2.1). Note that each coworker rated each item separately in the survey; in the report the pairs are brought together.

Ella had a very similar result on the second pair of items. Almost everyone gave her a "too much" rating on "Steps in" and almost everyone gave her a "too little" rating on "Trusts other people to handle problems." The results on these first two pairs of forceful and enabling items could hardly paint a more sharply etched picture of lopsidedness.

The verbatim comments lined up with these ratings. Her immediate superior wrote, "She is too involved with her team and from what I can tell her subordinates don't feel empowered to run their own functions." From a direct report came this representative comment: "While there's a positive side to her detail-orientation, the ability to delegate is crucial for a senior executive, and to dive deep on every single item is impossible, so Ella needs to focus more on delegation."

This is someone who is much too forceful and not nearly enabling enough, but not across the board. The third and fourth pairs of dimensions don't follow the pattern set by the first two pairs. In fact, the forceful scores go completely the other way: she *under-does* "Sets stretch goals" and "Holds people accountable."

How to make sense of the divergent patterns? It turns out that she put too big a burden on herself and expected too little of her staff. A staff member said, "I don't think she expects enough of her people." And someone close to her had this insight: "I think she's too hard on herself and not hard enough on her staff." Like other managers who move up the ladder, she continued to apply what worked in lower-level jobs and hadn't yet seen that the formula for success had changed.[8]

Ella's Lopsidedness on Strategic and Operational Leadership

Ella's results on the eight strategic and operational items tell an equally straightforward story (see Table 2.2). For example, 10 coworkers rated her too little on "Focuses on the long term," and the same number rated her too much on "Focuses on the short term." Her proven ability to deliver results is a great strength, although taken too far it has led to a short-term orientation. While her credibility as a leader rests on her organization's quarter-by-quarter performance, her head-down pursuit of short-term performance had come at the expense of attention to strategy. It is even reflected in her reading habits: "I read operational memos rather than a big document with strategic value."

Note too that her too-little score on "Keeps people on track" is consistent with not expecting enough of her team.

We now can see better what the in-house 360 survey missed. For instance, her high scores on "Drive for results" and "Bias for action" mask the fact that she overdoes it in those areas. And

Table 2.2. Ella Solo's Results on Strategic and Operational Leadership: Number of Coworkers Indicating "Too Much" and "Too Little"

| | Strategic | | | Operational | |
	Too Little	Too Much		Too Little	Too Much
1s. Focused on long-term strategy	10	1	1o. Focused on short-term results	0	10
2s. Big picture, thinks broadly	8	1	2o. Detail-oriented	4	8
3s. Entrepreneurial	5	2	3o. Focused on customers' immediate needs	0	5
4s. Uses inspiration to sell vision	11	0	4o. Keeps people on track	9	1

although her lowest scores on the in-house survey were on "Strategic thinking" and "Delegation," the fact that they were in the upper-3s hardly drove home the problem. Also, the competency profile did not make the link between what she did too much of (that is, "Bias for action") and what she gave short shrift to ("Delegation").

Ella's Strengths

Which scores, you may ask, indicate Ella's undiluted strengths? She received a very good score on "Makes herself available—responsive when her people need help" (Table 2.1). Of 15 people rating her, all but 2 indicated she does the right amount. Her score on "Focused on meeting customers' needs" is also quite good.

Although at first blush it may not look like it, her scores on the two taking-charge items also indicate a strength. Clearly, she possesses that ability, which certainly not every manager has. Because she takes it too far, she doesn't get full credit for it. But it is undeniably an asset. The same is true of her focus on short-term results and her attention to detail. Recall the subordinate who remarked that "there's a positive side" to her detail orientation, even if she did tarnish it through indiscriminant use. How she uses these strengths is what is getting in her way.

Maps of Strengths and Deficiencies/Excesses

After going over her report with her, I deliberately departed from the field's standard practice of proceeding directly from feedback to goal setting. Instead, I stopped, as my colleagues and I regularly do, to build a bridge between the raw data and action planning. Together Ella and I turned her list of strengths and her list of deficiencies and excesses into two hub-and-spoke maps.[9] The challenge in creating the maps is identifying the core, the hub, an integrative leap. She and I distilled the list of strengths down to "A high-energy, take-charge leader who knows the business and gets results." And we distilled the other list down to "Too deeply involved in getting short-term results." Taken together, the two maps, which appear in Figures 2.4 and 2.5, show clearly that Ella was so thoroughly engrossed in her team's day-to-day implementation of near-term plans that she (1) took her eye off the strategic ball and (2) deprived her staff of the autonomy it needed.

Figure 2.4. Ella Solo's Strengths as a Leader

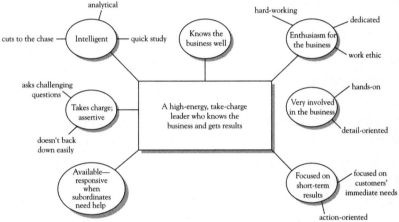

Figure 2.5. Ella Solo's Deficiencies and Excesses as a Leader

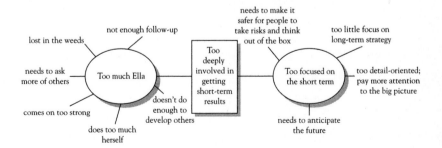

Potent Clarity

Never had the anatomy of Ella's leadership been more distinctly drawn for her, nor had the need for realignment been made so apparent. She could now clearly see that her overdeveloped short-term orientation squeezed out attention to the long term, and that her taking on too much cramped her staff's style and unduly burdened her. However well her style of play had worked at lower levels, and even then it had taken a toll, she understood that to make the grade as a senior manager she would have to realign her approach. By itself that recognition, potent as it was, might not have pushed her over the threshold. As I will show in the next chapter, to gain a clarity sharp enough to precipitate change, she also needed to understand and address what drove her to lead the way she did.

Coincidentally, Ella had recently taken up tai chi and was discovering that her intense drive to perform also hampered her in that very different activity. As she strained to execute tai chi's flowing movements, her neck jutted forward. Her teacher told her: "You are so intent on doing this well that your body is stiff. It lacks flexibility. There's so much tension you can't possibly flow." While applauding Ella's desire to do it right, her teacher encouraged her to relax. "When you rush, you lean too far forward. Lead from the center of your body. The idea is if you're moving forward, stay aligned and balanced, solid and fluid at the same time."[10] Whether at work or in a recreational activity, Ella had her developmental work cut out for her.

Developing Yourself, Coaching Others

Highlights

1. The leadership field has soldiered on for decades without assessing excess in leaders. Surely, it is time to correct this glaring omission, which somehow has escaped notice.

2. It isn't rocket science to build an assessment tool that detects excess and lopsidedness. To capture excess, all the tool needs is a rating scale with a provision for too much. In order to assess for lopsidedness, the tool also must define leadership requirements in terms of pairs of complementary dimensions.

3. Feedback delivered in terms of too little and too much will make it instantly clear what you need to do to improve. "I'm overdoing X. I need to tone it down." "I'm doing too little of Y. I need to turn up the dial."

4. Note the silver lining in excess. True, it looks terrible when 10 of 15 coworkers rate someone like Ella Solo as doing too much on "Takes charge." But buried in her attention-grabbing excess is a strength, a capability that hardly every leader possesses. Extreme behavior, especially when it is off-putting or frustrating, distracts us from recognizing the underlying strength.

5. Get a hand with your assessment report—from your supervisor, an HR professional, or a development specialist. A skillful person willing to put in the time can (a) bring an otherwise blurry picture into focus; (b) help you put the worrisome parts in perspective, that is, neither take them too lightly nor blow them out of proportion; (c) generally bring to life the written material otherwise sitting lifeless on the page; and (d) energize the improvement effort.

continued

continued

Questions for Reflection

1. Are you aware of the ways that people see you as going overboard?

2. When a staff member turns you off, do you consider the possibility that the behavior is actually a derivative of one of the person's strengths, for example, being a stickler for detail.

3. Have you found a way to hold a mirror up to your staff members' excesses? It can be as simple as asking their coworkers: "What would you like this person to do less of?"

4. Do you give your staff members a hand with their 360-survey feedback? Don't equate feedback with development.

Chapter Three

Know Your Own Strength

"Great talents are a rarity, and it is rare that such people recognize themselves for what they are."

—*Goethe*

In the last few years, a strengths movement has sprung up. The argument goes something like this: There's been entirely too much emphasis placed in our performance-driven culture on what's wrong with a leader's skill-set, not enough on what is right about it. So let's put much more focus on taking account of a leader's strengths and making the most of them.[1]

Valid as far as it goes, the argument overlooks the fact that strengths can be taken to an extreme. It comes as no surprise then that the tool used by a chief advocate of this movement only identifies strengths and gives no indication of whether you use any of those strengths to excess.[2]

Another thing that the strengths movement as well as much of the rest of the world has missed is that many leaders underestimate their strengths. Not appreciating how strong they are has a profound effect on their behavior, as we shall see in Ella Solo's case.

Ella Solo Revisited: Effects of Underestimating One's Strengths

It emerged in my discussions with Ella that her weaknesses were much more prominent in her mind than her strengths. She already knew she was self-critical, but she didn't see the impact it had on the way she led or how it would hold the key to improved performance. Her self-ratings on the Leadership Versatility Index were revealing. Although they went in the same direction as other people's ratings— she generally knew what the problem areas were—her self-ratings were more extreme, sometimes much more extreme. On several items shown in Figures 3.1 and 3.2, she gave herself a +3 or –3, scores not often selected by raters, and on some items not included in this excerpt from her full LVI report, she even gave herself a +4 or –4.

The pattern was the same on the ratings of effectiveness. She and her coworkers were asked to rate her overall effectiveness on a 10-point scale where 10 is "outstanding" and 5 is "adequate." On average her coworkers rated her 7.5, just about average for our firm's population of senior leaders. She, on the other hand, gave herself a lowly 4, definitely a failing grade and several standard deviations below the average. I've learned that any time managers rate themselves a point lower than coworkers on our 10-point scale of overall effectiveness, it usually means they are selling themselves short, and when the gap is 2 points or more it's a dead giveaway. The 3.5 point difference in Ella's overall self-assessment is a huge discrepancy and it betrayed something fundamental about the way she saw herself and her leadership.[3]

Whereas she readily accepted the LVI feedback on her behavior, Ella did not immediately see the significance of her severe underestimates. "Yeah, I know I have very high expectations of myself," she said. So it didn't surprise her that her self-rating was low, and lower than others' ratings of her. In that sense the gap taught her nothing. It took a second conversation for it to dawn on her: "It's true, I place more emotional weight on my weaknesses than on my strengths." She began to see that the unequal distribution of emotional weight put enormous pressure on her and made her overanxious to perform. That was why she intruded on her subordinates and did their work for them. That was why she took an otherwise admirable focus on results too far. That was why she "over-revved," as she put it.

To help her discover for herself the connection between her underrating and her behavior, I asked her a series of as-if questions, beginning with: "Let's say a manager seriously underestimated herself. What effect would that have on her?" She answered:

"The person would work harder."

"She would be much more demanding of herself."

"It would be easy for her to take the blame. In her mind: 'I could have done that better.'"

"She couldn't do enough."

"And she would be action-oriented, say put in twenty hours a day."

All these things were true of her! One step removed, she had understood the ramifications of downgrading herself.

The maps of her positives and negatives, shown in Figures 2.4 and 2.5 in the previous chapter, were two sides of the same coin glued together by her emotional makeup, by this stance toward her positives and negatives.

Not knowing their own strengths, then, leaders can react by doing what? Overdoing it. But that is not the only distorting effect.

The Distorting Effects of Not Knowing Your Own Strength

What attribute do you think managers most often underestimate in themselves?

When I ask a group of managers this question, they come up with perfectly good answers—power, people skills, strategic ability, presentation skills, and so on. Rarely does anyone suggest intellectual ability, which more than any other capability is, in my consulting experience, the one that bright senior managers fail to see in themselves. One such individual, whose trademark in his company was intellectual leadership, told me, "I always had the feeling that people around me were brighter and I was fortunate to be fairly bright."

Figure 3.1. Ella Solo's Average Ratings on Forceful and Enabling Leadership

Forceful and Enabling — Average Ratings

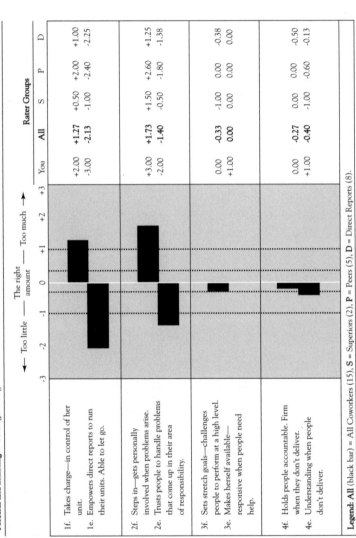

		Rater Groups			
	You	All	S	P	D
1f. Takes charge—in control of her unit.	+2.00	**+1.27**	+0.50	+2.00	+1.00
1e. Empowers direct reports to run their units. Able to let go.	-3.00	**-2.13**	-1.00	-2.40	-2.25
2f. Steps in—gets personally involved when problems arise.	+3.00	**+1.73**	+1.50	+2.60	+1.25
2e. Trusts people to handle problems that come up in their area of responsibility.	-2.00	**-1.40**	-0.50	-1.80	-1.38
3f. Sets stretch goals—challenges people to perform at a high level.	0.00	**-0.33**	-1.00	0.00	-0.38
3e. Makes herself available—responsive when people need help.	+1.00	**0.00**	0.00	0.00	0.00
4f. Holds people accountable. Firm when they don't deliver.	0.00	**-0.27**	0.00	0.00	-0.50
4e. Understanding when people don't deliver.	+1.00	**-0.40**	-1.00	-0.60	-0.13

Legend: All (black bar) = All Coworkers (15), **S** = Superiors (2), **P** = Peers (5), **D** = Direct Reports (8).

Note: Our norms and statistical research suggest that scores between −.33 and +.33 indicate a strength. Scores between −.33 and −1.00 (or +.33 and +1.00) indicate a likely performance problem and scores below −1.00 and over +1.00 are areas that cause signivicant problems. These guidelines are indicated in the middle of the report.

Figure 3.2. Ella Solo's Average Ratings on Strategic and Operational Leadership

Strategic and Operational — Average Ratings

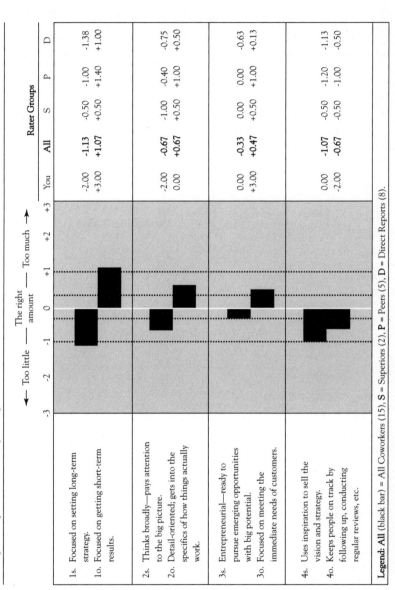

| | Rater Groups | | | | | |
	You	All	S	P	D
1s. Focused on setting long-term strategy.	-2.00	**-1.13**	-0.50	-1.00	-1.38
1o. Focused on getting short-term results.	+3.00	**+1.07**	+0.50	+1.40	+1.00
2s. Thinks broadly—pays attention to the big picture.	-2.00	**-0.67**	-1.00	-0.40	-0.75
2o. Detail-oriented; gets into the specifics of how things actually work.	0.00	**+0.67**	+0.50	+1.00	+0.50
3s. Entrepreneurial—ready to pursue emerging opportunities with big potential.	0.00	**-0.33**	0.00	0.00	-0.63
3o. Focused on meeting the immediate needs of customers.	+3.00	**+0.47**	+0.50	+1.00	+0.13
4s. Uses inspiration to sell the vision and strategy.	0.00	**-1.07**	-0.50	-1.20	-1.13
4o. Keeps people on track by following up, conducting regular reviews, etc.	-2.00	**-0.67**	-0.50	-1.00	-0.50

← Too little — The right amount — Too much →

-3 -2 -1 0 +1 +2 +3

Legend: All (black bar) = All Coworkers (15), **S** = Superiors (2), **P** = Peers (5), **D** = Direct Reports (8).

When leaders underestimate how smart they are, what effect do you think that has on their behavior?

You might suppose that they try too hard or strain to show how smart they are. Or you might say that they avoid activities with high intellectual content like computer systems or strategy. In either case you would be right because both effects occur (see Figure 3.3).

Whether you underestimate your overall ability or a specific ability like smarts or detail orientation or treating people well, the impact on your behavior can go either way. It can cause you to overcompensate for the perceived shortfall, or it can cause you to shy away from the thing you think you're not that good at.[4]

> "I don't think we managers truly understand that our strengths affect our weaknesses. They go hand in hand but sometimes we treat them as separate silos."

Figure 3.3. Possible Effects of Underestimating Your Intellectual Ability

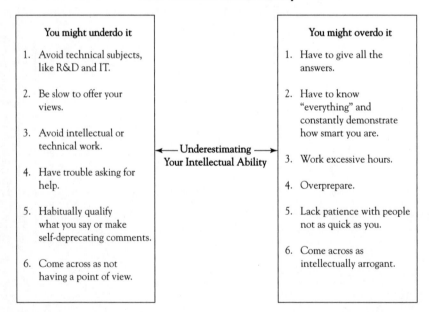

You might underdo it

1. Avoid technical subjects, like R&D and IT.

2. Be slow to offer your views.

3. Avoid intellectual or technical work.

4. Have trouble asking for help.

5. Habitually qualify what you say or make self-deprecating comments.

6. Come across as not having a point of view.

◄—— Underestimating ——► Your Intellectual Ability

You might overdo it

1. Have to give all the answers.

2. Have to know "everything" and constantly demonstrate how smart you are.

3. Work excessive hours.

4. Overprepare.

5. Lack patience with people not as quick as you.

6. Come across as intellectually arrogant.

An up-and-coming middle manager took one look at his data—both his excesses and his blatant tendency to underrate himself—and exclaimed, "Underestimate—overdo!"

Equally, however, underestimate—underdo.

Note that *overestimating* yourself also creates problems, potentially deadly problems. Over-raters

> An astute senior manager said this about the CEO: "If he internalized his strengths, a lot of his weaknesses would go away. It's because he doesn't accept his strengths that these weaknesses exist."

tend to be the weakest performers, have an inflated sense of themselves, and are most likely to derail.[5]

Underestimate—Overdo

Not appreciating that they are already strong in a certain area—not knowing their own strength, as it were—leaders frequently overuse that quality or over-invest in what is already a strong suit. This is how strengths come to be overused. This is the reason behind the frequently uttered truism, "Strengths taken to an extreme become weaknesses."

The reader might object: "Isn't it true that managers who underrate themselves are more effective than their counterparts who overrate themselves?" Yes, out of a need to make up for a perceived deficit, the under-raters, anything but complacent, work harder. But by misgauging their ability, these under-raters also distort their leadership. They may be more effective than over-raters, but that doesn't mean they are as effective as they could be. Be careful not to glorify underestimating yourself or confuse it with modesty of a healthy sort.

Take the case of Steve Sharp. The people he worked with very much admired his intellectual ability, but his own estimate of it was substantially lower, and the discrepancy mattered.

Asked, "What are Steve's major strengths as a leader?," twelve of the sixteen people interviewed mentioned this gift of his. Many people used superlatives.

The CEO said: "He's highly intelligent. Very, very bright. I'm sure he has a very high IQ. I think he is a very bright light bulb."

Three peers remarked: "He is clearly very, very smart." "First of all, he's brilliant." "I think his greatest strength is his intelligence."

Three direct reports each had the same high opinion of his brainpower: "I think he is very intelligent. Extremely intelligent." "I'd say his major strength is his intelligence." "I would say his greatest strengths are that he is very bright and quick on his feet."

When he was interviewed, Steve himself had cited "above-average intellect" as one of his strengths. But when he heard the feedback he resisted the view that he was gifted. "I am surprised at the comments about brilliance and about being very, very smart. I rank myself as [only] above average." At the office he actually carried on a running debate with his close colleagues about how smart he was. He honestly didn't see what they saw in him. "I don't think of myself as that smart. It's a core belief. I do have a good-enough understanding most of the time, but that's not brilliance. It's personality and tricks."

Ironically, his failure to fully recognize his intellectual assets turned into a liability. He had a bad habit in his staff meetings of losing patience with a presenter or with someone having an exchange with him. He was given to saying, "I'm not that smart and I get it right away. What's wrong with you?" This was a prime example of what people called his abrasiveness.[6]

Underestimate—Underdo

The flip side: leaders underdo the thing they underestimate. They avoid what they think they're not good at.

A direct consequence of feeling inadequate intellectually, for example, is that the manager avoids functions that require intellectual ability (thereby hurting his or her chances of ever getting good at those things), for example, technical functions like information technology or R&D or even finance. Underestimate—underdo.

Several times I've run across the following pattern. Growing up, the younger brother or sister of, as one manager put it, "an obnoxiously overachieving older sibling," evidently despairing of ever winning in that arena, doesn't try hard at school. The result of course is that his or her grades suffer. And what do children who adapt that way conclude? That their lackluster performance is evidence of not being smart! Even more striking is how long this twisted thinking persists. I have known top executives who, thirty or forty years later, still carry around the painful idea that they are not smart, while overlooking completely the circumstances under which that idea took hold and failing to recognize how successful and capable and, frankly, intellectually adept they now are.

Ella Solo Continued: How She Addressed the Distortion in Her Self-Concept

Attempting to help Ella see the distorted lens through which she viewed her leadership profile, I continued the as-if exercise by asking her, "What's the mind-set of a person like that [someone who underestimated himself]?" Brilliantly, she instantly came up with a striking analogy.

"Almost like an anorexic person looking in the mirror saying, 'I put weight on.' Because she doesn't see herself as skinny."

I then thought to ask her, "How would you help this person?"

"Help her realize how valuable she is and how much she's contributing and help her get a better picture of herself and the value she brings."

Intuitively, Ella knew that such a person needed to take in what he or she is good at, what good he or she did.

Closing, I had her apply her one-step-removed reasoning directly to herself. "What's the take-away for you?"

"Be easier on myself. Focus more on the parts of the glass that are half-full. Don't put so much weight on the glass half-empty."

And then, true to form, she added, "But I need to do more about the half-empty part."

The veil lifted. And Ella immediately saw how she could ease into a new mode of leading. "This process has helped me because I now appreciate my strengths better and that's helped me to move away from the fray more and pick my battles better." As soon as she reduced the internal pressure that drove her to be too involved in her people's work, she found it natural to back off. When I asked her three months and twelve months later, she reported that the realization had held up. The mental shift ran deep.[7] Several months later I had occasion to meet her spouse, who told me, "She's happier."

Obstacles to Overcome in Knowing Your Strengths—Resistance to Positive Feedback

Many leaders don't know their own strengths. You might use this four-step process to determine whether you are underestimating yourself in any respect:[8]

1. Begin by making a list of your strengths. Base the list on a recent 360-degree survey or find some other way to see your strengths as others see them. The more the merrier; there is no need to be brief.

2. Be sure to put texture on each item on the list. Don't just put down one-word answers like "Integrity." If it's "Extremely high integrity," say so. If it's "Exceptionally bright," write it down that way. It's important that the degree to which other people credit you with a strength comes through.

3. Go down the list item by item and put a star next to any that you don't see in yourself or that you don't see to that degree.

4. For each of those that you beg to differ on, look into why. In each case, write down your reasons. Be on the lookout for suspect reasoning like, "I'm not that bright, but I'm bright enough to know I'm not that bright."

You might think that hard evidence would persuade leaders that their estimates of their strengths are pegged too low. But frequently the data does not do the trick. So whether it is you or someone you work with, be prepared: there are many slips between the cup (of positive feedback) and the lip. First, leaders can be categorically dismissive of positive feedback. Second, they have just as hard a time facing up to their assets as to their liabilities. Third, each has reasons for finding praise threatening.

One of the best ways to change a person's mind about his or her strengths is to administer a heavy dose of positive feedback. My colleagues and I go about this by first gathering plenty of material about the person's strengths. Second, to concentrate the dose of positives, we pull a list of categories out of the data and then move every comment and every rating into the category where it belongs. So rather than have the many mentions of something like visionary ability scattered across the several sections of the assessment report, all of the verbatims on that appear under one heading. In so doing we boost the power of the positives and stand a much better chance of getting through to an individual about a strength that he or she underestimates. (We do the same thing with the negatives.)

To see, however, is not necessarily to believe. For managers to capitalize on their strengths, they first need to internalize them, a not inconsiderable task. I often encounter a confusion when I bring up the importance of internalizing strengths. The immediate response I often hear from the other party, eager to show that he or she understands what I mean, is: "Right, capitalize on strengths." No, I say, this is different. This is the step prior to capitalizing: seeing them as strengths in the first place.

The Gravitational Pull of the Negatives

Leaders typically think the real value of feedback resides in the negatives. The very idea that positive feedback offers great leverage for development runs smack into this cultural headwind.

When presented with the choice of pleasure or pain—pleasure in the form of good news about their leadership, pain in the form of bad news about it—which would you imagine that managers select? Despite what Freud said about the pleasure principle, they reach for the hairshirt. I've seen this so often in feedback sessions that I am beginning to believe I can predict human behavior!

> A manager said about reading his assessment report: "Part of me didn't listen to the positives because I thought they were just a setup for what was coming next so you wouldn't go to the bathroom and slit your throat!"

- A young up-and-coming executive and I are going over the many highly favorable comments about his leadership, but he doesn't seem fully engaged. I ask him if he is distracted. "I'll be more energized by the weaknesses because I'm anxious to improve," he explains. And when we do turn to the section on his weaknesses, he perks up. "This is where the gold is!," he exclaims.

- The moment a senior manager finishes reading the section on strengths, he turns the page to the section on weaknesses. Wise to this impulse in managers, I tease him about rushing off from the positive feedback. He protests his innocence by claiming he *was* truly interested in the positive feedback. His wife, a full participant in the session, genially countered, "Then why did you underline the heading to the weaknesses section and not the heading to the strengths section?"

Many a leader will brush past the positives as if they're not worth their time. They champ at the bit

> A veteran manager counseled: "An important message for managers is to learn how to coach their own people on strengths, not just weaknesses."

to get to the section on negatives. It is the managerial attitude: let's fix the problems. Furthermore, it is not just leaders who succumb to the gravitational pull of negative feedback. Experts in leadership development are also susceptible. I too used to regard positive feedback as something to fortify managers to deal with the negatives, not anything that required real work on their part. Believing that the leverage, my leverage, lay entirely in what was wrong with their leadership, I was initially left at a loss any time a manager I was working with received a highly favorable report. Like many consultants, I assumed that without plenty of negative feedback I was virtually helpless.

If you take your car to a mechanic, you're not that interested in learning that all the pistons still move, the radiator holds water, the fan belt remains taut. You want to know what repairs the car needs. "The brake pads need to be replaced." "The front end is out of alignment." The same is true of a physical exam. Sure, we like finding out that our knees are intact, that our pancreas is working just fine, but it's the bad news that gets our attention, that has the emotional impact, that requires us to act. "Your cholesterol is too high and you'll have to change your diet" or "You've got polyps in your colon that will have to be removed."

Leaders know that there's leverage in negative feedback. That's why they gravitate toward it. What they don't realize is that there is just as much leverage in positive feedback. That's why leaders and those responsible for helping them improve have to bring a balanced perspective to the value added by the positives and the negatives.

Looking a Gift Horse in the Mouth: "I Know Better"

You might imagine that leaders, upon being informed that they are better than they think they are, would drink thirstily from that vessel. But, no, it's not as simple as that. Actually, the resistance to positive feedback shouldn't be surprising. Think about how many of us have trouble accepting a compliment. We deflect it or give the impression that we accept it graciously while privately discounting it—anything but truly internalize it. Beyond being made uncomfortable by praise, some managers actively distrust it, believing that you grow with criticism and that praise makes you lazy.[9]

Presented with the data on their strengths, managers can be just as defensive about it as they can be about criticism. "I can't focus on this," one said to me, "because the business is in trouble and that's what I've got to focus on." Another manager told me that the reason he couldn't take in the affirmation was "I'm in too much pain because my boss is down on me." Never mind that the appreciation for his strengths might have been just the tonic that his bruised ego needed. In explaining away praise, managers can be quite ingenious. One manager dismissed several global compliments about his capability by invoking the statistical tendency for extreme scores to regress to the mean: "People at the extremes in how they view me will converge toward the middle of the range."

Steve Sharp actually put up a fight when I suggested that his colleagues might be right about his level of intellectual ability. "I don't want to adjust my view of my intelligence. I think that would be bad. The reason why is I think I play in an area with truly brilliant people, and if I viewed myself as equivalent, I might think I don't have to work as hard. I might relax."

He had taken this view on purpose: "Throughout my life a tool I've used is the idea that I'm handicapped. I always consider myself as at the lower end of the group I'm working with."

Steve's experience as a child gave him multiple reasons to feel one-down. He was young for his grade in school. He got average grades until high school. ("I think I may have been traumatized in school because I wasn't a good student," he remarked to me.) And his family moved a lot.

A great debater, he clinched the argument with me by saying, "Why wouldn't I devalue what I have and value more what I don't have?!," as if that is the only way to look at it.

Leaders with Steve Sharp's outlook actually believe in feeling inadequate. They depend on it to spur them on, and it has the side effect of closing them off to positive regard.

For years I had taken it for granted that managers took to the favorable comments like a duck to water, and so I made relatively short work of the report's strengths section. I've since learned to check out the individual's reaction to the data on strengths. "Do you buy what people are saying?" Often I find at least one strength about which the individual begs to differ.

Personal Reasons Why Leaders Find Praise Threatening

When leaders resist the data that clearly supports a more favorable view of them than they hold, there is always a reason. In probing, I've been surprised at what I've found. A fear of complacency. An assumption that self-confidence equates to arrogance. Praise experienced as a burden. Such are the beliefs and emotional reactions that must be overcome if managers are to embrace corrective positive feedback.

Fear of Complacency. Rich Bauer, featured in an earlier book of mine[10], had trouble giving praise, and he was equally uncomfortable receiving it. The reservoir of praise in him was so thoroughly stopped up that when he set himself the goal of complimenting his people he failed utterly.

He was leery of positive reinforcement because he was afraid that it would make people, himself included, complacent. He worried they would lose their edge.

Unable to praise people to their faces, he resorted to writing them notes.

Fear of Arrogance. Mark Modesto's assessment report clearly showed that he underrated himself. On our 10-point scale of effectiveness, his coworkers rated him a 8.25, yet he gave himself a 7, more than a full point lower. On a 98-item 360-degree survey, he rated himself as definitely needing improvement on fourteen items that everyone else marked as a clear strength.

After calling the under-ratings to his attention, I said: "Imagine you bathed yourself in the high praise, really internalized it."

"See, I have trouble doing that."

His response took me aback. "Why?" I asked.

"People would view me as egotistical. I don't like people who are like that."

Mark resisted taking in the evidence of his strengths for fear that he would get a swelled head. The problem was that he equated confidence with arrogance.

"Have you known this was an issue, that you don't recognize your strengths?," I asked.

"No." Then he warmed to the idea of a stronger sense of his strengths. "If I do this, will these weaknesses go away?"

"Money-back guaranteed!"

Fear of Having to Keep Up Superior Performance. The higher the praise, the higher the implied expectation. A new CEO held an off-site meeting with the two individuals who had been peers, who had also competed for the job, and who would now report to him. After a series of discussions about business issues and personal values, they told him, in what was a sacred moment, that they were ready to sign up for his team. The CEO said nothing and the conversation moved on.

When I asked him privately how he had felt at that moment, he said, "It felt great; fantastic. But I immediately felt the pressure of their expectations."

His parents burdened him as a child with their grandiose aspirations ("You can be president of the United States"). Now as an adult he had, as he put it, a "terror" of meeting expectations.

Another executive experienced positive reinforcement as pressure to raise the level still higher. Projecting how he would react to the data on his strengths, he said, doing back-flips in his head: "With mixed feelings. You want it but you get it and say, 'They're exaggerating,' and 'They don't really mean it,' and, 'Uh-oh, now I have to do better than that, if they're mentioning it. Now it's out in the open and not in some secret Swiss bank account.' So with praise it's like, 'Wow, the only way I will get praise from here on is to do even better.'"

For leaders like this, positive feedback is a double-edged sword. They interpret affirmation not so much as a reward but as a punitive expectation to continue performing at an exceedingly high level. For them praise is unwelcome pressure.

Thus, the surface onto which positive feedback is poured is not necessarily porous. And to open your pores you may have to contend with anxiety-tinged beliefs that keep your strengths from sinking in.

Developing Yourself, Coaching Others

Highlights

1. It is your strengths that will make you great. Start by knowing clearly what they are, all modesty aside. And don't worry that staring straight at them in the mirror will make you lazy, weak, or arrogant. Truly appreciating your strengths for what they are—no more, and no less—builds not a big ego but a strong ego,.

2. Be on the lookout for an upside-down version of the emperor's new clothes. You may think you're "naked" while the crowd sees you as fully, indeed beautifully clothed.

3. Don't bark up the wrong tree. Attacking your weaknesses head-on may never fix them if what's caused them is that you have underestimated your strengths.

4. Just because a person's stand-out strength is obvious to you and to everyone else doesn't mean that he or she recognizes it. Therein lies a golden opportunity for growth, one that many leaders, as well as leadership-development specialists, routinely overlook.

5. Praise given is not necessarily praise received. It can be just as hard for managers to get good news through their thick skulls as bad news, and sometimes harder. It takes effort and ingenuity and patience on the supervisor's or coach's part to reach the individual on his or her good points.

Questions for Reflection

1. Do you really know your strengths? What are they? Have you made the connection between your strengths and your weaknesses?

2. Do you underestimate any of your strengths? Do other people think more highly of any of your attributes, such as intellectual ability or the ability to take charge, than you do?

3. Have you ever gotten a heavy dose of the positives that other people see in your leadership? If not, you might have your staff "bombard" you with the things about your leadership they appreciate. (They can also suggest areas for improvement, but later.)

4. Do you coach your people on their strengths, not just on their deficiencies?

5. When you deliver positive feedback, do you check out how the other person received it? Rather than assume that he or she takes it at face value, ask questions such as:

   • "What's your reaction to the list?"

   • "Any surprises?"

   • "Any of these you disagree with?

   • "Do you feel good about what's on the list?"

6. Do you understand that taking in their strengths is just as useful for the development of leaders as facing up to their weaknesses? If not, re-read this chapter!

Chapter Four

The Impact of Mind-Set

Learning the Inner Game of Leadership

"What is life but the angle of vision? A man is
measured by the angle at which he looks at
objects."

—*Ralph Waldo Emerson*

Leaders have form just like athletes do. They may not swing a bat, drive a golf ball, or go to the basket with the other hand. Yet, as with athletes, sometimes their form is good and sometimes it is not. And when their form is off, so is their performance. When Shaquille O'Neal steps to the free-throw line, along with other basketball fans, I can tell whether he is likely to make the shot from the way he releases the ball. In any skilled activity, form is integral to performance. It's the form in per*form*ance!

The word form originally meant beauty. In and of itself, good form is beautiful to behold and, for anyone with a practiced eye, it also holds appeal because it is likely to lead to a good result. Poor form hurts the eye because it's contorted and awkward; even before we see the outcome, we fear it won't be good.

When a player's form is off, the question naturally arises: What throws it off? Why is the star shortstop in a prolonged hitting slump? Why is the pitcher having control problems? Why did Tiger Woods go through a stretch where he had trouble keeping his drives on the fairway? Likewise, why does a newly appointed CEO give short shrift to strategy? Why do a supervisor's direct reports not take his requests seriously? Why does a functional head have generally good relationships with the people on her team but strained relationships with her peers?

Among professional athletes, it is pretty well established that a player's psychology matters, not just skills. The book, *The Mental Game of Baseball*,[1] written for players and their coaches, takes it as axiomatic that in the major leagues what distinguishes the best players from the merely average is not skills. Everyone at that level has exceptional physical ability. It's the inner game, the ability to concentrate intently but not too intensely on hitting a pitch or fielding a ground ball, to take in stride the inevitable mistakes and setbacks and not go into an emotional tailspin when you strike out or make a bad throw—in general, to handle the pressure to perform. *The Mental Game of Baseball* is chockfull of stories of players who broke through to a higher level of play by learning to manage themselves better.

Leaders who follow sports, whether it's football or figure skating, baseball or gymnastics, skiing or tennis, men's college basketball or women's soccer, are used to hearing about how the athlete's psychology comes into play. They have no trouble seeing how the mental game makes a difference in sports. Yet somehow they don't as easily take that perspective in their own line of work.

> A development-savvy senior manager who read an early draft of this book surprised me by saying, "The chapter on the impact of mind-set I thought was good. I never thought of that."

But apply it does. Leaders wanting to raise their level of play must factor in what inside their heads influences their play. Certainly they need to pay attention to their behavior but not to the exclusion of what thoughts and feelings drive their behavior. Who you are is how you lead. What shows up on the outside is a reflection of what is inside. So in taking stock of your game, it's only practical to look inside too. Why leave leverage on the table?[2]

> Who you are is how you lead.

The Roots of Deficiency and Excess

The beauty of defining "off form" as doing too little or too much—and assessing managerial performance in these terms—is that it ever so naturally raises the question of what throws it off. That simple question is a door to the manager's inner life and usually a nudge is all it takes for the door to swing open. It is only natural to ask a manager who slights part of her job, "So what keeps you from doing more of that?" Working with someone who chronically overplays his hand, it is not the least bit jarring to him to say, "Do you know what drives that?" In helping managers factor in their internal drivers, it's helpful to have other clues about an individual's make-up, from a battery of personality tests, for example. But, rather than in any way pigeonholing individuals or imposing a psychological theory on them, I find that the best way for managers to understand their psychology is for them to discover it for themselves.

> ". . . you always have to look on the inner and outer sphere as being parallel or, rather, as being interwoven."
> —Goethe, *Maxims and Reflections*, p. 33

When leaders peel the top layer off their behavior, what do they find? Over and over they come face-to-face with crooked thinking or a trigger point, which, acting alone or in concert, are in many cases the hidden agents of off-kilter managerial form (see Figure 4.1). A manager had an action orientation that drove her from pillar to post. What prompted her? "To me inaction is bad," she said.

Crooked Thinking

Never assume that smart, rational leaders are completely free of off-base notions about their work. Scratch the surface of a deficiency or excess, either in yourself or another person, and you are almost sure to find a distorted belief about leading.

Figure 4.1. Two Factors That Throw Off Leader Performance

Crooked Thinking
Off-base operating assumptions, misplaced values, a faulty gauge
Trigger Points
Sensitivities, unwarranted fears

Leaders can be deficient in an area just because they haven't needed to learn it.[3] They might still be learning the ropes after a jump in responsibility. One newly minted executive, catching on, remarked, "Oh, I didn't realize that my job is no longer so much making decisions as it is managing the process by which decisions get made."

"A mistaken idea is all very well as long as you are young; but it's no good dragging it on into middle age."
—Goethe, *Maxims and Reflections*, p. 12

It also happens that a leadership function, even an obvious one, just may not have made it onto a leader's mental map. Despite being quick on the uptake, one senior manager in his early forties came to this revelation: "I've always believed that being effective means knowing things and getting things done." It's not that he had no idea that he needed to work with other people. It's that the interpersonal part of his job didn't figure prominently in his mental model, and, guess what, relationships were his weak suit.

Often I find that, when a leader's form is contorted, the reason is that earlier in life the individual adopted a belief that that no longer applies. One manager learned in his assessment report that day to day he wasn't engaged enough with his staff. They reported he didn't spend enough time with them, didn't take enough of an interest in what they were doing, didn't understand their work in enough detail, didn't get involved enough when they needed him. All along he had believed he was doing the right thing by giving his staff plenty of autonomy, but to his surprise they felt neglected. What prompted him? He had related to his staff exactly as he preferred to have his own superior relate to him, and it never occurred to him that they might want something different from him. This is a common mistake, to carry over an assumption derived from past experience and to assume unthinkingly that what works for you works for everyone else.[4]

> A newly promoted middle manager had this insight: "I used to think that doing great work was enough. The hardest thing I had to learn is to give it away. You have to have great people and be able to walk away from it."

Place low importance on a leadership function and you're bound to underdo it. Likewise, place inordinately high importance on it and you're liable to go overboard. One individual made a fetish of preparation. A colleague said, "His idea of being ready is to overprepare. He feels like he has to answer every question, think of every angle, and he doesn't." Thoroughness is a virtue, but this individual took it to an extreme. The culprit was a faulty standard of performance, an unrealistically high expectation, a perfectionist belief that your work will be scrutinized very closely or judged harshly.[5]

A manager decided to teach himself the piano, and after a year of practicing regularly he sent a tape of his playing to two professional pianists he knew. Their response, he told me, was: "Great, but you're playing three times faster than you ought to be playing." He realized, "I was looking for an affirmation that fast was good, and it wasn't."

I asked him, "Why did you believe playing fast was a virtue?"

"It was the idea that I ought to play as fast I can and be able to hit all the notes. You somehow think if you're doing something faster that you are doing it better."

"So you made a virtue out of fast and took it to an extreme."

"Yes. I've tried playing slower and I like it better. I play better and enjoy it more."

Stemming from inexperience as much as anything, the naïve belief in the virtue of speed yielded easily to expert guidance. Its roots were shallow and therefore easy to pull up. Other times the root mass of distorted thinking wraps itself around the individual's core sense of self and so it's no easy matter to remove it.

Probe a strength overused and you often find the assumption that more is better. A manager who believed fervently in hard work did a poor job of setting limits on the hours she worked. An individual with an intense drive for results believed in giving completely unrestrained expression to it. A friend who discovered running in his forties made a point of doing four or five miles every day, ignoring the advice of his daughter, who was on the cross-country team, that it is a mistake to run every day. It took a painfully sore knee, which sidelined him for several months, to get my friend to moderate his demanding regimen. It is tempting to maximize whatever we deem well worth doing.

> "As in a building, if the original rule is warped, if the square is faulty and deviates from straight lines, if the level is a trifle wrong in any part, the whole house will necessarily be made in a faulty fashion and be falling over, warped, sloping, leaning forward, leaning back, all out of proportion."
>
> —Lucretius

In one variation of crooked thinking, the leader's gauge is off, leading the individual to believe that the volume is higher or lower than it actually is. One manager was puzzled as to why staff members didn't respond to his requests in a timely manner. I suggested we do a role play. He would make a request of me, taking the part of a direct report. He spoke softly and without any edge to his voice. So I asked him to try again, with feeling. This time he spoke slightly louder. I asked him to turn up the dial even higher. In an aside to me, he said, "This is hard," and then managed to raise his voice and speak with authority. "What were the settings on the dial?" I asked him. "Three, five, eight," he said. "My reading," I said, "is two, three, five." He had exhibited much less vocal power than he thought because his gauge was giving him false readings. For him to do a better job of giving direction he had to recalibrate his gauge or at least take into account that it was off. Evidently, he was so concerned not to be overly aggressive that he overestimated how much he was asserting himself.[6]

The same sort of calibration problem can result in overdoing it. Several executives I've worked with overpower other people but are oblivious to it. They have big voices, they talk a lot, they're intense. Having a conversation with them is "like drinking from a fire hose," as one bowled-over coworker put it. The playing field so easily tips in their favor that the other party struggles to have a voice. But, remarkably, they typically don't know their own power, sometimes due to a faulty gauge. It's like getting caught for speeding only to find that your car's speedometer reads 15 mph slower than the car is going. (Or if you are under-powered, your speedometer gives you a false reading in the other direction, which explains why other cars are always passing you.)

When your form is off, this particular type of crooked thinking may be responsible.

Trigger Points

Scratch the surface of off-kilter behavior and you may find a hot button, a sensitivity that triggers either overkill or avoidance.[7] It's a fight-or-flight response, a reflex reaction. A middle manager acts much too quickly. Why does she rush to closure, truncating the discussion? It's not just her standing belief that inaction is bad. In the moment a fear kicks in, an unconscious fear that she won't earn her keep and she'll be fired.

A functional head, although respected for his technical ability, discovered that the business heads were critical of him for not keeping them informed and for, stylistically, being "underwhelming." A sensitivity was at work. "I find it distasteful when people put themselves forward." And if he were to advocate for his function, an anti-boastful voice in his head would object: "Don't talk about yourself all the time. You're not the only one in the room. You didn't do all this by yourself anyway. What about the other people? That's great for you, but don't think that what's good for you is right for everybody. Don't make other people feel small by making yourself big."

In heeding this fearful voice, he hobbled himself.

He came by the compunction honestly. "I realize that this is one of the ethics I grew up with," he said. "My family had a strong negative reaction to boastfulness." He was afraid of becoming the egotistical personality that his parents had disapproved of in others.

This story is typical of leaders who err on the side of doing too little of an important part of their jobs. Out of a fear of "putting themselves too far forward," they

> A manager said about her golf game: "If I worry about the water, I hit it in the water."

unwittingly hold themselves back. Worried about going too far, they come up short. To the world, they are limited, under-equipped, even handicapped. In their own minds, they are exercising admirable self-restraint.

A trigger point can throw off behavior in the other direction too. Afraid of not going far enough, leaders end up going overboard. The world sees them as constantly pushing the limits; they see themselves as making sure they are doing enough. In either direction, fear is a vector that bends the trajectory of the leader's behavior.

In combination, a wrong thought and a needless fear often conspire to throw leaders off. A senior manager possessed a lovely ability to connect personally with people, yet he hardly ever walked the halls. What held him back? His HR manager suggested to him: "I think it's that you don't know what will come up."

He agreed: "I might not remember a name. Or I might not know what the person is working on and so he or she would feel: 'He doesn't know the freaking project I'm working on!'"

"So you think people expect you to know everything?" I asked.

"Yes. Otherwise I'd leave the person deflated. I say to myself, I should know because that is how I would want to be treated."

"How would it reflect on you?"

"Negatively. I'd come across as aloof, unaware, out of touch."

"How bad would this be?"

"Unacceptable to me. Not okay. I would avoid the negative part."

At one level, a faulty operating assumption kept him from circulating. Obviously, he didn't need to know everyone's names or what each of them was working on. At a deeper level, it was fear of rejection. In this instance, he was covertly governed by an anxiety-tinged belief that he only now unpacked.

Fear warns us off. As one manager said of another, "Like many of us, he will spend more time with things he's good at and comfortable with and ignore those things he isn't." It's a normal human tendency to avoid what you are afraid of, but you're better off knowing the fear so you stand a chance of managing it. It's the flight reflex. Of course, fear can also excite the fight reflex.

When leaders are lopsided, fight and flight act in unison—fight on the side you overdo, flight on the side you underdo.

What's Behind Lopsidedness? Why Too Much of One Thing and Too Little of the Opposite?

A manager had virtually dissociated himself from the frank exercise of power, and that also showed up on the tennis court. "I play more of a reactive game, a waiting game. Do I go for the kill often enough or early enough? No." His style of play, on the court and in the office, stressed defense and slighted offense. And though he seemed to recognize the warp in his play, at heart he believed in it and justified it as the exercise of careful, thoughtful choice. "I pick my spots. Every shot is designed to set up the next. I'm thinking all the time." Because of the great premium he placed on thinking and on tapping into others' thinking, he did not fully recognize what he was trading off. Nor did he see how much that tradeoff frustrated the heck out of his staff, one of whom said, "I just philosophically believe that leaders lead and don't seek consensus on everything. We avoid issues that are critical to the company because he is struggling to please a lot of audiences.

In sports and at work this leader's game is lopsided. What's behind his lopsided play? A one-sided mind-set.

Lopsided leaders resolve the tension inherent in a pair of opposing leadership virtues by opting for one side over the other. Rather than see the opposition as a complementarity, they turn it into a false dichotomy.

In his extreme relationship to the opposition of Breadth versus Depth, a general manager with a technical background offered a vivid instance of a one-sided mentality.

With an undergraduate degree in engineering and a graduate degree in computer science, he started his career in a technical function, information technology. But at the first opportunity he swung over to the business side. In his business capacity you might expect him to act as a bridge to technical functions. Instead he gravitated to the business directors on his staff and he was very chummy with the other general managers. "It's true," he said, "my most tense relationships are with the IT people." Instead of having an affinity for technical types, he kept his distance.

He embraced breadth, identified with it powerfully, and derived great personal satisfaction from his status as a line manager. And he distanced himself from the narrowness that technical depth connoted.

In high school he had excelled in science and math, hung out with like types, got an 800 on the math SAT, and was admitted to a highly selective liberal arts college. There, exposed to a wide range of talented peers, he redefined himself: "People were just a lot broader, and I think it triggered a desire in me to be broader. A lot of the things I've done in my career have been an attempt to be broad. That's why I prefer general management to technology. It's more worldly."

In a reflective mode, he could see how he polarized depth and breadth. "Clearly," he said, "I have a distaste for the techno-nerd. Certainly, I over-idealize breadth and I disparage depth."

This manager equated depth with narrowness, which he associated with being on the margin and being one-down. His bad associations went all the way back to childhood. He had been the ugly duckling. "I was an ungainly kid, on the dorky side, always a little overweight, not good at sports, and I was teased a lot. At some level I still think of myself that way." A childhood friend remembered him as "Awkward. He was on the chubby side, with glasses." So, in his words, he "became an academic kid," which gave him success but also fed into his sense of himself as marginal. In opting for a career in general management, he moved as far away as possible from depth as narrowness and marginality. That solution created a different problem, severely lopsided behavior fueled by a lurid one-sided mind-set.

The Peril of One-Sidedness

To be one-sided is to marry oneself to a principle, as if your life depended on it.

Ironically, maximizing a value corrupts it. Sherwood Anderson captured this well in his novel *Winesburg, Ohio*. One of the characters is an author himself who wrote about "grotesques," individuals who deform themselves by latching onto a single truth:

> "In the beginning when the world was young . . . all about in the world were the truths and they were all beautiful. . . . Hundreds and hundreds were the truths and they were beautiful.
>
> "And then the people came along. Each as he appeared snapped up one of the truths. . . .
>
> "It was the truths that made people grotesques. . . . The moment one of the people took one of the truths to himself, called it his truth, and tried to live by it, he became a grotesque and the truth he embraced became a falsehood."

This is how leaders become lopsided. It's not just by embracing a single truth; it's also by rejecting the opposing truth. It is a too-great attraction to one thing, and it is also an active avoidance of the opposing thing.[8]

Beset by unexamined fear and mistaken beliefs, leaders like the general manager who polarized depth versus breadth choose one side of an opposition over the other. They cling to their favored truth like a life preserver, never realizing that they need both complementary truths in an ever-shifting arrangement—forceful and empowering, strategic and operational—as circumstances require, in order not only to stay afloat, but to make headway in challenging seas.[9]

Developing Yourself, Coaching Others

Highlights

1. Who you are is how you lead. For better or worse, wherever you go your idiosyncrasies go with you.

2. See your operating assumptions for what they are, just assumptions. This is hard to do: we believe what we believe.

3. Make the link to your past experience. The child is father to the man, is mother to the woman.

4. Think mind-set. If a staff member's behavior is off, chances are that a trigger point or crooked thinking has thrown it off.

5. Confide in someone you trust. Solitary introspection will only carry you so far.

Questions for Self-Reflection

1. Working from the outside in:

   • Is there anything that matters that you are doing too little of? What keeps you from doing more of it? Do you worry about doing too much of it?

   • Is there anything that matters that you are doing too much of? What drives you to do so much of that? Are you afraid of doing too little of it?

   • Are you lopsided in any way? Behind that, do you detect a one-sided mind-set? Do you have excessive faith in one side and too little faith in the other?"

continued

continued

2. Working from the inside out:
   - Make a list of your cherished beliefs about leadership. What possible effect does each one have on your behavior?
   - Do you know what your sensitivities, your "hot buttons," are?

3. Working forward from career experiences:
   - Which three experiences have left an indelible impression on the way you lead?
   - What effect, good or bad, has each experience had on your leadership?

4. Working forward from childhood experiences. In a quiet moment away from work, or better yet at the beach or in the mountains, you might ponder questions like the following.
   - What were the "commandments" you took away from childhood? "I must do this," "I must never do that." For example: "No excuses!" or "Work harder than what you're paid: if you're paid $10, give them $20 worth."
   - In which ways do you take after your mother or your father?
   - Do you have bad associations that influence your behavior to this day, for example, being poor, losing a parent at a young age, chronic conflict in your family, being rejected by peers, not doing well at school?
   - Did being a star performer leave you feeling burdened by high expectations?

Part Two

Two Major Oppositions in Leadership

Of all the oppositions, dichotomies, polarities or dualities in leadership, two stand out as arguably the most important to a leader's effectiveness. They are: (1) forceful and enabling leadership, and (2) strategic and operational leadership.

Chapter Five

Forceful and Enabling Leadership

The Power of Both

"I don't think there's a finite amount of liquid for
forceful and enabling so that if there's more
forceful, there's less enabling. It's not a zero sum
game."

—*A senior manager*

The vast majority of leaders would recognize, at an intellectual
level, that forceful and enabling leadership both have value. Yet in
practice they tend to be lopsided.

This is one of the fundamental oppositions that leaders need to
reconcile. In the simplest terms, *forceful* leadership is taking the lead
and *enabling* leadership is creating conditions for other people to
take the lead. It is getting things done by directing the actions of
other people versus creating conditions for other people to direct
the action. It's being a force to be reckoned with and at the same
time allowing—better yet, actively arranging for—other people to
be forces in their own right. This distinction by one name or
another has permeated the academic literature on leadership for
decades.[1]

Forceful leadership is a virtue, and enabling leadership is
a virtue. The versatile leader puts either approach foremost as the
situation requires and rarely ignores one for the other for long.
The versatile leader's organization thrives thanks to the leader's
attention to both dimensions. There is no better example than a
senior leader who is a model for how to treat people, and yet when

business conditions or an individual's performance requires it, is capable of taking people out of their jobs, as much as it may trouble him or her to do so. One such individual put it this way: "Can you trust people and also go in with the knife when you really have to? You've got to have both, because neither by itself will work in our business environment."

Both Sides Are Virtues

Forceful leadership has unquestioned value. Assuming authority, making your presence felt, taking stands, holding your ground, setting high expectations, and making tough calls—in short, using personal power and position power to get things done—is for some people the very definition of leadership. But the list is not complete.

There is a companion set of virtues, under the heading of enabling leadership: empowering your people, delegating authority and responsibility, involving your direct reports in decisions, seeking their input, making it easier for them to push back, showing appreciation, providing support. In general, this approach amounts to creating conditions for other people to be forceful leaders in their own right, contributing their talent, drive, and ideas to organizational performance.

> A forthright manager was afraid that doing the "soft stuff"—giving recognition, providing emotional support— would take away from his directness and "edge." It later dawned on him: "I can do both!"

To be sure, the enabling side is not the totality of leadership either. In fact, neither side is complete without the other. They complement one another.

Despite the conceptual tension between the two sides, a versatile leader does justice to both. This is an approachable ideal, not an unrealizable dream. In fact, the more versatile a manager is, the more effective he or she is. This is one of Rob Kaiser's and my key findings:

executives who are rated higher on overall effectiveness are those who receive higher scores on an index of versatility (see our statistical findings below and in the Appendix). Other researchers have also concluded that on similar distinctions like "initiating structure" and "consideration" or "concern for production" and "concern for people," that high-high is best.[2]

Beneath the overall distinction fall pairs of specific dimensions. Again, can the manager perform optimally on pairs of dimensions that oppose each other?

> If .320 is a really good batting average, I am at .320 on the enabling side. And on the forceful side I raised my batting average from .120 to .250, and I don't feel like I've destroyed anybody in the process and they got the message about what needed to be done and they did it. That tells me my balance is better.

- Both take the lead *and* enable others to take the lead?
- Both take stands *and* be receptive to the stands that other people take?
- Both be decisive *and* participative?
- Both make tough calls *and* have compassion?
- Both push people hard *and* provide support and encouragement?

The question of versatility on the forceful-enabling pair plays out at this concrete level too.

Versatile Doesn't Mean Homogenous

Sometimes people hear "balance" or "versatility" and immediately think of a nondescript, mushy blend of the two sides, neither here nor there. One executive, for example, worried that the whole feedback craze would rob people of their distinctness:

"My view is that you need to leverage unique strengths rather than ask people to pull back from their strengths and suddenly get bland. I'd rather have somebody bipolar than bland, in the middle."

Other managers have raised similar concerns about becoming "homogenized," "normalized," "neutered." They worry that, in responding to feedback about their weaknesses, forceful types might bow to social pressure and lose their ability to lead.

This idea of versatile as being homogenous is plain wrong. To expand one's range on a pair of opposing virtues is not to average out the two sides into a shapeless blob. It is not forever hugging the middle of the range. Quite the opposite: the more versatile the leader, the greater his or her range. Forceful leaders who develop the versatility to be enabling don't lose the capacity to be forceful, even extremely so. They simply add to their range on the other side. All they give up is misplaced forcefulness. It is important to distinguish between going to necessary versus unnecessary extremes.

A take-charge leader needn't forfeit that capacity, only learn to use it more selectively. An outspoken manager who learns to listen better is no less capable of speaking out. To be more versatile, then, is not to be forever stuck in the middle. It is to roam more freely from one end to the other.

Versatility is freedom of movement. Imagine walking into a room that is empty except for a chair on casters. The wall to your right has "forceful" written on it in big bold letters; the wall to the left, "enabling." If sitting there you can roll freely all the way to the right and all the way to the left, you are versatile indeed.

Two Camps

It is not just leaders who lean one way on forceful and enabling leadership. Leadership consultants, coaches, and researchers frequently show the same bias to one side or the other.

The distinction between Theory X and Theory Y, introduced in 1960 by Douglas McGregor, had great staying power in the field.[3]

What McGregor did brilliantly was to expose the fallacious thinking behind heavy-handed leadership, which he designated as Theory X. Theory X holds that the average person doesn't like to work, avoids responsibility, and therefore must be directed and even coerced into getting his or her work done. What managers who subscribe to Theory X overlook, according to McGregor, is the self-fulfilling prophecy they set up, a reverse Pygmalion effect: put employees in limited, unsatisfying, low-paying jobs and, not surprisingly, they assume only limited responsibility, which then, in the manager's mind, justifies close, directive, controlling supervision.

Theory Y sets up the opposite self-fulfilling prophecy. It is predicated on the assumption that the average person is perfectly willing to work hard and to take responsibility and, given a chance, will act responsibly. The idea is to replace a vicious cycle with a virtuous cycle.

A carefully reasoned polemic against self-defeating over-control, McGregor's model of leadership contains a bias that is hard to miss. Obviously, Theory Y is the "better" of the two. Subtler is the favoritism embedded in another longstanding distinction—autocratic versus participative. Isn't it true that "participative" has a positive connotation and that "autocratic" is pejorative? How many managers would be honored to be known as an "autocrat"?

So much for the partisans of the enabling side. On the other side of the fence today reside academics who have serious misgivings about the empowerment movement and its de-emphasis on the power of the person in charge, which Abraham Zaleznik saw as deriving from America's love affair with fraternal leadership, with leader as brother.

In a book subtitled *Restoring Leadership in Business*, Zaleznik argued that strong, charismatic leadership is critical to organizational effectiveness. He contended that, as long as it is not self-serving, "personal influence *is* leadership."[4] By personal influence, Zaleznik means the forceful action of the individual. In pointing out how the empowerment movement and the quality movement went too far in reducing the importance of forceful leadership, however, Zaleznik himself overcorrected.

I have run across executives who feel the same way as Zaleznik. One such individual, whose company had championed quality for ten years with considerable success, expressed grave concern about the muffling effects of a strong orientation toward process. What gets lost, he thought, was "personality and leadership."

> "This company has been caught up in the bad, terrible part of process, which implies lack of edge, lack of accountability, lack of consequences, lack of responsibility. And when you focus so much on process, you tend to forget the role of personality and leadership."

In bemoaning the overemphasis on process, the executive failed to acknowledge its benefits.

Another executive also spoke to the need for tough-minded leadership:

> "This corporation needs people with more of an edge, more of a bite. A whiff of brutal clarity, if it's based on reality, is an essential component of leadership."

To this leader, organizations can't remake themselves without strong leadership.

> "If you have a change agenda, you have to overweight the agenda to get it going. You have to overweight it since you're up against inertial tendencies. That's where passionate energy and leadership are required."

He complained: "This corporation is full of round-worded, nice people who don't make a change."

A third partisan of strong leadership spoke derisively of "get-along, go-along types," who in a misguided effort to avoid inflicting pain on people hurt them even more in the long run. "There is a tendency," he said, "to try to be 'kind' when employees aren't making it and you end up being unkind." He expressed his sneering misgivings about the soft-hearted approach this way:

"I don't trust feel-good. When people have to execute, they can't. If you don't deliver, what's it all about?"

It comes as no surprise that the advocates of strong leadership are typically over-weighted in that direction.

Although in the minority, some leaders camp out on the other-oriented side. One individual with this outlook told me:

> "This business is large and complex and there isn't any one of us who can have all the answers. Given that, I've worked really hard to hire really smart, hardworking, insightful, driven people, and I listen to them. That's the main thing that has gotten me to where I am today. It's my conviction that talent, wisdom, insight come from any corner of the organization—from a board member or someone who is down on the factory floor."

And it is no surprise that, like this manager, individuals in this camp typically fall short on the forceful side of leadership.

Both camps tend to discredit and be dismissive of the other. In reality, each critique has more than a grain of truth in it. McGregor is right about the self-defeating effects of extreme control-oriented leadership, just as critics on the other side are right about extreme employee-centered leadership. What each camp misses in these leadership-culture wars is the value of the other approach, used effectively. Each equates the other school of thought with its excesses and in the process misses the things about the other side that work.

You don't have to fall into either of these traps. Without a lot of difficulty, you can avoid being one of those managers who see the forceful-enabling distinction as "either/or" and who commit themselves to one side or the other as "the right way." All you have to do is be practical about what the situation objectively requires of you and then act accordingly, even if it gets you out of your comfort zone!

What is needed in organizations and among leadership experts is a style that permits travel back and forth. Practicing managers are better off if, as needed, they are able to place a foot in both camps.

Lopsidedness on Forceful-Enabling Leadership

The key to understanding the anatomy of lopsidedness on forceful-enabling leadership is to define the excessive version of each pair of virtues. In the two middle columns of Table 5.1 are listed several pairs of specific forceful and enabling attributes. For the moment the columns at either end have been left blank. You might try your hand at identifying what it means to take each virtue to a counter-productive extreme.

Table 5.1. Forceful and Enabling Leadership, Virtues Only

Forceful Leadership		Enabling Leadership	
Taken to an extreme	*Virtues*	*Virtues*	*Taken to an extreme*
	Takes charge, in control of his/her unit.	Empowers subordinates to run their own units. Able to let go.	
	Lets people know clearly and with feeling where he/she stands on issues. Declares himself/herself.	Interested in where other people stand on issues. Receptive to their ideas.	
	Makes tough calls, including those that have an adverse effect on people.	Compassionate. Responsive to people's needs and feelings.	
	Makes judgments. Zeros in on what is substandard or is not working in an individual's or unit's performance.	Shows appreciation. Makes other people feel good about their contributions. Helps people feel valued.	
	Holds people strictly accountable.	Understanding when people are not able to deliver.	
	Forces issues. Puts tough issues on the table, even if it makes people uncomfortable.	Fosters harmony, contains conflict, defuses tension.	
	Sure of himself/herself. Speaks authoritatively.	Modest. Aware that he/she does not know everything; can be wrong.	

Table 5.2 below contains my version of the extremes.

Table 5.2. Forceful and Enabling Leadership, Both Virtues and Vices

| Forceful Leadership | | Enabling Leadership | |
Taken to an extreme	Virtues	Virtues	Taken to an extreme
Dominant to the point of eclipsing subordinates.	Takes charge, in control of his/her unit.	Empowers subordinates to run their own units. Able to let go.	Empowers to a fault. Gives people too much rope.
Other people don't speak out, aren't heard.	Lets people know clearly and with feeling where he/she stands on issues. Declares himself/herself.	Interested in where other people stand on issues. Receptive to their ideas.	People don't know where they stand.
Insensitive, callous.	Makes tough calls, including those that have an adverse effect on people.	Compassionate. Responsive to people's needs and feelings.	Overly accommodating. Nice to people at the expense of the work.
Harshly judgmental. Dismisses the contributions of others.	Makes judgments. Zeros in on what is substandard or is not working in an individual's or unit's performance.	Shows appreciation. Makes other people feel good about their contributions. Helps people feel valued.	Gives false praise or praises indiscriminately.
Rigid; demoralizing.	Holds people strictly accountable.	Understanding when people are not able to deliver.	Tender-minded. Lets people off the hook.
Confrontational. Lacks finesse. Abrasive.	Forces issues. Puts tough issues on the table, even if it makes people uncomfortable.	Fosters harmony, contains conflict, defuses tension.	Avoids conflict. Shies away from confronting performance problems.
Hard for others to state their views. Arrogant.	Sure of self; speaks authoritatively.	Modest; aware that he/she does not know everything.	Self-effacing. Self-deprecating.

If you are like the majority of managers my colleagues and I have worked with, you orient yourself more to one side of the forceful-enabling pair than the other. And that orientation might have made it easier for you to come up with excesses for one side and more difficult to imagine what the excesses are on the other side.

My colleagues and I regularly encounter lopsidedness on forceful-enabling leadership in the senior managers we work with. And Rob Kaiser and I have encountered the same pattern in our analyses of ratings on the Leadership Versatility Index. In seven different samples totaling more than 550 target managers, we found a sizable *negative* correlation between the two sides.[5] In other words, managers who are rated "too much" on forceful are likely to be rated as "too little" on enabling, and conversely. This is a very robust generalization: we have found the "polarity effect" in every one of our samples. For example, the graph in Figure 5.1 displays the scatter plot of forceful and enabling scores of 107 managers. The correlation is quite high, −.64, and it is an inverse correlation,[6] meaning that managers who were rated as overdoing forceful leadership tended to be rated as underdoing enabling leadership, and conversely. The pattern could not be clearer.

Research to date has turned up almost exclusively positive correlations between these two factors, roughly forceful and enabling leadership, and usually sizable positive correlations at that. In fact, a recent study that used "meta-analysis," a statistical technique, to summarize over one hundred independent studies of a prominent version of this distinction calculated the correlation between the two sides of leadership to be +.46.[7] Several researchers have noted that this correlation is not what would be expected and have speculated that it may be due to rater bias. No one has suggested it may be an artifact of the instrument, or, specifically, the rating scale.[8]

Figure 5.1. Inverse Relationship Between Enabling and Forceful Leadership

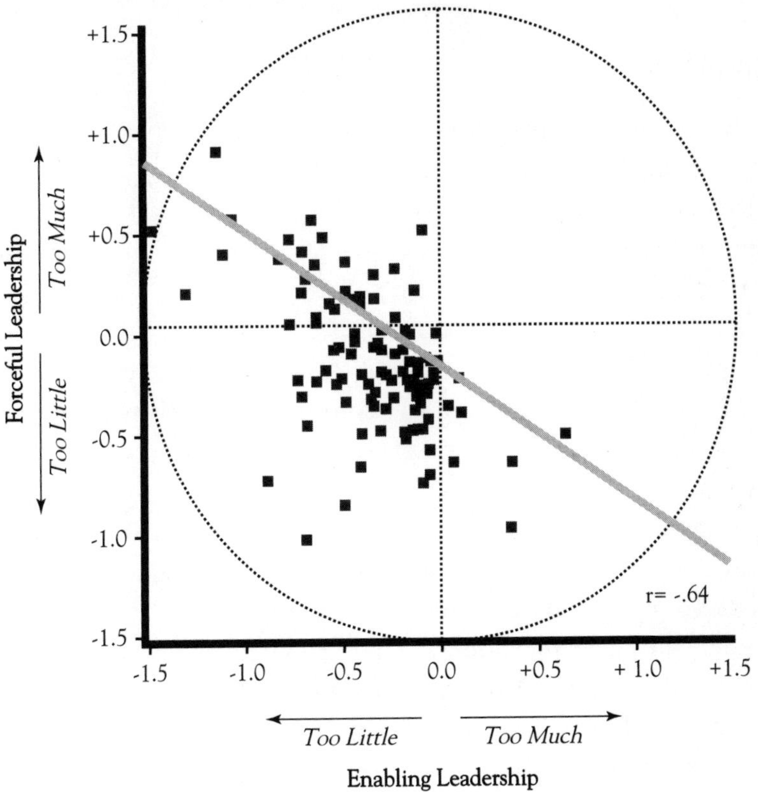

Since this inverse relationship makes perfect sense, it will come as a surprise that this is not what numerous studies of these two factors, known by several different sets of names, have found over the past fifty years. If anything, the correlations have been positive. How could this be? We can only conclude that it was the failure of previous research, conducted over the last seventy years, to employ a measure of excess. Without it, it is impossible to identify lopsidedness, which is a type of excess.

To bring to life the inverse relationship between forceful and enabling leadership, let's look at two lopsided leaders, both composites drawn from real people. The first individual leaned heavily to one side; the second leaned heavily to the other side.

Sara Central

In her ten years as president of a prestigious liberal arts college, its first woman president, Sara Central was a high-profile leader who left her mark on the place. Within a few months of taking the post, she launched an ambitious three-year capital campaign that, through her Herculean efforts and aggressive salesmanship, reached its goal and met its deadline. With those funds in hand, she presided over the remaking of the school's physical plant and made her school the first in the country to wire all the dorms for high-speed Internet service and to equip all entering students with laptops.

Sara Central was the epitome of a leader who led off her own intellect and energy. She fairly reveled in her efficacy. If it is true that the secret to fulfillment is to use one's powers fully, she had unlocked that secret. She was given to saying, "Self-actualization comes from the impossible dream achieved."

Without revealing the exact details of Sara's upbringing, I'll simply say that she was born into difficult circumstances that made furthering herself an uphill struggle. Underneath it all, she felt wronged. It could have been race, religion, ethnic, or socioeconomic background, or the way she was treated by her parents. Some individuals succumb to adversity. Sara overcame it with a vengeance. Her ambition didn't gel right away though. She was a lackluster student through high school and it was only after nearly flunking out of college that she "snapped out of it" and transformed herself into a star student, graduating magna cum laude and going on to a first-tier graduate school. Throughout her career, her nagging sense of being "one-down" fueled her rapid ascent.

The downside of Sara's leadership was that she didn't do nearly as well at tapping into the intellect and energy of other people. Her leadership was "Sara-centric," the provost said. In her staff meetings, she was the undisputed hub: all the action revolved around her. She didn't begin to exploit the "rim." A staff member once told her that he likened these staff meetings to a game show:

> "Being in a meeting with you is like playing 'Jeopardy.' I've got my finger on the buzzer, but you always hit the buzzer first. So I never get to feel smart. If I had another second or two, I'd come up with the right answer, but I never get the chance. We all know that you're smarter than us, but that doesn't need to be proven. If you let people have a chance, the organization could develop more confidence."

The dean of students came up with this image to capture how Sara could redress the imbalance:

> "She is extraordinarily capable—talented to the max. But she could do less and be more effective if she would let those that she works with work with her. She is a shining star. She's a nova. But there are some other stars in the galaxy that she could work with in a really nice harmony."

Her scores on the Leadership Versatility Index threw into bold relief the extent to which she over-weighted the forceful side and under-weighted the enabling side. Table 5.3 below contains a simple count of the number of times her coworkers gave her a rating of too little or too much. (Twelve coworkers rated her on nine forceful items and nine enabling items, for a total of 108 ratings on each. Not shown is the number of times raters indicated right amount: 43 on Enabling and 60 on Forceful.)

Table 5.3. Sara Central's Lopsidedness

	Enabling	Forceful
Too much	0	46
Too little	65	2

The pattern is a familiar one among managers. Although her talent made her a valuable asset, the way she deployed that asset degraded it. Her effectiveness rating was a respectable 7.9, but it fell far short of her potential.

Among several members of the administration, her approach bred resentment: "You want to dictate the solution; I'll play along but not wholeheartedly." Among the faculty she excited decidedly mixed feelings. They grudgingly acknowledged what she had done for the college but resented her centrist, non-collegial approach with them. Having won many admirers but few friends, she put herself in jeopardy: "You've got to be the star; go ahead, but if your star falls don't expect me to help out or care."

To take her play to the next level, she needed to enable others to be powerful in their dealings with her and to shine in their own right.

Billy Peoples

Billy Peoples was known in his own organization as a "positive people leader." His staff and those at lower levels appreciated that of course, but senior management, populated by "locker room types," broad-shouldered guys who had played football in college, had reservations. They couldn't argue with Billy's track record, but they also couldn't help looking somewhat askance at his style and perhaps even his slight build.

Everyone who knew him, family included, remarked on his ability to relate to people. "He really connects well," said one direct report. He was genuinely interested in what people were doing and it showed. You didn't get the sense that you were just a cog in the machinery. Speaking for many others, a hotshot on his staff made the point that, "After a conversation with Billy, I've always come away feeling better about myself!"

The key was that Billy was an exceptionally good listener. Operating on the assumption that other people had a lot to offer, he was truly interested in what they had to say. For a "guy" he possessed unusual empathy: he was uniquely good at seeing things from the other person's point of view. And he didn't wait for people to come to him; he went out of his way to solicit their input.

Along with that, Billy was a great believer in the power of the group. One staff member observed: "He doesn't figure out solutions by himself; he gets others to collectively figure out what should be done. He builds consensus."

Summing up his motivating effect on the organization, a staff member said:

> "Billy has an ability to relate to people at all levels in his organization and to energize them and make them want to be a part of his team. They don't want to let him down, which leads to the ultimate goal of success in the marketplace. He naturally engages with you to change the world."

He wasn't just good at relating to people. He was a winner; always had been. All along he had received excellent grades in school and he had been a starting infielder on very good baseball teams in high school and college. As an adult he remained an intensely competitive athlete.

Along with raising him to be a high achiever in school and on the playing field ("Be a winner," they told him), his parents also sent another strong message: "Be humble." Under the second heading, Billy could rattle off a long list of his parents' dictums. "Don't win at someone else's expense." "Don't run up the score." "Be a good sport." "Play by the rules." "It's the team that wins." "Help your teammates out." "It's not important to be the star."

Billy's devotion to the other person, along with the premium he placed on the team, came to be responsible for his shortfalls. It's a shame that goodness on that order was not only rewarded. His modesty, claiming nothing for himself and calling no attention to himself, went way past being a simple virtue. That was coercive. It kept him from fully asserting himself and from taking his full and rightful place at the head of the table.

He did such a good job of giving other people a voice in decision making that his own voice was lost or at least muted. His people weren't sure, for example, where he stood strategically. It seemed to his team that the strategy was essentially a group product. On the Leadership Versatility Index, all eight coworkers who filled it out indicated that he didn't declare himself enough, and four of the eight, including some of his direct reports, rated him as too receptive to other people's ideas, including their own.

His boss took him to task for giving his people too much choice: "You let your marketing head choose between two jobs when you knew that she would do better in one of those jobs." His boss was

> Billy People's initial reaction to his 360-degree survey results, which showed plainly how lopsided he was and which carried the implication that he should be more forceful: "I'll be damned if I'll become an SOB because I don't like what it would do to my leadership or to my personal life! I *like* being an enabling manager."

also critical of him for being too slow to make changes: "You choose to live with situations that aren't working, and you're tolerant of people who just don't cut it!" If a touch of the locker-room attitude crept into his manager's perception, it largely fit with the widely shared experience of Billy People's leadership.

Table 5.4, which contains a count of the number of times any of his coworkers gave him a rating of too little or too much, paints a clear picture of his lopsidedness. (Eight coworkers rated him on nine forceful items and nine enabling items. Not shown is the number of times raters indicated right amount: 36 on Enabling and 20 on Forceful.)

Table 5.4. Billy People's Lopsidedness

	Enabling	Forceful
Too much	29	3
Too little	7	49

Although he definitely leaned to one side, on average he didn't lean *very far* in that direction. Even if not extreme, however, the lopsidedness hampered his effectiveness by impeding his ability to drive organizational change. The CEO was afraid that Billy's inclusiveness kept him from pushing the enterprise-wide strategic agenda hard enough. The CEO and the HR head asked each other, "Can a guy this nice run the company?"

Four Variations

When my fellow consultants and I began using the Leadership Versatility Index, we expected to find lopsidedness, and we did. We also found a pattern of scores that we did not anticipate—the tendency for a manager to be rated as not forceful enough *and* not enabling enough. With respect to managing conflict, for example, the manager doesn't: he or she neither forces issues nor fosters harmony. It is an opting out, a disengagement.

Larry Little, who appeared in the last chapter, is a case in point. A person with an ostensibly strong personality—he had a resonant voice, a firm handshake, a confident air—he was strangely marginal in his own team meetings. A stranger would not have been to tell that he was the team leader. Two of the three general managers and the human-resources director were stronger presences than he was. They said more and took stronger positions. While he led the organization ably otherwise, in this respect he abdicated his role.

There is a passivity to this pattern, an opting out on both the forceful side and the enabling side. The term connotes a benign neglect.[9]

The disengaged pattern, also known as laissez-faire, is a benign neglect. But it is not so benign because it injures the leader's effectiveness. It depressed the rating of Larry's overall effectiveness. It was a low 7, well below average.

Impact on Effectiveness

So far in this chapter we have identified three configurations on the forceful-enabling duality:

- Versatile, or doing the right amount of both forceful and enabling
- Lopsided in either direction (too forceful/not enabling enough or vice-versa)
- Disengaged, or doing too little of both

As Figure 5.2 shows, there is a fourth possible pattern, doing too much of both. This, however, is a null set. Possible in theory, this pattern does not exist in nature. In all of our samples—including about 350 executives and 200 middle managers—there is not a single recorded case of a manager whose overall profile fit this pattern. This is not surprising: a manager who is too quick to take the lead is unlikely also to empower too much. A leader who comes on too strong is not going to be too receptive to other people's ideas. A manager who is too critical of others is not likely also to express too much appreciation. Likewise, it would be hard for someone who expects too much of others at the same time to be overly supportive and overly encouraging.

How do the four configurations that are found in nature compare on effectiveness? Managers who on the Leadership Versatility

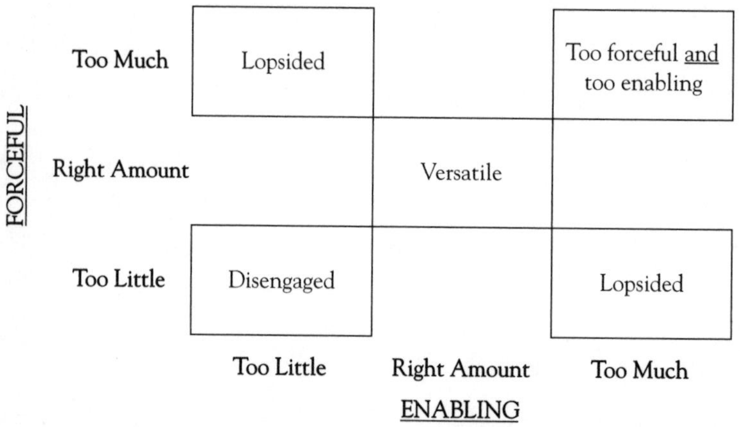

Figure 5.2. Four Leadership Styles and a Null Set

Index qualify as versatile receive the highest ratings of overall effectiveness from their coworkers. Those categorized as disengaged are rated the lowest. And those classified as lopsided—it doesn't matter in which direction—receive effectiveness ratings in the middle.

Subpairs: A Deeper Look

On the ladder of abstraction, half way between the high-level forceful-enabling opposition and quite concrete pairs of dimensions represented by the LVI items, reside three distinctions. Rob Kaiser and I derived them the research literature.[10] These three mid-level pairs appear in Table 5.5.

"Takes charge" is about establishing yourself as the head of your unit, as opposed to "Empowers," which refers to granting people the authority to run their own units. "Declares" has to do with stating your views clearly, even emphatically, as opposed "Listens," which involves being open to others' views, even when they run counter to your own. "Pushes" has everything to do with holding people accountable and being adequately direct and firm about that, as opposed to being "Supports," which involves being responsive to people's needs for consideration, compassion, and appreciation.

These subpairs are useful because they help to differentiate individual leaders' profiles, which don't necessarily fall out the same way on all three subpairs. You might remember, for example, how Ella Solo tipped decidedly in one direction on the first subpair (took charge too much and empowered too little) yet tilted the other way on the third subpair (fell short on making demands).

Table 5.5. Forceful and Enabling Subpairs

Takes charge	Empowers
Declares	Listens
Pushes	Supports

Clearly, it is advantageous to be versatile on forceful and enabling leadership. Added power goes to those who can employ each side in the right proportion for the circumstance. To become more versatile, leaders also need to factor in the psychology of lopsidedness. As discussed in the last chapter, a one-sided mind-set is often responsible for lopsided behavior. All of this applies to the strategic-operational pairing, the subject of the next chapter. You might think of strate-

A manager who has made a study of dualities observed: "It's easy to go one way. Everyone has a personal flow and goes in one direction. And so you don't see the other side. Once you know it, it puts the monkey on your back, to do the other side too."

gic and operational as the *what* of leadership—what leaders work on—and of forceful and enabling leadership as constituting the *how*—how they go about it.

For a pictorial array of what it takes to be a versatile leader, see Figure 10.2 in Chapter 10, which lays out the forceful-enabling and strategic-operational dualities, along with their subpairs, and maps them in terms of too little, the right amount, and too much.

Developing Yourself, Coaching Others

Highlights

1. On forceful leadership and enabling leadership, you *can* do both, you *must* do both.

2. If you lean to the forceful side and have misgivings about becoming more enabling, open your eyes to the circumstances that require a leader to be enabling, for example, when it is vital to know what is on other people's minds or when staff members who are senior in their own right want the same leeway to do their jobs as you do.

3. If you lean to the enabling side and have misgivings about becoming more forceful, be clear in your mind about what types of situations require a leader to be forceful, for example, when you owe it to staff members to let them know your concerns about their performance or when a discussion has gone on long enough and it's time for you to cut it off and decide.

Questions for Reflection

1. Can you equally well:

   - Take charge *and* let others take the lead?

   - Declare yourself *and* listen well?

   - Hold people's feet to the fire *and* be sensitive to their needs?

2. Do your beliefs or attitudes deprive you of versatility?

   - Are you ambivalent about power? Is taking too much power the last thing you would want to do—be dominating in any way?

continued

continued

- Do you believe strongly in being egalitarian?
- Is it your idea that leaders have to be strong at all times? Do you have a horror of being weak?

3. If you are a forceful leader, do you get frustrated with staff members who lack forcefulness? Contain your frustration. It won't help those individuals develop forceful qualities.

4. If you are an enabling leader, are you intolerant of staff members with strong personalities? Rather than judge these types for lacking what you have, help them improve.

Chapter Six

Strategic and Operational Leadership

The Power of Both

"For every thing there is a season, and a time for
every matter under heaven: A time to plant and a
time to pluck up what is planted; . . . time to break
down and a time to build up."

—*Ecclesiastes*

If forceful leadership and enabling leadership have to do with *how* people go about their work, strategic and operational leadership is about *what* they work on. These, I believe, are the two most basic dualities in leadership. This is not to say that the large footprints made by these two pairs cover the entire domain of leadership. They don't include, for example, the distinction between functional leadership and general-management leadership—depth leadership versus breadth leadership, if you will. Leading versus managing may seem like an opposition that lies beyond the pale but, in fact, it overlaps quite a bit with strategic and operational leadership.

The question is, can you do justice to both sides of the strategic-operational pair, despite the tendency to favor one over the other, a tendency as natural as being right-handed or left-handed? Can you resolve the tension contained in this pair by embracing both sides?

Strategic leadership is about positioning your unit, however big or small it is, for the medium to long term. *Operational* leadership is about getting results in the short term. It puts a premium on executing a few carefully selected priorities and using disciplined processes to focus the organization on those.[1]

By strategy I don't mean a pie-in-the-sky, futuristic vision. Whatever the size of your unit, strategy is the very practical real-world idea of where you want it to be three to four years from now. The strategy in question could be a grand, enterprise-wide shift, like Thomas Watson, Jr., taking IBM from calculators to computers, or a more mundane change like achieving six sigma quality in a manufacturing process, improving customer service, or reducing the number of lost workdays due to accidents.

Both strategic and operational leadership are indispensable, and at the same time they stand in opposition to each other.[2] It is no mean feat for a manager to build a repertoire that encompasses both. But, as our research shows, the most versatile—and effective—leaders turn from one side to the other as the season dictates.

The question of versatility on the strategic-operational duality applies not only to the overall distinction but also under it to a series of specific distinctions. In each of these distinctions is contained a tension, which it is the leader's challenge to resolve.

Can you:

- Take both a long-term *and* a short-term orientation?
- Take a broad view of the organization *and* get into operational detail?
- Track trends in the outside world *and* keep your finger on the pulse internally?
- Set direction *and* drive for results?
- Think out of the box *and* employ tight discipline to get things done?

To those managers who are ambidextrous, as it were, go the spoils of superior effectiveness. As with forceful-enabling versatility, there is a strong statistical association between versatility on strategic-operational leadership and ratings of overall effectiveness.[3]

> Said one CEO: "A lot of CEOs are great at focusing on operations, but they don't get the balance that must be struck between efficiency and growth. I say you can do both and you must do both. Great CEOs know how to balance improving efficiency with spending time and energy to stimulate growth."

To be versatile on this opposition doesn't mean employing both sides in equal measure at all times. Hardly. If you are a plant manager or the person in charge of the back office of a bank, you must bring a full measure of operational leadership to the assignment but only a limited amount of strategic leadership, however able you are strategically. If, on the other hand, you are doing a tour of duty as head of strategy or mergers and acquisitions, it's strategic ability that's needed, and for the time being you can park much of your operational side (unless of course your job includes the company's annual strategic planning process, a highly operational process).

The Propensity for Lopsidedness on Strategic-Operational Leadership

To get into the right frame of mind, you might pause for a moment to turn the virtues listed in Table 6.1 into vices. Taken to an extreme what does each virtue become?[4]

Table 6.1. Strategic vs. Operational Leadership, Virtues Only

Strategic Leadership		Operational Leadership	
Taken to an extreme	*Virtues*	*Virtues*	*Taken to an extreme*
	Focused on setting long-term strategy.	Focused on getting short-term results.	
	Thinks broadly and pays attention to the big picture.	Detail-oriented; gets into the specifics of how things actually work.	
	Expansive; aggressive about growing the business.	Respects the limits on the organization's capacity to grow.	
	Entrepreneurial; ready to pursue emerging opportunities with big potential.	Focused on meeting the immediate needs of customers.	
	Uses inspiration to sell the vision and strategy.	Keeps people on track by following up, conducting regular reviews, and so forth.	
	Steps back to reflect on direction.	Action-oriented. Has a sense of urgency.	

Table 6.2 fills in with the extremes as I see them.

Table 6.2. Strategic vs. Operational Leadership, Virtues and Vices

Strategic Leadership		Operational Leadership	
Taken to an extreme	Virtues	Virtues	Taken to an extreme
Too much looking down the road.	Focused on setting long-term strategy.	Focused on getting short-term results.	Tunnel vision. Myopic.
Hopelessly conceptual. Lost in the clouds.	Thinks broadly; pays attention to the big picture.	Detail-oriented; gets into the specifics of how things actually work.	Bogged down in details.
Too ambitious; at risk of strategic overreach.	Expansive; aggressive about growing the business.	Respects the limits on the organization's capacity to grow.	Conservative; too respectful of limits.
Too ready to jump; not selective enough.	Entrepreneurial; ready to pursue emerging opportunities with big potential.	Focused on meeting the immediate needs of customers.	Completely caught up in meeting current needs.
Too much cheerleading; too much talking about future possibilities.	Uses inspiration to sell the vision and strategy.	Keeps people on track by following up, conducting regular reviews, and so forth.	Inflexible; oppressive.
Engages in navel-gazing.	Steps back; reflects on direction.	Action-oriented. Has a sense of urgency.	Ready-fire-aim.

Supporting the idea that managers lean one way or the other on strategic and operational leadership, a recent study compared two key roles in creating a new business—coming up with a bright idea ("Ideator") and implementing the new idea ("Implementer"). In the company studied, people tended to gravitate to one role or the other and were almost never proficient at both. And the personality profiles associated with success in each role were exactly the opposite. "Visionary Ideators" were more intellectually curious, more independent/nonconforming, and less methodical. The opposite was true of the "Implementers," who were less curious, more conforming, and highly methodical.[5]

It is worth noting that, based on Leadership Versatility Index data, the commodity in shortest supply among managers seems to be strategic leadership.[6] This certainly doesn't mean it can't be over-done, as Sam Menza's over-expansiveness will show.

Strategic and Operational Leadership in Action

Sam Menza was over-weighted on the strategic side; Pete Powers on the operational side.

Sam Menza

Soon after making partner at the Boston Consulting Group in his early thirties, Sam Menza decided it was time for the next adventure and accepted a client's offer to become the financial officer of one of its biggest businesses. Two years later he was promoted to general manager.

His strengths cohered around strategic leadership. He brought the "broadest perspective," and he made it a priority to keep his knowledge refreshed by, for example, checking in every year with seminal thinkers in every corner of the industry. He had superior insight into the dynamics of the marketplace. But beyond that he had a gift for extrapolating into the future. Admiring colleagues used phrases like "sees over next hill" and "sees trends before they occur." Within months of his arrival, the corporation made a major acquisition that had worked out well and that would never have occurred if it were not for Sam's strategic sense.

A considerable intellect, honed by the many years he spent with the cream of the crop in college, business school, and the strategy-oriented consultancy, greatly aided his strategic thinking. "Cerebral" someone called him. Someone else credited him with "general brainyness." He navigated easily through abstract material, and he was a "fast synthesizer," good at taking in lots of input and integrating that into a larger thought. He would say to his team, "What business do we want to be in, and don't get that confused with tactics or with the underlying strategies."

Because he entered corporate life as a middle manager, however, Sam Menza had missed out on assignments that would have built up his ability to run things. It also left him with a bias: "To me the bigger picture is more important and has more leverage than the day-to-day detail." His mentor disagreed: "A great leader has to do both." Yet, although Sam soared easily at 100,000 feet, he rarely dipped down to ground level. A chorus of voices in Sam's feedback report appealed to him to pay more attention to detail. "He has to get into the nuts and bolts," a direct report said.

He certainly did not ignore operations completely. On the contrary, he expected his line managers to deliver on their commitments and showed his displeasure when they failed to do so. He conducted operations reviews once a quarter, so he was not out of touch. But his staff could tell from what he got excited about that he didn't have his heart in the operational part of his job. He could spend hours at a time with the young super-bright staffers in the marketing, strategy, and finance functions mulling over industry trends and doing blue-sky thinking.

He knew his predilections well enough to put strong, experienced people in operational slots. He failed to appreciate, however, that he still had an operational role to play. The monthly one-on-ones with these managers had a way of getting cancelled. Truth be known, he didn't care for what he called the "drudgery" of running an operation. As a result, his senior people had trouble obtaining the minimal guidance or the chance to talk over a problem together that they definitely needed.

Seeing him as "a better starter than finisher" and as "not grounded in the realities of implementation," his boss worried that Sam's hands-off operational style was hampering the division's efforts to hit its financial targets consistently. He did have a tendency to over-promise, but that wasn't the problem. He just didn't do his part to fully work out the intermediate-term plan and keep the organization focused on grinding out steady progress towards annual objectives.

It is dangerous to be a Sam Menza. Out of a combination of not fully understanding the operations and not truly caring, you unintentionally communicate to 75 percent of the organization, all those people producing the operational results, that a lot of what they do doesn't really matter. That implicit message distances people and breeds a sense of being peripheral and a collective demoralization: "You don't know what we do on a daily basis, and when we tell you, you don't show much interest." It creates a bifurcation between the supposed brain trust and what to the leader are the drones. That posture does not do what senior leaders need to do: invite everyone in the organization to put their shoulders to the wheel and strive to do their parts.

Pete Powers

Like Sam Menza, Pete Powers was a general manager new to his company, but the resemblance stopped there. Characteristically, Pete had gotten up to speed quickly on the organization's inner workings. He had, as someone said, "extremely high understanding of the detail; he gets under the hood." Armed with that commanding practical knowledge, he made it crystal clear to everyone working for him what he expected of them. Likewise, his three, just three, improvement priorities for the business each year were no less clearly drawn. In discussions, he expressed himself in short, punchy sentences; you never had to wonder what he meant.

Focus was his trademark. "Extremely focused in getting the orga-nization to perform" is the way one of his peers put it; "an absolute focus on the key issues." He was also very organized and brought tight process discipline to the organization. It manifested itself in the way he ran his staff meetings and monthly operational reviews. "He is very organized, methodical, rigorous," as someone described him. In general, he "makes sure that things don't fall through the cracks."

His admirably focused, disciplined approach had drawbacks, however. He had blinders on. The tightly structured way of running things went hand in hand, it seemed, with his tendency to cut off discussions of new ideas. And his knack for selecting just a few objectives for the year and limiting the organization's attention to those—a gift for narrowing the field—morphed into a failure to take a broad enough view. His intense interest in short-term per-formance came at the expense of any real attention to, or patience for, long-term thinking.

The Pete Powers of the world run two risks. The first risk is to their organizations: a possible impairment in the future of the orga-nization's ability to evolve, a possible delayed reaction. The second risk is to themselves. They can easily become typecast as good mid-dle managers who lack the breadth to move into top roles. Since they don't talk conceptually and broadly the way many CEOs do, they may leave the impression that they are not bright (not that Sam Menza's brand of book-smart strategic thinking is the only way to be strategic). Nor do they credit themselves with intellectual ability—street smarts, perhaps. They are regarded as the people who bring in the profits and, even as they are being rewarded for that, they are getting boxed in.

Subpairs

The broad distinction between strategic and operational breaks down into three mid-level distinctions, which at this stage in Rob Kaiser's and my thinking are those listed in Table 6.3.[7] As with the

Table 6.3. Strategic and Operational Subpairs

Direction	Execution
Growth	Efficiency
Innovation	Order

forceful-enabling opposition, managers do not necessarily fall out the same way on all three subpairs. A manager who excels at planning and at growing the organization isn't necessarily innovation-minded, just as someone who is results-oriented and good at setting priorities won't necessarily do as well at taking an orderly approach to getting results.

What could be more familiar than the first strategic-operational subpair: (a) looking down the road to what adjustments the organization will need to make to remain viable and (b) putting a head-down focus on getting the organization to deliver results in the near term? The third subpair, Innovation-Order, captures the tension between breaking with the established order to come up with new services and products, and using consistent practices for getting things done.

As a practical managerial challenge, the second subpair, Growth-Efficiency, is a familiar tradeoff, and the tension lies between launching numerous initiatives inside and outside of the organization and concentrating available resources on a select few priorities. As an idea, this duality goes all the way back to Pythagoras.[8] At the top of his Table of Opposites, Pythagoras placed Unlimited versus Limited. Operationally oriented individuals are admired for limiting their focus, for having their feet on the ground, for systematically driving the organization down the field to a preset goal line. And they are faulted for tunnel vision and for a lack of strategic boldness. One such leader, in fact, set a goal of soaring higher and staying in the air longer. On the other hand, strategically oriented senior leaders disdain the short-yardage ground game, and much prefer to put the ball in the air. Expansion-minded, they push the limits. They fly majestically but aren't sufficiently grounded in the realities of what can and cannot be done. Ego is a factor.[9] Bold strategic leaders tend toward a brash egotism; prudent operational leaders tend toward humility (interesting to note that the root of the word humility is the earth, the ground).

Napoleon, as portrayed in Emerson's short biography, possessed a fabulous ability to get it done on the battlefield. Blessed with a combination of great practical aptitude and superior intelligence, not to mention exceptional vigor, Napoleon "knew what to do, and he flew to the mark; he would shorten a straight line to come at his object. . . ; he saw only the object; the obstacle must give way." Having delineated Napoleon's gifts as a leader, a broader set than mentioned here, Emerson changed course: "I am sorry that the brilliant picture had its reverse." Napolean's desire for conquest knew no bounds, and in the end he overstepped his bounds. In him the Unlimited held sway until the Limited defeated him.[10]

Larger-than-life examples aside, every manager has characteristic postures on all three strategic-operational dichotomies. Do you know yours?

What Throws Off Leaders' Form on Strategic and Operational Leadership?

Certainly the accumulation of experiences can tip managers one way or the other. Take, for example, those individuals who, like Sam Menza, in mid-career move from a consulting firm into high-level management positions. Lacking experience in operational jobs, they almost inevitably fail to appreciate what is actually involved in undertaking major organizational change ("To think it is to make it happen"), and they lack respect for those pragmatic types who do make it happen. Likewise, managers who specialize in running operations, and whose jobs don't ask much of them strategically, almost inevitably lean the other way.[11]

Personality, no doubt influenced by experience, leaves its stamp too. Carl Jung believed that individuals prefer either "sensing" (getting into the details and rigorously examining the facts) or "intuition" (taking a holistic approach and trusting your instincts). The Myers-Briggs Type Inventory, a personality test based on his theory, picks up individual differences on that pair of dimensions, among others. In addition, Michael Kirton developed a test to measure individual differences on "adaptive" versus "innovative" problem solving, being inclined to improve the existing system versus being inclined to introduce fundamental change.[12]

Spurred by our preferences, we seek out, and are selected for, jobs that fit our interests and abilities.[13] As we gain experience in a type of role, we become more and more proficient at it, and if we are not careful we may get stuck in it.[14]

Crooked thinking also comes into play. Take the CEO who, like Sam Menza, focused harder on strategy than on the operational part of his job and maintained that that was the right thing to do, despite the consensus among his direct reports that he should be more involved operationally. He insisted: "The bigger picture is more important and has more leverage." His too-little ratings on "Detail-oriented" and "Keeps his finger on the pulse" didn't sway him: he equated attention to detail with being bogged down in it.

Sensitivities—an unwarranted sense of intellectual inadequacy, for example—can also throw off a leader's form on the strategic-operational opposition. Some senior managers whose jobs demand strategic thinking of them nevertheless give short shrift to it. Apparently, it is the intellectual character of that work that intimidates them. Puzzled, dismayed, frustrated, the people around them have no idea what causes the executive to veer away from that critical part of his or her job. If the individual happens to know the reason, he or she is not about to divulge what amounts to a dark secret.

Strategic and Operational Leadership: In Search of Versatility

It would be hard to find leaders who wouldn't say that both strategic leadership and operational leadership are important. Yet it is not easy to find managers who are truly good at both. The vast difference in the two sets of skills makes this balance very difficult to achieve. Presented with two halves of a whole, managers tend to migrate to one, like a parent who can't help treating one of two children as the favorite.

What recourse do leaders have? It's different for strategic-operational than for forceful-enabling. For the latter, many functions reside in the person of the leader, and there is no alternative to having that person perform them. Therefore, to redress an imbalance it often falls to the leader to change personally. The only way to talk less is to talk less. The only way to be show more empathy is to do just that. When it comes to self-assertion or compassion, there is no finding a substitute.

Strategic-operational leadership is different. In addition to making up deficits by learning and changing personally, managers can bring in reinforcements. The character of the strategic and operational functions makes them much easier to hand off. If you aren't an out-of-the-box thinker, you can recruit one. If you are not a tightly organized person and have no appetite for running a disciplined system for tracking progress and tackling deviations from the plan, you can assign someone else to do it. If you know you are prone to taking big strategic risks, you can use your team or your superiors or the board to check you on this tendency.

There is one condition. Although your personal repertoire need not be balanced, your perspective on the two sides must be. Whatever your predisposition, you must give each its due. (For a picture of how the subpairs on both the strategic-operational and forceful-enabling oppositions come together, see the model in Figure 10.2 in Chapter 10.)

Developing Yourself, Coaching Others

Highlights

1. On strategic and operational leadership, you can, with help, do both; you must do both.

2. Strategy is part of your job, even if you are not a senior manager, even if your job description does not explicitly mention strategy. Your responsibility may not be so much to look ahead as it is to apply that forward look to your unit as it operates today: "Here, in light of the longer-range plan, is what has to change right now."

3. Operational leadership is part of your job, even at senior levels—if to do nothing more than make sure the operational leaders under you receive whatever guidance and regular involvement they need from you.

4. Connect the strategic part and the operational part. Strategy constantly has to pull the operational piece, or your unit will be stuck in the mud. At the same time, the operational piece has to act as a reality check on strategic thinking, or people will say it's pie in the sky.

5. Bring in reinforcements. You can't easily delegate being forceful or being enabling. But if you are not strong strategically or operationally, you can readily bring in surrogate strategists or surrogate operators. What you can't do is disparage that function or the people who perform it.

continued

continued

Questions for Reflection

1. How versatile or lopsided are you on strategic-operational leadership?

   - Do you pay good attention to longer-range planning *and* focus hard on meeting near-term objectives?

   - Do you look to strengthen or expand your unit *and* respect the limits on the unit's capacity to absorb change?

   - Do you encourage innovation *and* practice operational discipline?

2. Are you more comfortable with one side or the other? Would you rather think about strategy than get into the nuts and bolts (or conversely)?

3. Do you show appreciation for people in both strategic and operations roles? Or does one group feel more valued by you?

4. Do you take into account how your career has affected your leanings on strategic-operational leadership.

Part Three

Prescriptions for Development

This part offers ways to correct overdoing it, underdoing it, and the combination of both, lopsidedness. All three chapters describe the outer/behavioral work of development and the inner/personal work of development. The book concludes with an elaboration of an ideal of versatility, which if not a destination that most leaders will reach can nevertheless serve as a direction for their development.

Chapter Seven

Throttling Back

"Excess is not success. Excess is false success."
—*Harry Kaplan*

Adults can if fact change, despite what some people believe. But typically it is difficult, whether it is you who is trying to improve or whether you are trying to help someone else improve. There are no formulas to follow, no sure-fire methods of effecting the desired change. In fact, the halls in organizations are littered with stories of nagging performance problems that persist over the years despite everyone's best efforts. But there are things you can do to increase the probabilities. There is leverage that can be applied—to temper strengths overused, for example.

A throttle controls how much gas vapor flows into an engine's cylinders. Leaders who over-rev in one way or another need to throttle back—stop putting excessive energy into that function. This may seem like an obvious point, but the field of leadership development hasn't put the same emphasis on tempering strengths overused as it has on making up deficiencies.[1] The explanation is simple: organizations can't very well develop what they don't assess.

Your own success depends on learning to restrain characteristic strong tendencies that have long stood you in good stead and acquiring true hair-trigger control of your reflex actions, even during times of great stress. That way you won't waste energy and therefore will have plenty of it available to you when it is most needed.

There are three ways to throttle back: (1) *catch yourself*, that is, restrain yourself through sheer willpower or though a process meant to buttress willpower. This is the outer work of development; (2)

change your mind-set. This is the inner work of development, contending with the crooked thinking or trigger points that fuel the excess; and (3) to the extent that you are not yet able to contain your excesses on your own, or while you are still learning to do that, another option strongly recommends itself: *use a counterweight,* usually a person or group that offsets the excess.

Let's also remember that the problem of excess is a good problem to have. You don't have to acquire a capacity or build one up. You already have a plentiful supply of the talent, skill, knowledge, motivation—all the strengths you could possibly need. All you have to do is learn to regulate them better.

This chapter and the next tackle diametrically opposite developmental tasks. Just as this chapter is about easing up a little on the gas pedal, or if necessary tapping on the brake, to keep from over-revving, the next chapter is about the opposite fuel-feeding function, revving up. Yet, as Table 7.1 shows, both chapters are organized around the same three developmental levers:

> A manager confided: "I don't trust myself, so I'm constantly having to prove my worth. Internally I'm constantly churning, telling myself I've got to turn the intensity up, which explains the throttling, the over-revving."

> A senior manager made this observation: "No one touts moderation. But I know I've got to not mindlessly pursue any single goal, not overemphasize any one value."

1. The outer, or behavioral, work of development;
2. The inner work of development; and
3. The use of others to deal with deficiencies or excesses.

Although the emphasis in this chapter and the next is on what you as an individual can do to change, I don't want to leave the

Table 7.1. Ways of Throttling Back and Revving Up

	Throttling Back	*Revving Up*
Outer Work of Development	Catch yourself	Force yourself
Inner Work of Development	Contain your urges	Overcome your inhibitions
Use of Others (where development falls short)	As counterweights to "catch" or balance you	As complements— to compensate for your limitations

impression that change happens in isolation. To the extent that you make adjustments, other people may also need to adjust. If you stop taking more than your share of responsibility and delegate more, some people on your staff may struggle with the additional responsibility and need your help in adapting to it. On the other hand, if you stop filling your space and some of theirs too, they may simply breathe a sigh of relief!

Catching Yourself: The Outer Work of Throttling Back

Leaders who set out to correct for excess often describe the correction as catching themselves. It is an act of willpower exercised at the moment that the urge to go too far is about to kick in. While there is often an inner aspect to catching yourself—some self-awareness—nevertheless the emphasis in this outer work is on directly managing your behavior.

Throttling back starts with the realization that you need to tamp down your excesses, along with a commitment to do just that. Since willpower is hardly a sure thing, it's smart to bolster your efforts. Of the many tactics you can employ either to throttle back or to rev up, I cover four in this chapter and the next: (1) choose a swing thought, (2) know the signs, (3) adopt a regimen, and (4) build in feedback loops (see Table 7.2). In no way intended as a complete compendium, these tactics are simply meant to illustrate the outer work of development.

**Table 7.2. Tactics for Outer Development:
Changing Your Behavior**

1. Choose a "swing thought" — a single correction to your form that is easy to keep in mind

2. Know the signs—often physical cues of an impending reflex reaction

3. Adopt a regimen—a program for bringing out the changed behavior.

4. Build in feedback loops— cuing, scorecards, surveys.

Choose a Swing Thought

A "swing thought" is a golfer's term for a single correction to your form that you keep in mind as you stand over the ball. A swing thought keys on a very specific behavior that stands for the shift you are seeking to make. The idea is that to try to make several adjustments at once is a setup for failure. Sara Central, all too ready to take center stage, learned that she inadvertently pushed other people to the periphery. Her swing thought: "Let the other person finish." Although there is a lot more to being enabling than letting people complete their thoughts, for Sara, not interrupting was a start and stood for the larger goal.

A swing thought is most likely to be effective if it is grounded in feeling and not just a pointer or technique. This was never more apparent than in a manager whose general tendency not to be forceful enough carried over to his relationship to top management, with whom he was too deferential. He had tried and failed to approach his superiors more or less as peers. A role play changed that. In demonstrating for me how he would make his point with a more senior person he, in effect, genuflected, and it repulsed him.

He chose the swing thought, albeit a negative one: "Not on bended knee!" When he went off to a meeting with top management, it fortified him to have the thought and the feeling of disgust in mind.

A swing thought, then, is a simple device for building momentum, and it works best if it represents something you badly want to do or be.

Know the Signs

If you are to succeed in catching yourself, it helps greatly to become familiar with the indications that you are about to overdo it.

Often the signs are physical. One manager discovered that his left leg would begin to bounce moments before he made a too-pointed comment in a meeting. Another "got hot" (he could feel his face flush) moments before he was about to let a subordinate have it for disappointing him. Someone else, who was given to entering a room with an exuberance that, as a coworker put it, "would turn over the apple cart," realized that at those moments he felt like a "spring wound too tight."

> A middle manager who worked on his form at work and on the golf course had concluded: "Positive swing thoughts are much better than negative ones. A negative swing thought such as 'Don't try to crush the ball' or 'Don't move your head' tells you what not to do and focuses your attention on not messing up. A positive swing thought focuses you on a right thing to do to improve your game."

The idea is to interrupt the reflex reaction. If you learn to recognize the signs of an impending overreaction, you can pause for a moment to find an alternative to your customary knee-jerk reaction. You can bleed off the urge to blurt something out by writing down what you were about to say. If you find yourself wound too tight at the start of a meeting, you can take a deep breath and calm yourself. That way other people won't have to gird themselves against your over-exuberance or excess intensity and can more freely partake of your contribution. It is learning to do what great performers in any line of work do—slow down the action so that you can, in a Malcolm Gladwell "blink,"[2] modulate your exquisite natural reflex reactions.

You can only use these signals, physical and emotional, if you tune into them. Many leaders do not. As my colleague Lawrence Stibbards says, "We live in our heads." So it helps to get better acquainted with your moment-to-moment emotional life and more conversant in the language of your body.

Adopt a Regimen

To turn insight into sustained change, many leaders need discipline, the same tight discipline that they bring to any important initiative. If they don't buttress the edifice of their ambition for improvement, it can easily topple to the ground. A regimen is one such support.

To rein in a tendency to give her staff too much autonomy, one manager set aside two hours—thirty minutes for each direct report—every Tuesday afternoon for check-ins and progress reports. Using this simple regimen, she got in the habit of connecting with her people and shaping their work.

Managers driven to work endless hours benefit from restraints that they impose on themselves. An irresistible force will only be denied by an immovable object. To contain his overweening drive that tipped his life decidedly toward work, one individual made a commitment to leave the office at 5:30 p.m. twice a week when he wasn't traveling so that he could have dinner with his wife and two young daughters. He told his wife about it, naturally, so she wouldn't fall off her chair when he arrived early. And he told his assistant so she could shoo him out of the office at 5:15. How did he do? He couldn't sustain the twice-a-week regimen, but he did institutionalize a weekly practice. It may not seem like much, but there was a world of difference between getting home in time for dinner once a week versus not at all.

Another manager put himself on a program to moderate his high intensity, which he had always believed was the key to his success. Now, however, the high intensity had begun to take a toll. No serious health problems, fortunately. But he had grown weary of his nervous energy and near-frantic way of going about his job. From time to time, his wife had expressed concern, but he hadn't taken it seriously because he didn't want to tamper with a winning formula.

In an effort to be less tense, less agitated, he started doing a formal relaxation exercise, using a tape that walked him step-by-step through a thirty-minute program.[3] That way he could at least know what it felt like to be relaxed. Also, he bought an audio version of Dale Carnegie's *How to Stop Worrying and Start Living*, replete with instructive stories of people facing serious problems who nevertheless learned to relax, and he listened to the tape on the drive back and forth to work. "When I get to the end of the tape, I start over," he told me (how is that for intense?!). He did this for months on end in an attempt to drill a new mantra into his head, overwriting a script that was no longer serviceable. By tackling an improvement goal in his customary disciplined way, he could not guarantee the outcome, but he certainly increased his chances of obtaining it.

In attempting to throttle back, rather than depend exclusively on your good intentions, you are usually better off if you devise simple practices, processes, or mechanisms that bring out the desired behavior on a regular basis. The principle is consistency.

Build in Feedback Loops

In addition to picking up on internal cues, you can have other people cue you when you overdo it.[4]

Over-talking has to be one of the most widespread types of managerial excess. Going on and on, sometimes in a monotone and sometimes with great gusto, some individuals seem to have no awareness or no self-control. One such person enlisted a peer and a direct report to signal him in the different meetings they attended when he slipped into that mode, and if necessary to interrupt him.

Another individual "deputized" his assistant to intervene when the manager monopolized in his staff meeting. He actually gave her a plastic sheriff's badge (a children's party favor, no less) that the assistant could humorously flash.

Just as useful as getting feedback in the act of overdoing is receiving it shortly after the fact. One manager had each person on his team "adopt a weakness"—in most cases an excess—that it was his or her responsibility to stay on the lookout for and bring to his attention.

Feedback loops of this kind have an additional advantage. By making your commitment public, you increase your chances of making the change.[5]

Feedback loops are a way to hold yourself accountable for making the change and a way of getting support in your efforts to change. Note that a feedback loop in human form is not quite a counterweight. Although it brings instances of excess to your attention, it stops short of a determined effort to dissuade or deter you.

By whatever outward means—sheer force of will or mechanisms for bolstering it—the goal of the outer work of development is to curb excessive behavior, to keep from crossing the line. Of course, as you try out new behavior, that experience becomes grist for the inner work of development.

Changing Your Mind-Set: The Inner Work of Throttling Back

Improving your mental game rounds out your repertoire for effecting genuine, lasting change.[6]

Effort is a critical attribute for players in any line of work, and extra effort distinguishes high performers from all the rest. But woe to the person who, overanxious to perform, tries too hard, has too tight a grip on the baseball bat, golf club, or tennis racket or, for that matter, on the meeting he or she is running. Phil Simms, the former New York Giants quarterback who guided his team to a SuperBowl victory, completing twenty-two of twenty-five passes, has said that "over-gripping is the most common mistake."[7] A tensed arm can't throw the football well. On the same principle, golfers speak of holding the club like a bird. When intense becomes tense, athletes and leaders alike impair their performance.

By itself, a purely behavioral approach often isn't enough to tame excess. It only makes sense that leaders also work on their mental game, because in many cases that is what has thrown off their performance in the first place. You can think of the inner work of development as increasing your emotional intelligence, as Daniel Goleman called it, or your emotional competence, as Edgar Schein called it. Since change is such a chancy thing, why not raise the probability of success by taking both outer and inner approaches?

Table 7.3 contains a list of three approaches to changing your mind-set, which apply to both throttling back and revving up. By no means do these three exhaust the possibilities.

Straighten Out Crooked Thinking

If it is hard to imagine adjusting the gearing in your head or in anyone else's, here are four concrete measures you can take: (1) recognize when more is less; (2) alter your idea of the switch; (3) moderate the sky-high value placed on a strength; and (4) moderate unrealistically high expectations.

**Table 7.3. Tactics for Inner Development:
Changing Your Mind-Set**

1. Straighten out crooked thinking

2. Defuse trigger points

3. Own your strengths

Recognize When More Is Less. "What do you mean?" is the retort I sometimes get when I tell a manager that his high-as-possible score on a prized dimension such as Results Orientation could mean he or she is taking it too far. For that individual, in that respect there is no such thing as too much of a good thing. The maximum is the optimum. No surprise, I suppose, in a land of supersized meals and oversized vehicles.

A couple of days after his feedback session, a manager who was high-powered to a fault came to to this realization: "I see: I don't have to give up my fastball. I just don't have to throw it all the time!" A baseball fan, he told me the story of Sandy Koufax, the brilliant Los Angeles Dodgers pitcher who didn't become a great pitcher until he stopped throwing his fastball so hard and so often. Koufax came into his own when he took his catcher's advice to "stop trying to blow his fastball by the hitters, to try more curves and change-ups, and to throw his fastball less hard and more accurately."[8] The Dodgers' manager, Walter Alston, said that Koufax was less effective when he pitched with "all muscle and no finesse, trying to use 100 percent of his strength, when his experience taught him he is most effective when he uses 90 percent of it in a steady, rhythmical pattern." Koufax achieved greatness when he learned to govern his power.

You may know better than to believe that more is better, but that doesn't protect you from slipping into that frame of mind on something near and dear to your heart. As the "fastball-throwing" manager discovered, the key is to learn to use an overdeveloped strength selectively. It is learning to discriminate between the right amount and too much.[9]

Alter Your Idea of the Switch. One reason that leaders have trouble turning down the volume on an overused strength is that they think of the volume control as an on-and-off switch. But what they imagine is an on-and-off switch turns out to be a rheostat. This is what Sara Central discovered: "My big learning on 'too much Sara' has been, let's call it, modulation. A year ago when I got the feedback,

I took it to mean throw an on-off switch. But now I see there are more than two levels. It's more like a volume control. It's continuous."

When it comes to a strength you rely on heavily, the rheostate allows you to fine-tune it without any danger of losing it completely.

Moderate the Sky-High Value Placed on a Strength. When we attach inordinate importance to a skill or attribute, we become poor judges of how much is enough, and through our feverish eyes too much looks like just the right amount. As one manager said, "Some people fall in love with what they've emphasized, and it becomes a religious thing." This extreme emotional attachment is what leads to the idea of the switch as on-and-off.

Many leaders become incredibly attached to their own intensity, and can't think clearly about lowering it. There is an element of superstition. They don't want to tamper with a winning formula. As the Southern saying goes, "Dance with the one who brung ya." One young senior manager got credit for "taking the edge off," which enabled him to listen better. Yet giving up some of his intensity felt wrong to him: "I'm used to going 110 miles per hour and so I feel guilty for only going 80."

A closet pride is often at work here. Long hours become a badge of courage.

Think of it as a "more-than" attitude. "I am more—fill in the blank—conscientious, or analytical, or results-oriented, or straightforward, or principled, or kind than everyone else." This was true of a manager who prided himself in his "servant leadership," which to him meant putting others' needs ahead of his own. Although it made him a wonderfully supportive, empathic, development-minded boss, he couldn't recognize that he took it to extremes nor could he see what he traded off. In general, that unconscious superior attitude is an obstacle to seeing excess for what it is. Often a more-than attitude originates in childhood when, in a position of vulnerability, the child adopts it to feel special. Adults, in a much stronger position than children, do well to drop the conceit in favor of accepting themselves as they are.[10]

The danger for all of us is that we value certain leadership properties to the nth degree and don't know it. Our job is to take the blinders off.

Moderate Excessively High Expectations. When you expect too much of yourself—how many hours you work, how well-written your memos are, how responsive you are to your boss, how well-armed you are with facts for a presentation to the board, how quickly you will advance—you run a serious risk of doing too much. We all have them—unrealistically high expectations, potent "shoulds" and "should not's" that acquire the status of unquestioned truths or absolutes and exert extraordinary power over us.[11]

Who could ever argue with a strong sense of responsibility? But in some managers it is overdeveloped. One senior leader discovered that subconsciously he was afraid the organization would crumble if, Atlas-like, he did not personally hold it up. The drawback was that, without meaning to, he usurped the authority of his direct reports, senior managers in their own right. He had his developmental work cut out for him because of how he came by his motivation. He and several other leaders with the same profile were all first-born sons who at young ages lost their fathers. Having had to assume a heavy burden of responsibility prematurely, they overlearned the lesson.

Expecting too much of themselves, managers frequently expect too much of others. Woven into the fabric of their being, their expectations don't seem excessive to them. To them it is the right and proper way to be. Up to a point, their personal example is motivating. But it is also oppressive. One manager was hardest on the coworkers she was closest to. "I treat them the way I treat myself," she explained.

Perfectionism can be harmful not just to performance but to the person's health and well-being. Vince Foster, the deputy White House counsel in the first Clinton administration, placed an unwavering value on honesty and integrity. However, during the investigation of the so-called "Travelgate" scandal, in which he was blamed for alleged improprieties in the dismissal of White House travel office staff, his integrity was called into question on the national stage. His diary entries around that time show evidence of increasing distress, obsession, and a mounting fear of public humiliation. And his suicide note makes it clear that the pressure became too much for him to bear. No question that high integrity is a virtue. Little question, it seems, that Vince Foster's attachment to an idealized image of himself cost him his life.[12]

What's needed is a retooling of your excessively high expectations that dictate how much work you must do and how good at it you must be. The challenge is to stand outside of your tightly wrapped system of thought. If you can achieve some emotional distance on these unrealistic expectations, you can take some of the power out of them, for your sake and the sake of others.

Defuse Trigger Points

A trigger point is a fear that touches off a reflex reaction, usually an overreaction, one that is difficult to control because it fires instantaneously and therefore easily escapes your notice. But if you can defuse that trigger point, that is, better manage the fear or outgrow it, you can avert the overly strong reaction. To do that, however, you must acknowledge your fears to yourself, something that managers, especially male managers, don't make a habit of doing.

A middle manager became incensed any time he witnessed unfairness and found it difficult to see his (over)reaction as anything but justified. Unfairness usually meant that someone, a service person such as an airline ticket agent or waitperson in a restaurant, was, in his view, taking advantage of him or of someone else. Even though these incidents usually took place away from the office, they mattered to his effectiveness because the coworkers with him were made very uncomfortable by how quickly and unnecessarily he escalated the situation. Presented with this feedback, he held to his position and insisted, self-righteously, that it was his job to put a stop to the unfairness not just for his sake but for the good of society. Upon reflection, he was able to distinguish between *what* he made an issue of and *how* he went about it. And he seemed to soften his position a little when he made the connection between his hot button and the rough treatment he had endured as a child.

Not all trigger points result in an instant reaction. Some are responsible for a chronic tendency to overdo a part of the job. A middle manager admitted to me that he spent way too much time composing emails. The reason, as he reflected on it, was that he was afraid of losing other people's respect. He gathered that he could cut down on the time he spent polishing emails if he somehow worried less about the impression they would make.

Similarly, when managers live in fear of not having enough of a prized attribute, growth consists of

> A manager identified this reflex reaction in himself: "If one of my people asks a question, I'll immediately give him the answer, rather than turn the question back to him to get him to think about it. I see now that when I answer the question, it's selfish. I'm meeting my need to be productive and to show that I'm smart."

allaying the fear. Billy Peoples, widely taken to be cooperative, decent, and honorable, nevertheless worried that he wasn't enough of those things. Hearing this, a peer pointed out to him: "You carry around a bucket of 'good-guy capital.' Good-guy capital spills out of that bucket, it's so full." The peer went on to say, "And your 'bad-guy capital' bucket is empty." In other words, Billy had accumulated so much "good-guy" credit that he had plenty of leeway to take the unpopular stands that he had shied away from.

To know your fears puts you in a stronger position to catch yourself before they push you overboard. A manager prone to outbursts in his staff meetings peeled the onion and discovered that fear was the trigger, fear of not knowing enough about the organization he was running, fear that his team would fall short in this respect. The moment he sensed that a subordinate was unprepared or was trying to fake it, he panicked and promptly shot his mouth off. Knowing this about himself gave him the opportunity to "press the pause button" when he began to panic and to interrupt the reflex.

Fear also comes into play when leaders contemplate turning down the volume on a highly valued trait. The manager described above who was concerned about lowering his intensity from 110 to 80 miles per hour actually called me right after the assessment to ask, "If I don't work quite as hard, is there any danger that I'll get lazy." I asked him, "If you set out to be lazy, could you do it?" Of course, "No" was his answer. He later realized that his fearful thinking had been unwarranted. "At the start of the process I worried that the good part weakens. But no, the bad part weakens, and the good part strengthens." Incidentally, I've heard the same anxious question from an overly nice manager who saw he needed to be more tough-minded. He called me on the phone to ask, "If I make this change, will I stop being a nice person?" I asked him, "Could you if you tried?" He admitted he could not. Leaders need to reassure themselves that by modulating a cherished strength they will not lose it.

If you live in fear of not having enough of a skill or attribute, then you probably have trouble seeing straight about how much of that attribute you in fact possess, in which case the following intervention recommends itself.

Own Your Own Strengths

A very useful device for modulating a strength overused is positive feedback, and plenty of it. For ten years my colleagues and I have deliberately used it as leverage for development, as described in Chapter 3, and we have repeatedly seen it work. When affirming comments make an impression on a manager, a typical response is: "I don't have to worry about that any more." A senior manager said precisely that upon learning that everyone credited him with impeccable integrity.

A manager who forever strained to justify his existence came to this realization after reading the positive comments in his report: "You don't have to always prove you know everything. People accept that you're smart and knowledgeable. You don't have to prove it every day. People know you're the leader. They know you're the boss." Able to relax a little on this point, he now felt able to give his people more space to talk and demonstrate how smart and knowledgeable *they* were—and to grow. He reduced his intention to a simple dictum: "Let other leaders lead."

You might think that what's most needed to fix a problem such as abrasiveness, which is being critical or confrontational to a fault, is negative feedback that brings the problem forcibly to the individual's attention. But negative feedback is overrated. If anything, managers need to resist its pull because it distracts them from positive feedback, a non-obvious cure for an issue like abrasiveness. You can try clamping down on the bad behavior, but that's merely treating the symptom. Better to go after the root cause, which can turn out to be a failure to recognize the extent of an asset.

Steve Sharp, who in Chapter 3 showed himself to be very resistant to feedback about how smart he was, had a bad habit of being rough on people who didn't "get it right away." Fine to challenge people, fine to be direct about inadequate work, but he took those qualities to a destructive extreme. How did he break the habit? In a way that surprised me. This was a person who had a running argument with his staff about how smart he was. He insisted, "Not that smart." They maintained, "Off-the-charts smart." The feedback to that effect didn't sway him. A month after the feedback session, we presented him with a consolidation report with all the comments about each strength or weakness arrayed under the respective heading. When Steve finished reading the section on strengths, he said nothing, which was very unusual for someone as quick-witted as he. Finally I asked for his reaction. "Sobered," he said. That his intelligence was way above average had finally sunk in. Right away he could see that he needed to make allowances for his brainpower, that he had to be more patient with people who, although plenty smart, weren't as quick on their feet as he. Immediately after the session,

> The management thinker Peter Drucker has said, "Most American managers do not know what their strengths are."[13]

his offensive behavior for the most part stopped. It was as if that way of relating to people simply dropped out of his behavioral vocabulary.

To err on the side of underestimating yourself is to risk creating a most unfortunate situation in which your strengths, rather than serving as a boon to your organization, are experienced as a bane because you take them too far. When this happens, coworkers don't admire you for your capability; they wring their hands because what they get is a perversion of that capability.

When you recognize the full extent of your ability and stop worrying that you are not good enough, then you will be less likely to take that strength to a counterproductive extreme. By stripping away the excess surrounding a strength, you are left with the effective core.

Using Counterweights

Whatever self-regulating that managers learn to do for themselves, it is not realistic to expect all the curtailing of excess to come from them. To the extent that they can't contain themselves, they need help in doing it. Enlightened leaders who understand that they can't always trust certain of their instincts impose controls on themselves.

Put a Counterweight in Place

Joseph Stalin, a wildly extreme case of a leader who abused power in the most heinously destructive ways, is a stunning example of the complete absence of counterweights. For the twenty-five years that he ran the newly formed Soviet Union, he lacked anyone or anything to check his excesses. He was responsible for the deaths of millions of his own people, including scores of individuals in his own administration who fell out of favor. Under these conditions, very few were the individuals who would stand up

> A manager had concluded: "You have to know what the flip side of your strengths are so you can have a couple of people on your staff who tell you that you are full of crap, and help balance that."

to him. On top of his murderous tendencies, Stalin was intimidating in conversation. He had a brilliant mind, a tremendous ability to retain information, and a stormy personality to boot.[14]

One of a handful of individuals capable of opposing Stalin effectively, General Zhukov had Stalin's respect as well as the strength of character not to be cowed by him. "Firmness and humor with Stalin usually worked well," according to a recent biographer.[15] But Zhukov was the exception that proved the rule. Stalin almost entirely lacked a loyal opposition. He lacked it in the people at senior levels. And it was also missing from the country's governance structure. Stalin controlled the judiciary. He controlled the legislative process. He controlled the military. Since the Soviet government under Stalin utterly lacked checks and balances, his executive authority and personal power went virtually unchecked for twenty-five years. Whatever the advances—industrialization, a build-up of military power—under his leadership, it took a tremendous toll on government officeholders and on the population at large.

> An individual with a strong personality had learned: "I know I need a couple of temperate souls on the team, and if they find my presence too intense and difficult to approach, they can safely let me know.

In any walk of organizational life, those individuals who go way out of bounds will probably forever need a counterweight on certain of their behaviors. An extreme overdo score on the Leadership Versatility Index, two or more standard deviations out from optimal, indicates excess so pronounced that the individual, on his or her own, is not likely to rein it in any time soon. This was true of Sara Central, whose coworkers rated her +2.21 on the too-much side of the scale on the item "Takes charge," which statistically is a whopping departure from optimal. However mild or extreme your tendency to overdo it may be, it is worth your while to introduce a process, formal or informal, for knowing what your excesses are and installing a loyal opposition to deal with them. Here are two cases in point.

- I once consulted to an otherwise capable business leader who consistently had trouble coming to closure on high-stakes decisions because he was too analytical and he fretted that the course of action he chose would go wrong. To break the deadlock, this leader, collaborative by nature, decided that where possible he would involve his inner circle in the actual making of decisions.

- An otherwise effective manager and good person had overbearing tendencies that carried over to his relationship with his wife. To check himself, he arranged for her to say "red," in effect holding up a stop sign, when he came on too strong. They also agreed that, if he made a sarcastic remark at her expense, she was welcome to throw a wadded-up piece of paper at him.

Again, going to extremes absolutely has a place in leadership. The problem comes when those extremes go far beyond what the situation dictates.

Realistically, those leaders most in need of an offset are those whose psychology make them unlikely

> A top executive was wise enough to know he needed a counterweight: "I know I need other people to 'catch' me."

candidates to put one in place. This is where a higher authority may need to impose controls on a leader who lacks the ability to keep his or her own behavior in bounds. This is where peers or subordinates have a responsibility, as daunting or risky as it might be to discharge it.

Tolerate the Tension of Being Checked and Countered

It is incumbent on leaders to manage the tension between what their instincts dictate and what restraints the counterweight would place on them. A very high-powered individual badly needed strong, capable characters on his team who without a lot of difficulty could push back, disagree, or even say on the spot, "You're overbearing." Much to this person's credit, his own needs for dominance did not keep him from having, as one direct report put it, "forceful people on his staff," who could stand up to him.

A continuing tension between him and his team centered around how much change to take on. Ambitious for his organization and eager to improve its market position, he regularly proposed initiatives, projects, and new organizational processes. He wasn't noted for being realistic about what it would actually take to implement a plan or what the combined impact of several initiatives had on the organization. According to a team member, "When he wants to do something, he gets very focused and he's going to do it regardless of the consequences." This is where his team, closer to the action and more practical than he was, came in. As determined as he was and even though he could "occasionally steamroller over everybody," people "for the most part felt comfortable challenging him," and they had some success in influencing him. They did find that, instead of confronting him one-on-one, they were better off raising issues in team meetings.

Sometimes the tension between leader and would-be counterweight turns into a monumental struggle because the leader has his mind made up and the stakes are extremely high. I don't know of a better example in literature or in life than the scene in *Moby Dick* where Starbuck, the first mate, tells Ahab, the ship's captain, that they need to stop for repairs. It seems that precious whale oil is leaking out. No way is Ahab, believing that they are in range of Moby Dick, the killer white whale, willing to interrupt the pursuit. He orders Starbuck back up on deck.

Starbuck's face reddens as he moves further into the captain's cabin and "with a daring" that is "strangely respectful" delicately presses his point.

Ahab grabs a loaded musket and aims it at Starbuck.

Starbuck, "mastering his emotion," says, "'I ask thee not to beware of Starbuck; thou wouldst laugh; but let Ahab beware of Ahab; beware of thyself, old man.'"

After Starbuck leaves, Ahab says to himself, "Ahab beware of Ahab—there is something there!" And he orders the crew to make the repairs. By handling his boss with extraordinary skillfulness, a difficult-to-achieve blend of plain talk and deference, of intensity and emotional control, Starbuck prevailed this time. When leaders with strong personalities are hell-bent and determined, it takes a most delicately balanced opposition to sway them.

For leaders to benefit from a counterweight, they have to give credence to a lieutenant's opposing view. Ahab benefited in this instance because he allowed Starbuck's caution to scare him. It is a matter of permitting a responsible party to question your judgment and to be humble enough to know that your position, even though firmly held, could be wrong.

Developing Yourself, Coaching Others

Highlights

1. Leadership assessment and development is deficiency-oriented, much more focused on the need to rev up than to throttle back.

2. To throttle back you have to see moderation for what it is—drawing every bit of strength needed to meet a demand and not a dram more. Moderation has gotten a bad name. It has mistakenly come to mean less than full effort. But to moderate a strength is to remove the waste, the excess that works against what you want to do or that creates unwanted side-effects. Let's give "modulation" and "moderation" a respected place in the managerial vocabulary.

3. To temper a strength, start with the counterintuitive realization that more of a prized asset or attribute is not necessarily better.

4. By all means, try to catch yourself. Pause before you react in the usual way, and put structure and discipline to your exercise of willpower.

5. Also go to work on the assumption, value, expectation, or fear that sends you overboard. Make a list of your most closely held values or those skills or personal qualities that are most precious to you.

6. Don't limit yourself to *self*-regulation and *self*-development. See to it that other people help you stay within bounds.

Questions for Reflection

1. Do you have trouble conceiving of how, for certain of your behaviors, there could ever be too much of a good thing? In your own mind can you never be, for example, too principled, too honest, too hardworking, or too results-oriented?

2. Do you make a practice of having other people "balance" you in areas in which you go too far?

3. Do you have the strength of character to tolerate pushback? Can you bear the tension when another party responsibly attempts to keep you in bounds?

4. Do you personally act as a restraint on your staff members who go overboard? Because you can't be present all the time, do you make sure that dominating staff members have on their teams at least one other strong, outspoken person. However talented and productive someone is, it is important that he or she not get away with murder.

Chapter Eight

Revving Up

"Fear is the enemy of thought and action."

—John Lahr

If combating excess is like braking when you're going too fast, then overcoming a deficiency is like dealing with a reluctance to press down on the gas pedal. That is why leaders may have to *make* themselves do more of a behavior they underdo. This is apart from those cases in which managers simply have not gotten around to acquiring a skill or it hasn't yet been important to their work to learn it. Forcing yourself to do something or to do more of it is a direct intervention into your behavior, the outer work of development. Getting at the underlying inhibition is the other developmental track, the inner work.

Forcing Yourself: The Outer Work of Revving Up

Making yourself do more of something that you haven't believed in or have been afraid to do can contain an element of coercion, just as curbing excess contains an element of forcible restraint.

Many managers understand this intuitively, as these statements by two different individuals show:

- "I have to force myself to sit back and think strategically. It's harder for me because it's the sort of thing that takes a leap of faith."

- "When it came to public speaking, I was a wreck. But I knew that in my line of work I had to force myself to do it. I just had to push past my fears and learn to do it."

Force yourself you must, or you will never discover for yourself what the benefits of the neglected facet of leadership are.

Choose a Swing Thought

To reinforce a swing thought designed to bring out more of a behavior, it helps to find a symbol or metaphor or image that brings home its importance to you. It could be a photograph, a painting, a slogan, a poem, a found object.

- An enabling-style leader saw that he needed to be more decisive, concise, and incisive, all "cutting" functions. His swing thought was "Cut. Cut to the chase, cut out unnecessary discussion, cut out unnecessary verbiage." In a fit of inspiration, I handed him my stainless steel cigar cutter which, for many months, sat on his credenza.

- Dale Carnegie, whose swing thought was "Relax," left a sock on his desk because it stood for the inner limpness he was after.[1]

- For one manager it was a photograph of a group of people listening intently to a speaker. His swing thought: "Say your piece." Having a horror of being "an egotistical loud mouth," this individual sat on good ideas.

- Another individual, whose swing thought was "Take a broader view," put a miniature hot-air balloon on his desk. He decided to "go for regular balloon rides" to stop being so focused on his own patch and to take an enterprise-wide perspective.

For the artifact to reinforce the swing thought, it helps to display the artifact prominently—at work, at home, in your briefcase. Another way to keep your improvement goals front and center is to set up your electronic calendar to send regular "pop-up" reminders, a way of combating repression, a great inhibitor of change, the tendency to block out something uncomfortable or unpleasant.[2] Also, prompts are essential in the hectic managerial world where there is always more to do than time to do it. If the change agenda slips from your mind, it won't get done.

Know the Signs

We all know what it is like to be fearful. Your heart beats faster, your hands get clammy, your mouth dries out, your breathing gets shallow, you begin to sweat. It is your autonomic nervous system, outside of your conscious control, that is preparing your body to get out of harm's way. Fear is a bodily event.

An otherwise effective manager who was able to speak up with reasonable people like himself had a hard time bringing up issues with people he found intimidating. "I now notice when I'm anxious. My shoulders tighten up just walking into a meeting with one of these guys. That feeling used to silence me. Now I'm using it as a reminder not to go quiet."

Therefore, learn to recognize the signs that fear or discomfort is about to warn you off of an action worth taking so that your avoidance urge doesn't win out.

Adopt a Regimen

As we all know, the way to cement good habits is to put yourself on a program that has you practicing regularly. Ballerinas, gymnasts, wrestlers, golfers—all have their daily regimens. Peyton Manning, the quarterback, and Marvin Harrison, the wide receiver, of the Indianapolis Colts football team spend thirty minutes before every game going through "the tree." Harrison runs each pass route in the play book, starting with the short routes and working up to the longer routes. They go through several repetitions, making their form and actions second nature.

A regimen is also important to breaking out of a bad habit. Albert Ellis, one of the fathers of cognitive therapy, tells the story of how as a young adult he overcame being painfully shy with women. He made himself attempt to strike up a conversation with women he didn't know (130 over three months), and in the majority of cases he got a good response. By repeatedly doing what he was afraid of, he liberated himself from a potent inhibition.

The key is doing the thing that fear or prejudice has precluded, and doing it not once but over and over again. The cognitive therapists call this desensitization, a proven technique for helping people get over a phobia.[3] There is wisdom in stringing together a series of small wins that encourage you in the belief that you can do it and that it pays to do it.[4]

After six months of plainer speaking, a manager who had to overcome misgivings about being direct said, "I actually enjoy myself being more assertive." In addition to having a greater impact, the reward for him was the satisfaction of using his powers fully: "This sort of flexing around these issues feels good."

Another way to systematically bring out a flat side is to create a structure that requires you to act in a way you find difficult and then take your place in that structure. A manager received this advice on how to do a better job of holding people accountable: "Look, you and I are not table pounders and the only way we're going to be as tough as we need to be is to set up mechanisms that require us to be that way." Heeding this advice, the manager instituted bi-monthly operating reviews.

> "What I did, and I've always resisted this, is I put in place a way of monitoring to make sure things are moving. It had never been necessary in my career, never been necessary with the other teams I have had. So we now meet twice a month to make sure the basics happen. There are milestones, and if you miss a milestone we understand why and we deal with it. Not that I expect every project to succeed. I've had a long-time aversion to any kind of bureaucratic structures, but I had to get over it. My orientation is probably 70 percent strategic and 30 percent operational, and I think that at times that is a problem."

There is no end to how inventive and resourceful you can be in coming up with structures or processes that draw out behaviors you would not otherwise engage in. Structure enables.

Build in Feedback Loops

If you are serious about revving up in some respect, you owe it to yourself to evaluate your progress.

Technology can aid the effort at self-accountability. Every Friday afternoon, for example, your electronic calendar can be set up to ask you, "Have I done more of X this week?"

To keep yourself honest, obtain others' assessments too. You can ask people informally. You can send out a brief email survey or have it administered for you. You can re-administer relevant items from a 360-degree survey. On any behavior you are attempting to rev up, arrange to get rated on whether you are in fact doing more of it.

It is also useful to keep track each step of the way. One individual who was perpetually late to meetings hadn't realized how much he frustrated his people by keeping them waiting. To remedy his punctuality deficit, he arranged with his assistant to keep track of how many minutes he was late to every appointment, whether it was his meeting or someone else's. She computed a people-minutes index, consisting of the number of minutes he was late times the number of people kept waiting. At the end of the week, she gave him a report with a copy to me. With the aid of this tracking system, he greatly improved his record of on-time arrivals.

The manager who set a goal of speaking up in meetings designed a scorecard to help in the effort. He had a stack of scorecards printed up and kept them on his desk. At the top of each card was his swing thought, "Speak up." Underneath were five blank lines. Before important meetings, he took a few minutes to list the points he intended to make. As he made each point, he checked the box. Starting out with the goal of making one contribution per meeting, he quickly progressed beyond that. After a few months, he no longer needed to keep score, but he found it useful to continue to prepare for meetings this way.

A scorecard does two things. It keeps track of progress toward the goal and it functions as a constant reminder, whether it is you or someone else doing the scorekeeping.[5]

Changing Your Mind-Set:
The Inner Game of Revving Up

It's no easier to overcome an inhibition than it is to contain an urge that results in overdoing.

When managers succumb to an inhibition, they are in fact leading defensively; they are trying to *prevent* something undesirable from happening.[6] Skiing the Rockies three winters ago, a top executive attempted a double black diamond—a trail both steep and narrow—and she fell, tumbling all the way to the bottom of the slope. Luckily she wasn't hurt and was able to ski the rest of the way down the mountain. For the rest of that winter and all of the next, she avoided that trail. The third winter, on a sunny morning after six inches of fresh snow had fallen, she decided to try again, and this time succeeded. What made the difference? "When the conditions are good, I can ski as well as anybody. When the conditions aren't good and I tense up, I can't ski very well." Then she posed the big question: "So how can I stay relaxed in an environment that I consider hostile?"

In skiing it is the turn that matters. It is by turning that skiers control their speed down the mountain and avoid falling or running into the woods. When the trail is difficult for the skier, it is awfully tempting to lean back from the pitch, but that only makes it harder to turn, to shift your weight from the downhill ski to the uphill ski. In the same way, leading defensively works against the leader. This is the standard for all performers tackling difficult challenges: to not allow fear to corrupt their form.

Straighten Out Crooked Thinking

So much of what drives the behavior of leaders is the ideas in their heads about what it means to lead. If those ideas are off, then you can be sure their behavior will be off too. Leaders would be lost without their operating assumptions, but what can be done when an assumption is just plain wrong?

Of the corrective measures that can be taken, here are three (1) add a missing element to your mental model of leadership, (2) call into question your self-limiting assumptions, and (3) recalibrate a faulty gauge.

Add a Missing Element to Your Mental Model of Leadership. Planning ahead hadn't been on one middle manager's mental map. On reflection he understood why he had avoided it. He didn't think he was good at it, especially the conceptual part, and he much preferred playing to his strength, which was fighting the fires that came with his job. Still, being a responsible person, he had to admit that it was important to his effectiveness that he be more proactive. "How," he asked, "do I translate my intentions into action?"

Because planning ahead was foreign to him, he knew he had to put himself on a program. He dedicated half of his monthly meeting to looking ahead, and he arranged to be tutored by a senior manager who was an exemplary long-term planner.

Equally important was the change that occurred in his head: "I have to say that, looking back, being proactive hadn't registered, if you can believe that. So one change I've noticed is I now use the word. I see that it's one of the most important things for me to do." With the addition of "proactive" to his vocabulary, his repertoire expanded.[7]

Another manager, very sharp and technically gifted, had omitted a major leadership function from his idea of leading. He realized that, for him, being a leader had meant "knowing things and getting things done." Noticeably absent from his conception of the job was having effective relationships. Obviously,

> Heading a function is not just leading. It's also counseling your bosses, and you can't be hesitant to take a consigliore role. It took me a long time to learn that. You have an image of yourself that is too small. And you believe that the people at the top are masters of the universe. But in fact they are looking for your advice.

he knew that he had to work with others and he did it every day, but that function had not been important enough to be part of his tacit working definition of the job.

An anachronism can blot out an element of the leadership role. One young executive's hands-off policy with his staff was a pure projection of his own need for autonomy. As the child of self-absorbed and rather neglectful parents, he had learned to fend for himself, and without realizing it he attributed his need for self-sufficiency to his people, who he now learned felt neglected by him. He now saw that part of his job was to meet their needs for his help.

Filling in the vacancies in your mental model of leadership is the necessary precursor to adding it to your repertoire. If the skill isn't on your list, you won't develop it. It's as simple as that.

Call into Question Your Self-Limiting Assumptions. When leaders know very well the importance of a managerial function yet slight it anyway, a faulty operating assumption is often the reason. Even in otherwise clear-thinking people, it can live on for years unnoticed and unexamined, all the while throwing off their form.

One such manager knew he should circulate but avoided walking the halls because he wrongly assumed that people would be offended if he didn't know their names or wasn't aware of what they were working on. Tinged with fear of rejection, this assumption led him to give short shrift to a big part of his job—to be visible to employees and to stay in some kind of touch with them. It was unfortunate that he limited himself in this way because he had a real talent for relating to people. Fortunately, he was able to see the self-limiting assumption for what it was: "I realize now that people will give me more slack than I think. So I don't have to be so fortified or guarded." Freed somewhat of his fearful assumption, he could make better use of his talent.

Another example: An executive had two children whose late-afternoon soccer games she wanted to attend, but she would not permit herself to do it. Holding her back was an inviolate assumption: thou shalt not leave work early on weekdays. When she exposed this guilt-tinged assumption to the light of day and took into account her long hours and great dedication, she was able to consider making occasional exceptions to her ironclad rule.[8]

A concrete way to clear a path for change then is to rummage around in the attic of your mind for dusty supposed truths about leading that turn out to be merely half-truths or even dead wrong.

Recalibrate a Faulty Gauge. In attempting to rev up, managers are sometimes hampered by an internal gauge that gives them inaccurate readings. It misleads them into believing they are doing more than they actually are. Afraid of moving too far in the direction of the other side, they apply the brakes too soon.

A senior manager who had trouble being direct and directive

Newly promoted to the senior team, a manager unearthed this self-limiting assumption: "That's new for me, the idea of being on a par with the CEO. I'm used to thinking he must have better information, or a better perspective where he sits, or better judgment from years of making decisions like this. So after years of thinking the boss is right, now I realize that I owe it to myself to challenge his idea if I have the facts or grounding and I don't agree."

saw a connection to his basketball-playing days: "If you missed a certain number of shots during the game, the coach made you run laps and that made me a little more gun-shy." Hearing this in a follow-up session, I decided to do a little demonstration for him. I stood to one side of the conference room and told him that the wall right behind me stood for treating people well and the wall across the room stood for being direct and directive. I then placed a pitcher of water on the floor half-way across the room. Then backing up several feet toward the good-to-people wall, I said, "You're here. Then as you move toward being more direct and directive, you think you are closer to the mid-point, where the pitcher is, than you really are." He agreed: "This is one of those scales where I don't have a good handle on what the center point looks like."

If your calibration is off in this way, make a mental note that's a twist on the notice that appears on a car's rear view mirror: "The object is closer than it appears."

Delve into Your Trigger Points, the Better to Defuse Them

There is knowing the signs, emotional or physical, that signal the onset of off-center behavior, and there is becoming well-acquainted with the emotions that those signs signify. Often that means a person must face the fact that he or she feels threatened. Being aware of the fear as opposed to merely reacting to it has the advantage of giving the individual some choice in the matter.

One manager almost never showed up for social events for employees, customers, or vendors. Once he finished venting ("Those functions are a complete waste of time"), he admitted that he felt like a fish out of water. If he had no choice about attending a social function, he often left early and sometimes abruptly. The reason: "I panic." Never mind how much he had achieved. Never mind his standing in the organization. When he found himself in situations with no task, no structure, he felt at a complete loss. It was a sensitivity that he had come by honestly many years ago. His parents were careerists and socialites, and when they were home they had a way of finding him lacking. As he recounted the story and understood better the origins of his intense social discomfort, he gained a modicum of control over it. Rather than fleeing by reflex when he felt panicky, he decided he would try "pressing the pause button," and attempt to hang in there.

Bob Kegan, a student of human development, has devised a useful process for identifying the fears that can so easily thwart a leader's attempt to make good on his or her commitment to change. The process helps to expose what he calls a "competing commitment," a self-protective conviction that, unbeknown to the individual, stands in direct opposition to the vow to change.[9]

Responding to the fact that she dominated meetings, Sara Central made this commitment to herself: slow down enough to give other people a chance to express their views fully and to ask the extra questions. My colleague and I guided her through Kegan's process, during which she uncovered this competing commitment: "I'm committed to not be lost, to knowing where I am, to not be unsure, all of which makes me uncomfortable." And if she were to feel lost or unsure, then what? "All kinds of bad things would happen. The whole thing falls apart. The strengths fall apart. The foundation crumbles. I'm lost. I'm not in control. And if I'm not in control, only bad things happen. I don't achieve results, I'm not successful. It's a disaster." Her stated commitment and the underlying competing commitment were held in what Kegan calls a state of "dynamic equilibrium," where a lot of energy is spent pulling in opposite directions and things end up staying pretty much the same.

Call it a competing commitment, a trigger point, or a sensitivity, discovering what drives your behavior helps you change it. The often covert avoidant force is probably what you are up against when you attempt to overcome a deficiency. It's why you have to force yourself.

Own Your Strengths; You May Be Stronger Than You Think

Although its high value for development is widely overlooked, positive feedback is an excellent way for leaders to allay their anxiety that they're not good enough when the reality is that they are plenty good enough, and in that way remedy a deficiency. After all, many deficiencies are mere symptoms. Managers have work to do when they receive positive feedback, which is to give it credence and allow it to revise their underestimates of themselves upward.

It was in working with Rick Freed that I began to appreciate this overlooked leverage for development. Preparing for a feedback session with Rick, an upper-level line manager I had yet to meet, I was startled to see that his ratings on a 360-degree survey, predecessor to the LVI, may have been the best I'd encountered. I turned to the written comments, also collected over the Internet, and they were just as favorable. Five of the nine people responding offered high praise. To top it off, his overall effectiveness rating on a 10-point scale was a very high 8.8. I was floored. His report was so good that I found myself worrying, "Do I have anything to offer this guy? What am I going to do? Quickly go over the report, congratulate him, and end the session early?"

Rick Freed was an exceptionally effective senior leader. He got consistently good results and did it with practically all the right behaviors. What came out in our discussion, however, is that he hadn't caught up with how good a leader he had become.

His very high rating on overall effectiveness went hand in hand with his good grades on both sides of several classic dualities. His boss observed: "I look for people who can cover the waterfront. Rick has a lot of it. There is a small minority of people who have that ability." Rick did well on strategic thinking and on execution; on getting things done and on having good relationships; on being a strong leader and on empowering others; on having "mental toughness" and on caring about people; on contributing personally and on bringing out the best in others. He was intelligent, insightful, and a quick study. He set priorities effectively, he was well-organized, he managed conflict well, and he had high integrity.

The excellence of his leadership was also reflected in the comments made about him overall, for instance:

- I believe that Rick is one of the most consummate managers/leaders in our company.
- This is the best manager I've had in my twenty years with the company.
- Rick is the best leader and manager I have worked for.
- In my opinion, Rick has all the qualities of a great leader and has the potential to contribute to this corporation at a higher level. He is clearly a person capable of heading this corporation.
- Rick is a great leader whose potential has only begun to be tapped.
- I admire his abilities. He's been a role model for me.

The people around him knew just how good he was, but he had some catching up to do.

After we had gone over his report, he asked me, "How do I compare to other executives?" I said, "Very favorably," and pointed out how wide his leadership repertoire was, how highly he was rated and regarded.

His response: "The positives are overwhelming to me." Having slept on all this, he reported first thing the next morning, "The realization was very liberating."

Liberating is a striking word, laden with significance, especially coming from a no-nonsense businessman not given to using humanistic language. Liberated from what? From the constant pressure to prove himself: "There has always been this feeling within me that I didn't quite measure up. I've always put a lot of pressure on myself, even though there were outward signs I was very successful—accomplishments, promotions." Thanks to the positive feedback, the pressure abated somewhat: "Out of this report comes the reinforcement that it's okay to take a little of the pressure off."

Liberated to do what? "This experience has helped me recognize that there's a degree of relaxing that goes with this, which can help me in other areas, which will make other things possible." Chiefly, it freed him to become more of a factor in top management, to be more vocal and influential in the most senior forums. Rick had always run his piece of the business exceedingly well, but in meetings with the other top executives and the CEO and the COO he had taken a low profile. Three months after the feedback session he reported:

> "In the past my natural inclination with a group of senior people was to be cautious. I didn't enjoy being thrown in with other senior people, especially superiors. This is tangling with people. But I have started to step out more."

Now he spoke up more. Two years later he continued to enjoy a stronger voice in senior management meetings, which enabled him to have an influence on enterprise-wide decisions that he had not had previously. He reported:

"The greatest thing that happened to me was that this process allowed me to move into a strategist role in the company. I realized that I had a voice that was important and could be effective in shaping the corporation's strategy and that it was important to express that and not take as cautious an approach as I might have. So it helped me be a risk taker in unknown circumstances. It's a heckuva lot easier for me to be reserved than to be an outspoken person.

"I'm more effective upstream by 50 percent because I'm much more open, confident, willing to speak my mind, willing to take a controversial position, realizing that I don't always have to win the point. So from that standpoint, this experience has helped me greatly."

In the same way, he opened the valve with his own people and now communicated more freely and powerfully with them:

"Part of this is showing what you are passionate about and what you stand for. These are qualities that were inside of me, but they were suppressed because of this baggage I was carrying around. So this was saying I was okay and releasing."

His newfound openness also carried over to his marriage, but with his wife it took a different form. Where he now brought a certain hard openness to his relationships at work, with her he now exhibited a soft openness. He began to spend more time with her and he talked more personally with her:

"I can be vulnerable with her in a personal way. Here again it comes back to me feeling okay. Before, part of not feeling confident was you don't want to be vulnerable. You want to be in control. That's one of the things I'm working on. I'm not there. But I can recognize it and experiment."

It is fascinating how internalizing his capability generally freed him to be more open generally, both in the hard direction and in the soft direction. The shift he made was fundamental. He had evolved into a better leader and a better husband by more nearly being himself. As he put it, the realization "allowed me to relax into who I was, with a degree of self-assurance."[10] In retrospect he could see that he had been playing a role:

> "I fully admit that there was a facade. But the data said it's okay to let the facade go away. With maturity and age it's faded a little. If you spend a lifetime acting and suppressing, it takes a whole lot for you to make genuine change, and you do that through being more aware and releasing yourself to be a little more open and experiment. It's letting a little more of my natural self out. This is liberating. I think this release has helped me be a real person with people and a genuine person."

In saying he had relaxed, he hastened to add that he had not become lazy: "By relaxed I don't mean complacent or lackadaisical. This change releases you so you're not so pent up and you're not so tenuous." What had been tenuous? His sense of his self-worth. With a better hold on it, "you're not always walking on that tightrope, feeling that if you make a misstep you fall off that track." Now that he had a better hold on his capability and sense of self-worth, he could relax his tight grip on the wheel and drive even better.

Never one to claim more than he deserved, he added: "Let me assure you that I am a work in progress. I'm not there." But he was getting there, and he had positioned himself for an even higher-level role in the corporation.

If you find yourself underdoing or avoiding or inhibiting yourself from doing part of your job, consider the possibility that, like Rick Freed, you need to grow into your skin.

Using Others as Complements

En route to making up a deficit but still saddled with it, managers always have the option of tapping into that capability in others. Managers with an extreme deficit have no alternative to that. They have so far to go that in all likelihood they will never excel in that area. A manager whose LVI rating on "Makes decisions in a timely fashion" was −2.50 definitely had to compensate for that weakness if he was to be adequately decisive any time soon. In extreme cases, the individual is up against not an inhibition but a literal prohibition.

Nothing new here. "Compensate for limitations" is a familiar refrain in organizations. There is, however, an aspect that is not firmly planted in the collective mind: You can only compensate for something that you lack if you value it. Managers—like all humans—are liable to disparage what they lack. Asked what it would mean to pay more attention to strategy, a first-time CEO whose forte was operational leadership answered: "I'll have to spend more fluff time."

A CEO-COO pairing is a prime example of an opportunity for each party to compensate for the other's limitations. My colleagues and I regularly encounter the standard pattern of a strategically oriented CEO and an operationally oriented COO. That is as it should be because that is what the roles call for.

The different inclinations and skill sets of the CEO and COO, or co-CEOs, also contain the potential for them to disconnect or clash. In an arrangement that may be the closest thing to a work marriage, the differences can make the pair stronger than the two individuals taken separately or can drive a wedge between them. Some pairs are odd bedfellows who can never forge a true partnership. Others look like poor prospects for partnership but surprise everyone by working together well privately and by presenting a united front to the organization.

For the two individuals to compensate for each other's limitations, not to mention discharge the responsibility for the organization that they both share, the relationship has to meet two conditions. First, the two individuals need to connect personally. This means that each is satisfied with the other's personal character and that they develop reasonably good chemistry. Second, once that interpersonal foundation is in place, they need to be in regular contact, either informally or in regularly scheduled meetings, to keep each other abreast and to work through issues and come to a common view, or, failing that, to agree to disagree. Both conditions amount to a single requirement, that the two individuals make a commitment to the relationship and consistently nourish it with appreciable time.

To summarize: in contending with your deficiencies, it doesn't all have to come from you. In fact, it *can't* all come from you.

Developing Yourself, Coaching Others

Highlights

1. You are never going to get better at something that you don't think is important. The prejudicial attitude that kept you from using that skill or developing it in the first place will have to go.

2. The same prerequisite applies to compensating for your limitations. You are unlikely to recruit or make good use of talent to shore up one of your deficiencies unless you truly believe in the contribution of that function or role.

3. Grapple with any tendency to hold yourself back. Fear of failure or fear of rejection is often the reason.

Note: the next two points apply both to revving up and to throttling back.

4. Give the new behavior a try. Whether it's learning to do more or to do less, you can only underestimate the value of swinging into action. The cycle of action and reflection is the key to learning a new skill.

5. You must practice regularly and, to accomplish that, you need to enforce and reinforce the change effort (the same applies to anyone you're coaching).

   • Enforce the change effort by not leaving all the responsibility and accountability in your own hands. Put teeth in it. Tell others you have decided to make a change; put yourself on a program that has you practice the slighted behavior; appoint a watch dog; keep score.

   • Reinforce the change effort: seek others' support; use a confidant; take account of gains made; take pleasure in flexing underused muscles.

Questions for Reflection

1. Which parts of the leadership role do you slight?

2. Are you actively avoiding any part of your job? "Do I hold back for fear of. . . ?"

3. Is there a specific off-kilter attitude you need to change to make up a deficit in your leadership, for example, "To keep my boss informed of my department's achievements is bragging, and therefore wrong."

4. Are you willing to let other people know you are attempting to improve? Making a public commitment gives you added impetus to change.

Chapter Nine

Adjusting Both Sides

> "The art of executive leadership is above all a taste
> for paradox, a talent for ambiguity, the capacity to
> hold contradictory propositions comfortably in a
> mind that relishes complexity."
>
> —*Harlan Cleveland*

As we have seen in the last two chapters, leaders can work on over-doing or underdoing one at a time. But there is added leverage in conceiving of the combination of the two as a single performance problem and taking an integrative or holistic approach to solving it. Just as leadership is at its core heavily two-sided, so by definition must be leadership development.

But how likely are leaders to set two-sided improvement goals, when they are not assessed in two-sided terms? Not likely.

Beyond the mechanics of leadership assessment, I would go so far as to say that the central area for development in leaders is lop-sidedness. Central for two fundamental reason: first, lopsided lead-ership is everywhere and, second, lopsided leadership has at its root the basic human tendency to think in black-and-white terms, to be one-sided, to go either-or, to polarize.

This phenomenon is hardly restricted to leadership. We see garden-variety instances of it all the time in organizations. Depart-ments can't cooperate, they take a dim view of each other, and behavior and attitude feed into one another. Whether between people located in different nearby buildings, on different floors, or in headquarters and the field, a we-they dynamic sprouts as readily as weeds in a garden. More broadly, Republicans demonize Democrats and vice versa, and in the world's many ethnic and civil wars the demonizing of others has bloody consequences indeed.

In leaders this splitting plays out, less visibly, between their ears. Here it becomes me versus not-me. In the extreme case, leaders embrace one side of leadership, idealize it, only have eyes for it, assign great goodness to it, and distance themselves from the other side, cut themselves off from it, assign low value to it, are estranged from it, even nauseated by it. In extreme or mild form, this phenomenon is extremely common and it therefore needs to appear on leaders' development agendas much more commonly than it currently does. Once again, addressing lopsided leadership is best done both at the outer level and at the inner level.

To be faithful to the real action in leadership, development ought to be approached not in terms of single dimensions when you can muster greater leverage by approaching it in a two-sided way. The same applies to intervening not just on an outer plane but also on an inner plane:

> You can't just be one thing. You have to be big-picture and little-picture. You have to be a big power tool and sometimes a small screwdriver. You have to be able to zoom in and zoom out. And you can't just use one extreme quality to solve the problem.

let's not pass up the chance to go after the polarized mind-set that is responsible for lopsided behavior.

The potential always exists to reconcile seeming opposites and integrate them into a complex whole. This is the ideal for you to strive for—to embrace both sides of an opposition but neither side too tightly, to incorporate both sides in your repertoire without giving either too big a place, and, because there are no complete leaders, to honor what you lack so you can find it in others.

The Outer Work: Tackling the *Relationship* Between the Two Sides

At a purely behavioral level, it is useful to set improvement goals in pairs because a flat side that needs to be brought out often has an opposite number that you should tone down.

A two-sided approach to change on such a lopsided pair means making more selective use of a hypertrophied strength and building up capability on the complementary but atrophied skill. It means loosening your grip on a highly trusted approach and trying out what for you has been an untested way of leading. At the simplest level, the leader learns that it takes two wings to fly, and that he or she will not stay airborne if one wing is much larger and flaps more than the other.

Ahab stands out as a wildly one-sided leader. We know nothing about what shaped his leadership except the implied effects of his traumatic encounter with Moby Dick on the last voyage that left him with one leg and a one-track mind. As a result, he brooks no interference with his monomaniacal quest to exact revenge on the ferocious white whale—ignoring his crew's safety and his own. And remember the purpose of the voyage, to obtain whale oil, which was the investors' reason for financing the long voyage. After a two-year sail around the world, the Pequod finally finds the whale, gives chase, and harpoons him several times. Two days later, all they have for their extremely risky efforts are smashed whale boats and lost lives. But Ahab is undeterred, never mind that he lost his ivory peg leg in the mayhem. Starbuck, the first mate, appeals to him:

> "Never, never wilt thou capture him, old man. . . . Two days chased; twice stove to splinters; thy very leg once more snatched from under thee. . . . Shall we keep chasing this murderous fish 'til he swamps the last man? Shall we be dragged down by him to the bottom of the sea. Oh, oh—Impiety and Blasphemy to hunt him more."

Even as he acknowledges the bond the two had forged, Ahab declares, "Ahab is forever Ahab" and commands Starbuck, whom he addresses as "Underling!," to obey his orders [pp. 803–804]. No one, not even Starbuck, whose integrity, persuasive clarity, and candor had won Ahab's respect, could change his warped mind and alter his collision course. No believer in leadership development, Ahab is forever Ahab.

Lopsidedness in any leader is analogous to a see-saw with a heavy person pressing one seat to the ground, and a small fry perching high on the other seat, legs dangling in the air. You could intervene on one side or the other, but you have a better chance of correcting the tilt—let's assume they're seeking greater parity because it would make see-sawing more fun—if the two parties coordinate their efforts, if both make themselves behave differently in their respective positions on the see-saw, if the heavy person takes off some pounds, and the light one puts on a few.

An effort to curb excess on one side will benefit from a corresponding attempt to make up a deficit on the other. Catching yourself and forcing yourself often go hand in hand. Take work-life balance. If, like the manager in Chapter 7, you want to get home earlier on weekday evenings when you are not traveling, and you commit to leave the office by 5:30 p.m. twice a week, this is the force-yourself part. Nothing says you will not be able to keep this commitment, but you will have better luck, or at least experience less strain, if you address the complementary problem of taking on too much. Success depends on forcing yourself to leave at the appointed time, but it also depends on catching yourself as you are about to give in to your usual tendency to take a call as you are about to run out the door or you continue to load yourself down with so many commitments that it makes it well nigh impossible to keep your workload in bounds.

How Leadership Models Shape Development

To work in conjunction on two linked development needs, for example, too task-oriented and not people-oriented enough, it helps greatly to define them as linked in the first place. But most assessment tools don't make it easy. They don't juxtapose competencies in the report, so it falls to leaders or their helpers to make those connections and to define action steps in pairs. In the way a volleyball player sets up a team member to spike the ball, wouldn't it be advantageous for leadership models to pave the way for two-sided efforts to develop?

The Inner Work: Tackling Lopsidedness at the Root

The tilt in the leader's behavior starts with the tilt in his or her head. It originates in the individual's *imbalanced relationship* to the two sides, which in extreme cases is polarized. One way for you to remedy lopsidedness is to address that imbalanced relationship. Another way is to come to terms with the vulnerability, typically a sense of inadequacy, at its root.

Depolarizing Your Relationship to the Two Sides

In its crudest form, a lopsided relationship to a pair becomes one of "me versus not-me."

Dead Give-Aways. Notice the words or phrases other managers use in passing that are dead giveaways for their disregard for the side of leadership that loses out. For example:

- An extremely results-oriented senior leader referred to relationship-building as "schmoozing." What was this individual's weak suit? Relationships.
- A line executive who had a gift for visionary leadership tipped his hand with the phrase "operational gruel." Where did this executive fall down? On the operational side.

Stump the Stars. Leaders sometimes identify so thoroughly and completely with one side that they literally can't name the other side. They're stumped when I ask, "What is the opposite or complement?"

- A senior manager who believed strongly in being open with his team and who shared information to a fault had no idea what the complement is: Discretion, being discrete with sensitive information.

- In his meetings another senior manager was so aggressive about getting to the truth about the state of his direct reports' units that some people ran for cover. He came up empty-handed when I asked him, "What is the complement to digging for information so intensely?" The answer was an eye opener for him: Making it safe for people to come forward with the truth about problems.

- A highly principled manager who defined his leadership in missionary terms—service to others—and who wore himself out in the process was at a complete loss as to the complement: Taking care of himself.

- A spontaneous, freewheeling manager who most of all wanted to "flow" and who over-talked in meetings was left speechless when I asked him to identify the complement of flowing freely: A flow regulator.

The inability to even imagine what the opposing virtue is demonstrates that the slighted leadership quality in effect does not exist in the individual's mind. Having no place in the leader's mental model, it is absent from his or her repertoire.

Polarized on Principle. Beyond being absent, that quality can be literally anathema to the individual. A high-integrity senior manager felt compelled to object every time he detected what he regarded as hypocrisy. In an offsite meeting of the expanded senior team, he took on the CEO over the bad impression that buying new computers for that group would make on employees during a cutback. It didn't occur to him to take the CEO aside. His principled nature made it impossible for him not to speak up. A coworker made this observation about the manager's habit of principled confrontation:

> "He has no sand trap skills, and he doesn't like using the putter. He prefers the driver. If you have nine clubs in the bag, he hasn't perfected using the nine clubs and may actually look upon using all of them as a breach of his integrity."

Any time what he took to be a moral issue arose, and he was prone to see things in moral terms, this confrontational executive reached for his "driver," a forcing function, and was opposed in principle to using the "putter," finesse, a light touch.

One Manager's Attempt to Overcome an Aversion. Leaders can have an aversion to the other side; literally, they turn away from it. A case in point is a manager who had trouble displaying her forceful side because she had an aversion to "pushy" people and the last thing she wanted to do was to be one of them. As she began to gain perspective on her raging prejudice, she recalled her childhood experience of being the younger sister of a dominant older brother who was forever having run-ins with their father and who on rare occasions threw his weight around with her. She decided at a young age that she wanted no part of conflict like that and decided to "lie low."

As a manager she also took a low profile—too low—and had a distaste for outwardly powerful coworkers, which hampered her relationships with them. Her husband, she said, told her: "You're not taking advantage of what you're entitled to." She admitted, "I will generally scale down. I won't treat myself as a big shot." By going out of her way not to be aggressive, she had as a younger adult incapacitated herself: "Twenty years ago, just asserting myself in a store was intimidating." And what would happen if she used the other side? "I'm afraid I wouldn't be liked. It's tangled. I think I've been unidimensional on what it means to be liked."

Note the manager's use of the word "unidimensional." She as much as said that she was one-sided. In a case like this, reworking the relationship to the two sides meant depolarizing it, reducing somewhat the too-positive valence on the one dimension and removing the strong negative valence on the other side.

This manager came to understand that to change meant working on the relationship between the two sides: "I see that this has to do with reconciling being demanding with being nice. Right now those two things don't join." I asked, "Is the opposite of nice alien to you?" She said, "Yes, it's alien." She went on to say, "Being liked has too big a place." Pushing her hand down to indicate reducing the importance of being liked, she concluded, "I need to reclassify it."

> In the poem "Scrub" by Edna St Vincent Millay, she writes, "If I grow bitterly like a gnarled and stunted tree," it is because "a wind too strong bent my back when I was young" and "I fear the rain" will "blister me again."

Intuitively, this manager understood that she needed to "reconcile," as she said, the two sides that she had thought of as irreconcilable.

Another way to characterize the redefinition of the relationship is taking away some of the huge space assigned to one side and reallocating it to the other side. It is integration in the sense of making room for both sides where one had crowded out the other.

In her case, that meant relying less on the "soft" side of her leadership and making a bigger place for the "hard" side. On a hunch I asked her if the weaker part of her game was her forehand put-away shot. It was. A long-time recreational tennis player, she over-relied on a finesse game that depended heavily on her backhand, which was much better developed than her forehand. Her backhand shot with all the natural backspin on it was analogous to the soft side of her leadership, her finesse game. In general, her tennis game was undergunned. She told me, "A tennis friend once said to me, 'You don't go for the jugular.'" In conjunction with the goal of being more forceful at work, she set out to play a more versatile game: "I'd like to hit harder. I'd like to have more impact. I've been overcompensating with my backhand."

Her aspiration to grow as a tennis player ran perfectly parallel to her aspiration to grow as a leader, and her efforts in both arenas reinforced each other. "I want to round out my executive leadership style to create more power and impact while retaining my humanity,"[1] she told me.

Addressing the Vulnerability at the Root of Overdoing and Underdoing

To all appearances, deficiency and excess are diametrical opposites. When leaders overdo it, they pour themselves into the task at hand. Their involvement knows no bounds. When they underdo it, the flow of energy into a neglected part of the job slows down, gets constricted, sometimes down to a trickle. They either make no effort or it is only halfhearted. Where overdoing is a can-do attitude to a fault, underdoing is can't-do. Where one is overly expansive, the other is self-limiting. Where overdoing is under-socialized or under-controlled, underdoing is over-socialized or over-controlled. Where overdoing is fueled by a fear that I won't do enough to get what I want, underdoing is ruled by a fear that I will do too much and somehow overstep my bounds.[2] When leaders overdo it, they are in effect fighting back too aggressively. When they underdo it, they are doing too good a job of shielding themselves or being too quick to leave the scene.

Despite their different faces, these two classes of behavior share a common motive: self-protection. An instance of the fight-flight reflex, overdoing and underdoing are both aimed at contending with a common threat, the threat of not performing well, of not being accepted, of proving inadequate.[3] One manager caught a retrospective glimmer of this vulnerability and its effect on his behavior: "Ten years ago I worried about a lot of things. I see now that back then there was always a huge potential for panic. I worried about how people reacted to the decisions I made (and therefore was indecisive). Now I realize that you need empathy but you can't let others' negative emotion pull you down."

A way to remedy lopsidedness then is for you to get at the vulnerability that underlies it. The opportunity is to recognize and better manage in yourself the two-pronged impulse common to linked overdoing and underdoing: I protect my ego by avoiding "that" and by grabbing onto "this." It is a chance to manage the fear that would polarize your relationship to a pair of essential leadership functions and to understand in your own case how "fear robs people of the ability to deal with contradiction . . . and reduces them to black-and-white thinking."[4]

> One self-aware manager recognized the challenge of dealing with the continuous stream of little threats to his ego: "I worry about the moment-to-moment things that people do that question your authority, upstage you, take away your power or make you small. I worry about the temptation in me to react. It's a hazardous space. So I try to not react and still act robustly."

Case 1. A senior manager uncovered the fear that threw off his posture on the strategic-operational duality, loading down the operational side and shortchanging the strategic side. All these years he had specialized in having an up-to-the-minute grasp of the business, which served him well except that he carried it too far. Reflecting on this drive, he realized that he was driven by fear of intellectual inadequacy: "I'm afraid that if I'm meeting with my team or even people lower in the organization and something comes up that I'm not aware of, they'll think I'm stupid." The very same fear warned him off the strategic part of his job. It wasn't just the time he spent immersing himself in the inner workings of the business that took him away from strategy. Thinking of himself as not smart, he gravitated away from strategy because unconsciously he was afraid he wouldn't perform that function well.

Where did he come by the idea that he wasn't smart? Third-born, he had two older siblings who got straight A's, went to good colleges, and were regarded as "the smart ones" in the family. Abandoning that space to them, he developed a reputation in the family for being "good with people." The not-smart identity became a self-fulfilling prophecy. He didn't apply himself in school, and his lackluster grades fed into his reputation in the family and his idea of himself. The obscure college he went to symbolized for him his second-class status intellectually. Although he had suppressed this painful sense of himself, it lived on, silently shaping his definition of the job and his performance.

Nevertheless he was able to make a number of small adjustments that added up to appreciable change. For example, he had scored himself higher than average on the questionnaire item, "I am not as smart as other people think I am." It came home to him: "I might be right about that, I might be wrong, but what difference does it make?" In addition, he had a habit of feeling stupid when he thought he was taking too long to read something, and he learned to catch himself when he began to get anxious about being "slow."

He certainly hadn't arrived psychologically. When I asked him if he could take in the high praise that his colleagues heaped on him in a follow-up report, he said: "If I really did that, I'd have to feel a sense of self-worth. I had difficulty even saying the word self-worth. It stuck in my throat. Why do I feel uncomfortable with it? Maybe there's still a disparity between my self-image and what I'm hearing."

Yet he had gained enough sense of intellectual worth to add "smart" to his list of strengths. In the initial interview, he had not claimed it as one of his strengths. Now, two years later, in a kind of graduation ceremony, he took out the original list and hand-wrote it in.

In parallel with his inner evolution, he was also able to correct the lopsidedness in his leadership. He did in fact manage to pull back on his excessive involvement in operations and was able to put a greater focus on strategy. He helped himself by bulking up his senior team's formal mechanism for scanning the marketplace and for working through the implications for the business. The net effect was that he elevated his role. Not coincidentally, over the same two-year period the average coworker rating of his overall effectiveness went up quite a bit, from mid-7's to almost mid-8's.

Case 2. Even when an individual "gets it" at a deeper level, as this manager did, healing at the core is no sure thing. A manager who looked like an excellent prospect for a growth spurt remained mired in his historic way of leading and in the way he had long, painfully, viewed himself. A follow-up survey administered a year after the assessment indicated that he had made some progress but that there was at least as much ground left to gain. His original feedback had included a long, impressive list of positives, but his inhibitions kept him from making full use of them. He was respected for his brainpower, analytical ability, knowledge of the business, willingness to listen to all sides of an argument, fairness, and humility, but he took too long to make important decisions.

His meetings went on interminably long and, for his staff's taste, there were too many of them. His heavy use of participation was actually predicated on principle. It was an article of faith with him that no one in a large, complex organization is smart enough or knowledgeable enough to go it alone. The hitch was that the high value he placed on the contributions of others came at the expense of the value he placed on his own judgment.

Vulnerability underlay his lopsidedness, as the following exchange, which took place in the feedback session, makes clear.

He began by explaining why he (too) left smart off his list of strengths: "I find it hard to believe I am where I am because I didn't think I was smart enough to get there."

"Where did you get the idea you weren't smart enough?," I queried.

"I had a teacher in third grade who told me I'd never amount to anything. Yes, that hurt, absolutely. And it still has a strong influence. I was a kid who lacked self-confidence, and it took time to build that. But I don't consider myself as that smart. I view myself as smart—but not *that smart*."

"How does that affect your decision making?" I asked.

"I worry the decision will be a bad one and I imagine how painful that would be. Painful to my self-esteem. So the natural approach is to collect more data and to hold more meetings."

"Is your self-esteem on the line every time you make a decision?"

"For big decisions. And it's not always conscious."

"Such a capable guy, but there's a hitch."

"Yes. A kid who was fat and picked on. A kid whose parents got divorced in a small town where that didn't happen."

All was not lost. A year later when a new boss downgraded him for not being decisive and strongly encouraged him to trust his own instincts, he re-engaged with my colleague and me, this time with a still stronger commitment to adjust his leadership.

There is no easy or surefire way for leaders to alleviate the vulnerability that gives rise to lopsidedness. One approach, again, is to administer a concentrated dose of positive feedback that the individual manages to let seep into his or her sense of self.

Another is the accumulation of experience that gradually, eventually, eases the original hurt and shores up the structure of the self. Gaining experience can seem like a passive approach, something that just happens to you, hardly a course of action that you would choose to take if you were anxious to develop. It can, however, be active and intentional if you actively seek out those challenges, small and large, that represent the very thing you believe you are not good at: relationships, conceptual work, public speaking, self-assertion, personal discipline. The list is endless.[5] In a process of accretion akin to the way a coral reef grows, bit by organismic bit, even managers with chronic feelings of inadequacy can build up their faith in themselves. It can take a great deal of experience to reach into the deep, primitive part of the brain that humans have in common with other animals, where pain and sensitivities are lodged.[6]

To highlight how difficult it can be to outgrow vulnerability, let us briefly consult the worst case of being made to feel vulnerable:

torture. Outright torture, admittedly grim in this context, is extremely difficult to recover from psychologically. One victim later wrote that a tortured person becomes "a defenseless prisoner of fear. It is *fear* that henceforth reigns over him." It rules him in the sense that the individual can't help being afraid of being wounded again. The other thing that being seriously hurt in this gratuitous fashion does is to destroy the person's trust. As the same author wrote, "trust in the world will not be regained."[7]

If the chance that a tortured person will trust again is nil or next to nil, then what chance have leaders who as children suffered greatly? The deeper the original wound, the longer it takes to outgrow the vulnerability, the more developmental support that is needed, and the lower the probability that it will ever mitigate enough to straighten out the distortions in the person's leadership completely. Certainly, Ahab's tortured soul put him out of reach.

Even to avail themselves of developmental support is a tenuous proposition for severely wounded leaders. Their difficulty trusting applies to the relationship with the helping professional. It takes very little for such individuals to abandon the effort and the relationship. What to the consultant seems like a small misstep is experienced as a betrayal of trust. There is no margin for error.

Leaders with a troubled history do have an advantage as adults. They now have something they lacked as children—perspective and personal resources—and are therefore in a stronger position to revise those early patterns of adaptation.

Another option, beyond the reach of many leaders of this description, is to come to recognize the disturbance for what it is and to say out loud: "I am disturbed" and then, as a practical matter, to work with it and around it like any other problem. To acknowledge the disturbance, horrible as it is, opens the possibility of solving it, by adopting a program of self-management and self-development (swing thoughts included), by arranging for close colleagues to provide the emotional support and external controls you realize you need, and by getting professional help.[8] To admit the vulnerability to yourself, much less to your coworkers, to make it a habit of mind, takes extraordinary self-honesty and personal courage. To do so is an act of self-acceptance on the part of a person whose hardest daily challenge in life is to accept himself or herself. I have seen it done.

Developing Yourself, Coaching Others

Highlights

1. If there is a single basic area for development in leaders, it is the need to remedy lopsidedness. As F. Scott Fitzgerald famously stated, the mark of a first-rate intelligence is the ability to hold two ideas in your head while retaining the ability to function. This is a type of intelligence, dialectical intelligence, that many managers can stand to develop further.

2. Set improvement goals in two-sided terms. Don't just set a goal of toning down a strength taken too far. Look into whether the individual (you or someone else) is also doing too little of the complementary side. The same applies to setting a goal of doing more of something.

3. The acid test is, under the pressure of daily organizational life, to keep both ideas front and center in your mind. Can you keep the weaker side from being crowded out by the dominant side?

Keeping One Side from Crowding Out the Other

1. If you are a great believer in being open with your team, can you remember to be discreet with confidential information imparted by senior management?

continued

---

continued

2. If you are an aggressive change agent brought in from the outside who easily sees what is wrong with the culture, the business model, and the people who have been there for a long time, can you go out of your way to show genuine respect for what is right about the organization?

3. If you are a turnaround specialist who in short order pulls up a low-performing organization by its bootstraps, can you also be mindful of the limits on the organization's capacity to absorb change?

4. If you are a natural critic who finds it easy to disagree, can you remember to be encouraging when you hear a good idea?

5. If you are someone who lavishes attention on other people and who takes pride in being quickly and thoroughly responsive to their needs, can you remember to take good care of yourself?

6. If you are a team leader who doesn't hesitate to ask tough questions in meetings, can you remember to perform the complementary function and make it safe for your people to be open with you?

Chapter Ten

The Multi-Versatile Leader

"The survivors of any species are not necessarily the strongest. And they are not necessarily the most intelligent. They are those who are most responsive to change."

—*Charles Darwin*

"The wise man, when he works, works by all the virtues together—though one be most apparent—according to the nature of the action."

—*Montaigne*

"Oh Pan, and ye other gods that haunt this place, give me beauty in the inward man, and may the outward man and the inward man be at one."

—*Socrates*

To be versatile is to have freedom of movement on a given opposition and to draw freely but not too freely on either side as the occasion warrants. To be multi-versatile is to enjoy that freedom of movement on all the major oppositions, first and foremost, strategic-operational leadership and forceful-enabling leadership.

Will Stonecraft: An Approximation of Multi-Versatility

Will Stonecraft came close to the ideal. First of all, he was fluent both strategically and operationally. He never raised a tactical issue without having the strategy firmly in mind, and he never talked strategy without reducing it to its operational implications for that audience. In the forceful-enabling sphere, he had the singular ability to be absolutely direct and at the same time non-threatening and easy to take. Few people in or out of organizational life can do this. If they are direct and outspoken, they often lack tact and hurt people's feelings. If they are tactful, the other person doesn't know he or she has just been confronted. Will Stonecraft put people on the spot yet managed, through his tone of voice and the expression on his face, to use a light touch (the literal meaning of tact is touch).

In so many ways Will Stonecraft had the touch. His versatility index on both oppositions was in the low .90s, in effect an A– grade. Consistent with his versatility as indicated by the LVI and with the lively appreciation expressed in coworkers' comments, his overall effectiveness as rated by his coworkers broke into the 9 range on a 10-point scale, very unusual. Typical of the comments made about him were:

> "I do not believe I have met anyone during my business career who compares to him. He is a significant contributor to whatever challenge is presented to him, and his vision, leadership, and motivational skills are exceptional. I think he exemplifies what a leader should be. . . . I think your firm should ask him to edit your textbook. This is not a cute comment; I am sincere."

Another coworker pointed to his broad repertoire for influencing people:

> "I have seen him adeptly use every influence skill known to man to get things done, and he is equally capable of using his influence skills upward, downward, or sideways in the organization. He can fluidly move from 'model the way' to flattery, to alliances, to quid pro quo, to admonishment, to rewards and recognition. The trick is not only having the tools in your arsenal, but knowing when to use them. He does both."

In the following remarkable set of observations, a coworker spoke to this leader's ability to make the most of his strengths without going overboard:

> "He leads—without micromanaging. He teaches by example—without being didactic. He's supremely capable—without a bit of ego. He sets high expectations that people desperately want to meet—without browbeating anyone. He listens and understands—without being passive. He empowers—without over-delegating."

Note that this colleague called attention both to Will's repertoire and to his ability to call upon it adeptly. This aptitude may be the hallmark of versatility and high overall effectiveness—the eyes-wide-open, finely attuned ability to read and to respond adroitly.[1]

The same coworker topped off her commentary by speaking to Will's versatility with strikingly poetic language in precisely the two-sided sense used here:

> "His leadership style is steel forged of a series of opposites that usually trade off with each other, but he makes the sum greater than the parts. He wears a velvet glove woven of humility, compassion, and character that touches all those who discover they are better for having been around him."

Multi-Versatility on Display

The diagram in Figure 10.1 is both a circumplex model of leadership and a field on which to display Leadership Versatility Index ratings on both the strategic-enabling duality and the forceful-enabling duality.[2] Strategic in the upper-left quadrant opposes Operational in the lower-right quadrant. Forceful in the lower-left quadrant opposes Enabling in the upper-right quadrant. Likewise, each of the three strategic subdimensions sits across from its respective operational dimension—Vision and Execution, and so on.

Figure 10.1. Will Stonecraft's Results on the LVI

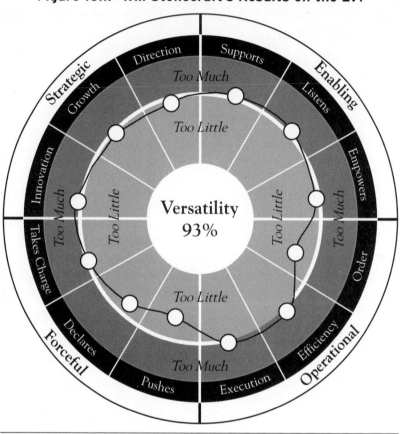

Note: Will Stonecraft's profile here is based on his average ratings across all of his coworkers who provided feedback. His versatility score, which appears in the middle of the display, is an index of how closely he approximates versatility on both strategic-operational and forceful-enabling leadership. (See the Appendix for details on how the index is computed.)

The diagram presents the leader's subdimension scores, which may fall in the too-much band, the too-little band or the right-amount band. Nearly all of Will Stonecraft's subdimension scores land in the right-amount band. The only two departures from optimal are his too-little scores on Demanding (he has trouble confronting direct reports about performance problems) and Order (he could be better organized).

If this diagram is the versatile leader's conference table, he or she can chair the meeting from whichever seat circumstances dictate. It is also like King Arthur's Round Table (which might not be the best note to strike given the fate of Camelot). But as long as every seat around the table was occupied by its proper holder, there wasn't "a more congenial spot," as Lerner and Loewe put it in their Broadway production, *Camelot*.

In the Eye of the Storm

This was the sense that a close colleague of Will Stonecraft's had of the foundation on which his versatility rested:

> "He pays attention to the signals—to what people are doing and what is really going on in the room. He's not thinking, 'What are other people thinking about me?' He is tuned into the other."

The lack of self-concern that frees Will to attend closely to the flow of events around him is, in effect, personal security. Secure in the knowledge that he is okay managerially and personally, he doesn't have to worry unduly about what other people are thinking of him. This explains his ability, mentioned above, to "fluidly move." This explains why he not only "has the tools in his arsenal" but also "knows when to use them." The same coworker suggested, "It's that base self-confidence."[3] Will's leadership rested on a solid base.

Leaders who approximate multi-versatility in their outward behavior possess on the inside an emotional steadiness, an equanimity. The more richly variegated their ability, the more that rests on personal stability.

Counterintuitively, that emotional steadiness is perfectly consistent with, and in no way precludes, a full range of emotional expression—passion, excitement, displeasure, anger, feelings of loss. Emotions are a vital part of effective leadership.[4] Whether it is passion, enthusiasm, anger, disappointment, what works is expressiveness under control. It is not getting carried away for more than a few moments by emotion, any more than it is being overly self-contained or repressed. It is the calm that Epicurus—who emphatically did not advocate, "Eat, drink, and be merry for tomorrow we shall die"—invoked as the ideal.[5] It is a state free of undue fears and excessive desires such as greed or over-ambition. It is a state that leaves the individual free to choose among the responses that best suit the situation, a state that neither forces him or her to respond in certain ways regardless of the situation or that denies him or her certain classes of response. It is being free enough of fears or desires—storms that throw the ship of leadership off course or immobilize it in the shelter of a harbor. It is intensity without undue tension, relaxed concentration, being completely engaged and yet utterly calm. It is the precious equilibrium that makes for the best performers in any type of skilled recreation. It's what enables athletes to "play heads-up ball," basketball players to have court vision. Ultimately, it is what enables leaders to calmly think things through under pressure. Mihaly Csikszentmihalyi calls this state "flow," a condition in which "attention can be freely invested to achieve a person's goals, because there is no disorder to straighten out, no threat to the self to defend against."[6]

> "The wise man, who has command over himself. . .; who has the strength and courage to restrain his appetites. . .; who has all within himself; a mind well turned and even balanced, like a smooth and perfect ball, which nothing external can stop in its course."
>
> —Horace

Possessing a state of calm during game conditions gives the managerial player an advantage. It stands in painful contrast to players in any walk of life who anxiously rush their shot. When she would have been better served to let a moment pass before responding, one manager was too quick with a retort when anyone criticized her unit and was too reactive to slights, real or imagined. She also rushed to judgment about business and personnel issues, and thereby undermined other people's trust in her judgment. It is greatly to a leader's advantage to sidestep the instantaneous, uncontrolled reaction and to pause just fractionally long enough to consider his or her options and choose aptly among them.

Joe Morgan, the Baseball Hall of Fame shortstop for the Cincinnati Reds and now a network sports announcer, said that the key to learning to hit major league pitching was slowing the ball down:

> "Instinctively, I had cut out a lot of preliminary hand and head movements at the plate. Suddenly I saw the ball as I had never seen it before. It was as though the ball came at me in slow motion."

This was the same player who, when he first came up to the major leagues and faced Sandy Koufax, the brilliant fastball pitcher, could not see the pitched ball: "I never saw it. I . . . heard it go by." The ability not only to see the ball coming but to "slow it down" so you can better read the type of pitch and its velocity comes with "a particularly high level of concentration." Note that he achieved that pure concentration when he stopped fidgeting nervously at the plate, when he calmed down during at-bats, when he was fully present and no longer distracted himself from the present challenge. He could then take pride in being one of a small group who "wound up hitting Koufax pretty well. . . . After a while. . . I actually could see (as well as hear) his pitches."[7]

The great race drivers always talk about slowing the race down so that they have plenty of time to brake at the last millisecond. The quarterback slows down the pass rush so that he can step through it and throw the ball to an open receiver. Barry Sanders, Jim Brown, skiers, surfers, sprinters, table tennis champions, I am sure there is no great athlete in any sport who does not experience this phenomenon of self-controlled management of time during competition.[8]

Versatility and emotional steadiness play off each other. Being versatile—having the capacity to respond proportionately to much of what the world throws at you—is a recipe for calm. And there is no better way to be versatile, to read situations accurately and neither overreact or under-react, than to be utterly calm, to have your wits about you in the face of a stiff challenge. Wobbly leadership and a wobbly state of mind go hand in hand.

Versatility and a firm personal foundation are a winning combination in another way. They make it possible to have a big enough view of yourself to easily conceive of playing all the cross-cutting leadership roles and yet a small enough view of yourself to keep from going overboard—to be both expansive and humble.

How does one come by a strong base? Either by growing up under favorable circumstances, favorable defined not as sheltered but as providing, along with emotional support, progressively bigger challenges that bring out capability and confidence. Or, as an adult, by outgrowing insecurity through a combination of a continuous stream of challenges, reparative close relationships, and perhaps also formal personal development or therapeutic work. Eventually the wounds heal sufficiently for the sensitivities to abate, the self-concern to diminish, and the structure of the self to firm up.

> "We must pity a good man with . . . torments unceasingly before him like a coursing fog that at times highlights the realities of the day's urgent business and at times obscures all that is present."
>
> —Goethe, *The Man of Fifty*, p. 63

As Will Stonecraft became surer of himself with experience, he found that he was decidedly quicker to achieve clarity about what he needed to do in a new assignment. Now in his late forties, he told my colleague and me, "I feel very confident but not overconfident." As a result, he recognized within a few weeks of taking over a division that was completely new to him that it was taking far too long to develop new products and bring them to market: "It was about velocity. I had clarity about that early." After a couple of visits to the Asia-Pacific region, he could see that the regional head wasn't up to the job and in short order established that with him and took him out of the job. He earned that clarity: "I was on the road every week getting out with people as much as I could—connecting with them, understanding their challenges, poring over the numbers so I could understand what potential the business had." In the past he had been somewhat slower to act out of a reluctance to be direct and out of a certain lack of boldness. The good news had been that he was down to earth, but that kept him from soaring like an eagle. Now he had expanded his range and converted himself from a good leader to an exceptional, and exceptionally versatile, leader.

A coda on calmness: Staying calm in a storm does not guarantee that you will use good judgment. If your perspective on the situation is warped, if your values are misguided, you can quite calmly do the wrong thing.

Can You Be Too Versatile?

By having the ability to moderate strengths you take too far, do you lose something? By having capacity on the other side, and by placing a value on that capacity, are you deprived of full extension on this side? In the face of a crisis or emergency, do you have the ability to be immoderate, to go to necessary extremes? Did the Soviet Union need a pathological leader like Stalin in order to industrialize the country rapidly? Without Stalin would the USSR have had a war machine capable of beating back the Germans on the Eastern Front and softening them up for the Allied invasion of the Western Front on D-Day? Would Rudy Guiliani as a mayor of New York City have had it in him to take the tough action apparently necessary to make the city governable again if he had tempered his super-aggressive mode of operating?

If you use "edge" with abandon, if you have little sympathy for the adverse effects on people, if you are numb to your own feelings, what can you accomplish that someone with compassion and compunctions cannot? You would be certain of not undershooting the mark on the tough, aggressive side of leadership. You would never make that mistake. But in camping out on the ragged edge, you would also regularly overshoot the mark. You would go beyond the necessary force that Machiavelli recommended. You would harm people when it wasn't necessary. Overkill would be your legacy. Over time the collateral damage would pile up. Everything that you traded off to get the result at any cost would catch up with you and, more importantly, catch up with the institution entrusted to you.

The question of whether leaders can be too versatile is reminiscent of the belief that great artists must be neurotic or worse. To do brilliant, innovative painterly work, an artist like Van Gogh has to be unbalanced enough to cut off his ear or one like Jackson Pollack has to be an alcoholic who in the end killed himself on a drunken joy ride. I don't believe that you have to be unbalanced emotionally to lead under adversity or to make bold, sweeping moves organizationally, any more than all great novelists, poets, scientists, or philosophers are tortured souls.[9] George Marshall's equilibrium did not vitiate his effectiveness, and it probably helped him in deploying formidable generals like Eisenhower and Patton where they were best suited.[10]

A class of leader sometimes mistakenly described as being too versatile is "the voice of reason," someone who can see both sides of every argument, who speaks in measured tones, who doesn't overreact or lose his or her objectivity. To be sure there is much to admire in this approach to leading. But by always being reasonable, this type lacks the capacity to be "unreasonable"; lacks the capacity to express anger even when he or she has every reason to be angry; lacks the capacity to come down quickly, firmly, and emphatically on one side of an issue when decisiveness is called for; lacks the capacity to expect "the impossible" from people who might just be able to achieve it. Rather than too versatile, these perpetually even-handed and even-tempered leaders are, in fact, not versatile enough. They are under-gunned on forceful leadership. The depressed ratings of their overall effectiveness reflect this limitation.

Another class of leader that may be mistaken for too versatile is the "chameleon," someone who tries to be all things to all people, someone who keeps changing their mind. What is his position on a controversial issue? It's whatever the last person in his office thinks. This type of leader is changeable. Versatile does not apply.

The Will Stonecrafts I know do not, by being highly versatile, sacrifice any appreciable ability to lead, even under very adverse business conditions. I don't know, of course, how they would perform in the worst of circumstances: as a general in war time, as the mayor of a city struck by a terrorist attack, or as a head of state in an intractable situation like Israel-Palestine or Northern Ireland.

Four Combinations of Lopsidedness

When, as is often the case, leaders are not multi-versatile, they can depart from the ideal in many different ways. Some leaders are generally deficient on both dualities. Others are versatile on one and lopsided on the other. When leaders are lopsided on both the strategic-operational duality and the forceful-enabling duality, there are four possible combinations, four distinct profiles, all easily recognizable (see Figure 10.2).

All four of these variations of lopsided leadership have a unique signature. They charge off, so to speak, to the four corners of the leadership cosmos. Only the versatile leader can command the whole cosmos from the center. Versatile leadership is not antithetical to any of the pairs. It is their summation; it reconciles all

Figure 10.2. Four Types of Lopsided Leadership

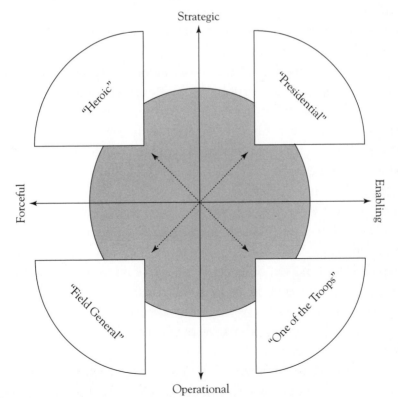

opposed pairs. The versatile leader experiences no contradiction between opposing sides.

In the upper left of Figure 10.2 appear those leaders, "heroic" types, if you will, who lean both toward strategic and toward forceful. They have a heroic cast because they boast expansive visions for their organizations and they possess the personal magnetism and force of personality to be inspirational leaders. Rich Spire is one such individual.

In the lower right is found the type that inclines toward both operational and enabling, the antithesis of the previous type, the kind of individual who pitches in, the player-coach, "one of the troops." This type is a rare breed. Forceful and operational are found together much more than enbaling and operational. Of the leaders featured in this book, Ella Solo, featured in Chapters 2 and 3, comes closest to fitting this type, but only roughly. She fits in the sense that, to a fault, she rolls up her sleeves and works side by side with her team, and in that way she is overly operational. Although, strictly speaking, she isn't overly enabling, there is an aspect of that in her not being demanding enough of her people.

In the upper right reside leaders with a "presidential" style, who err on the side of both strategic and enabling. No less strategic than the heroic types, they lean not toward ruling with a strong hand but toward taking a collaborative and participative approach. Sam Menza, described in Chapter 6 as strongly inclined toward the strategic, also employed a benign, enabling-oriented approach. Much more the leader than the manager, he believed in staffing his team and the level below with "A players," as he called them, and turning them loose, to the point of benign neglect.

In the lower left sits the "field general," the antithesis of the presidential type, who errs on the side of both forceful and operational. This is the sort of leader regularly found in the driver's seat of an operation that must perform consistently. Pete Powers, described in Chapter 6 as favoring operational leadership over strategic leadership, was also, in a coworker's phrase, "a bulldozer on tasks," too forceful, that is.

As you can see in Figure 10.3, Pete Powers' profile sags toward the forceful and operational functions. No doubt these strengths, albeit taken too far, are what propelled him up the career ladder. But now they may be weighing him down, preventing him from growing into a well-rounded leader. His versatility score is decent; 81 percent is a low B. But as the picture indicates, to become a grade-A senior leader will require that he tone down the forceful and operational functions and step up the strategic and enabling functions.

Boosting Versatility in Leaders

In this book we have identified several not-generally-taken approaches to boosting versatility and leveling out lopsidedness.

Figure 10.3. Pete Powers' Overall Profile on the LVI

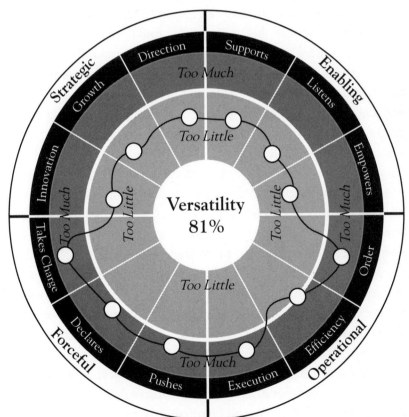

First, it turns out that leaders are routinely assessed for strengths and weaknesses but not for strengths overused. This despite the fact that leaders regularly go overboard. Is there any getting around the need to assess for strengths overused, not just deficiencies? Likewise, when it comes to development, moderating strengths overused belongs on the agenda. Think volume control. To be effective is getting the volume right, neither too low nor too high, for the situation.

Second, underestimating oneself has two opposite effects: it causes the person to avoid and underdo something or it causes him or her to go the other way and try too hard and overdo it. If, for example, you underestimate how smart you are, you are liable to either: (a) protect yourself by saying little in meetings or steering clear of intellectual work or (b) defend yourself by arming yourself to the teeth with information, preparing to the nth degree, and going out of your way to demonstrate how smart and knowledgeable you are. This is often how deficiencies and strengths overused originate. It is important to be mindful of this likely cause when we attack the effects.

Third, since overdoing and underdoing typically are linked in that overdoing one thing is accompanied by underdoing the opposite, complementary thing, it behooves us to define leadership in terms of opposing good things to do. To attain true versatility is to have the ability to call upon both sides of the many pairs of leadership dimensions, in the right proportion. It happens, however, that the competency models and 360-degree surveys in common use are unidimensional. No way then can leaders using this approach get a reading on how versatile they are in a two-dimensional sense. It is ironic that "balance" is on so many leaders' lips, and rightly so since managing those tensions is the crux of leading effectively, yet without realizing it they routinely submit themselves and others to assessments that utterly lack the capacity to appraise them in these terms. Should we not evaluate managers in the two-sided terms that many of them intuitively understand?

Fourth, in the great panoply of leadership skills, the dualities, strategic-and-operational leadership and forceful-and-enabling leadership, are absolutely central. And simply by placing leaders up against these two great pairs makes a fundamental fact clear: either/or won't work. You can do both, you must do both, whether by your own hand or with the help of others. This is one imperative. There is a second imperative: don't let one side of leadership dominate to the point of crowding out its opposite number. And a third one: cultivate the perceptive wisdom for knowing when to use which approach and develop skill at applying a wide repertoire of competencies in proper proportion. To accomplish that means not just bringing up the devalued side but also moderating the overplayed side.

Fifth, leaders, being the inveterate problem solvers they are, look upon feedback chiefly as a chance to identify the negatives that they can go to work on. For them the real value of feedback lies in the criticism. It turns out, however, in a way that most managers completely overlook, that positive feedback has developmental value that easily rivals that of negative feedback. There is serious developmental leverage in letting the strengths sink in, an overlooked way of toning down overused strengths as well as bringing up flat sides. It is just as challenging, however, to take in one's positives as it is to face up to one's blind spots.

Sixth, in seeking to improve, leaders are naturally inclined to intervene directly into their behavior, and there is a lot to be said for this outer work of development. But why pass up the equally useful leverage of inner development? It behooves leaders to adjust the mind-set that has given rise to underdoing and overdoing, for example, the one-sided perspective associated with lopsided behavior. An advantage of assessing performance in terms of doing too little or doing too much is that it quite naturally points to the leader's mind-set: what inside your head keeps you from doing more of this; what drives you to do too much of that? To regard the inner work of development as just as legitimate and practical as the behavioral work takes us full circle to underestimating one's strengths: what better way to correct for the distortions that arise from that than to own one's strengths?

Seventh, taking part in an assessment, leaders need potent data, enough of the right data for it to strike the individual as valid and credible. The goal of any assessment is for the leader to achieve potent clarity, a clarity sharp enough to spur him or her to change. But the data alone is in most cases unlikely to have that effect. To have the best chance of benefiting from a well-designed assessment, leaders also need potent help. Too often, however, managers receive scanty help with the feedback dropped on their desks. It is incumbent on those of us who administer 360-degree surveys to match quality data with quality assistance. The assistance, during assessment or implementation, can come from a supervisor, an HR or leadership-development professional, a peer, or a consultant—anyone who has the skill and will make the time.

In the end, the old rule applies to modern leaders: adapt or die. Although not as brutal as the survival of the fittest, the penalties are harsh: either grow or be moved out of the organization, or suffer complete career death, or survive but stagnate. For the majority of leaders, it comes down to whether they will have a sizeable impact or a negligible one, what the proportion of good versus harm they will do, and how much fulfillment versus personal strain will be their reward. Although different from natural selection, which takes vastly more time to play out and to replace one species with another one, it is a little like horticulture or animal husbandry in the sense that people can intervene and accelerate the process.[11] Whether you are concerned with your own development or that of others, why not sidestep the leadership field's blind spots and intervene with as full a set of performance-improvement strategies and tactics as possible.

Appendix

Research and Development of the Leadership Versatility Index[1]

Rob Kaiser

The purpose of this Appendix is to lay out the conceptual and statistical basis for the development and validation of the Leadership Versatility Index, the 360-degree measure of versatility that is integral to this book. We should acknowledge at the start that parts of this appendix may be too technical for the typical managerial reader. For those not interested in statistical methods or the detailed analyses, the findings have been summarized in plain language and, for ready reference, placed in sidebars.

Overview of the Instrument

The Leadership Versatility Index (LVI) grew out of "action-research," leadership consulting that doubled as research. The prototype was designed and first put into practice in 1993, and the tool as well as the theory behind it continue to be refined through statistical research and practical experience using it with managers.

Our conception of versatility is based on an observation made in the course of intensive assessment-and-feedback sessions with senior managers: they tend to be lopsided. That is, they place too much weight on one side and too little weight on the other side of "leadership oppositions" such as results-oriented versus people-oriented, assertive versus empowering, thinking versus doing, long-term versus short-term, and so on. For instance, some managers are too focused on results and not concerned enough about people, while others are concerned about people at the expense of the work. Relatively rare are leaders who do both well.

The LVI measures the two major pairs of opposites in managerial life: forceful versus enabling leadership and strategic versus operational leadership. Each of the four dimensions that form the two pairs—forceful, enabling, strategic, and operational—is further comprised of three subdimensions, shown in Table A.1.

Instrument Development

In the course of studying and consulting to executives, Bob Kaplan came to the realization that standard assessment tools employed rating scales that seemed to imply "more is better." Yet many of his executive clients' performance problems were the result of going overboard, doing too much of things like taking charge, pushing for results, introducing change, or even including people in decisions. Another shortcoming was that no assessment tools detected versatility or its counterproductive cousin, lopsidedness.

Table A.1. Definition of Leadership Underlying the LVI

Forceful Leadership	*Enabling Leadership*
Taking charge, asserting yourself, and pushing for performance.	Creating conditions for other people to take the lead, to be powerful in their own right, and to contribute.
Takes Charge	Empowers
Declares	Listens
Pushes	Supports

Strategic Leadership	*Operational Leadership*
Setting strategy, being expansive and innovation-oriented.	Focusing on short-term objectives, on efficiency and feasibility, and on processes for insuring performance.
Direction	Execution
Growth	Efficiency
Innovation	Order

Kaplan designed a prototype instrument for assessing forceful and enabling leadership in 1993. I joined him a few years later; we have together conducted a series of statistical studies, reviews of relevant research, and revisions to the tool that included the addition of strategic and operational leadership.

A New Response Scale

To capture excess as well as deficiency and optimal performance, we developed a new rating scale for the LVI, shown in Figure A.1.[2] Here the best score is in the middle, 0, flanked by deficiency to the left and excess to the right. Several features of the tool are designed to alert raters that the scale is not the usual linear type, where "more is better." Minus scores on the deficiency side and plus scores on the excess side call attention to these two different types of performance problems. And consistent with recent developments in the study of mental processes involved in ratings, the negative and positive numbers (and the arrows) also convey to raters that each side of the scale is distinct: low is not a lack of high; it is the opposite of it (Schwartz, 1999).

Pairing Opposites

Items on the LVI are written in pairs; each forceful item (for example, "Takes charge") also has an enabling counterpart (for example, "Empowers—able to let go") and each strategic item

Figure A.1. Too Little/Too Much Rating Scale

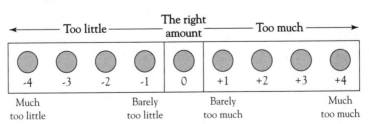

(for example, "Takes a big-picture perspective") also has an operational counterpart (for example, "Pays attention to the details"). This design principle ensures that there is symmetry at the behavioral level as well as at the subdimension and dimensional levels. In other words, the idea of mastering opposites is integral to the structural design of the instrument, from the ground up.

On the LVI survey, items are presented one at a time. Raters first rate all of the forceful items, then the enabling items, then the strategic items, and finally the operational items. But on the feedback report, results for each pair of opposites are presented side-by-side.

Grounded in Executive Development

Each item pair was inspired by one of our executive clients, either as a positive or negative role model. The material used to generate items came mostly from interviews we conducted with our clients' bosses, peers, and subordinates to gather developmental feedback. We harvested examples where individuals mentioned overdoing a particular behavior or being lopsided on a particular pair. In this sense, the method we used is similar to the critical incidents technique (Flanagan, 1954). Furthermore, taking the behavioral cores directly from these assessment interviews builds in relevance and content validity. By using the language managers themselves use to characterize each other's performance, we built in a degree of linguistic familiarity to make the rating task easier and the feedback more meaningful.

Conceptual Structure

The structure of the LVI refers to the grouping of items to subdimensions and subdimensions to dimensions. We used two methods, one empirical and the other theoretical, to determine the structure of the present instrument. First, we have induced structure by analyzing item ratings from previous versions of the tool using a statistical technique called exploratory factor analysis. This procedure identifies the most parsimonious way to group items to maximize similarity within groupings and to minimize overlap between group-ings. We have also used confirmatory factor analysis using different samples to test the adequacy of the structures derived inductively. This is discussed further below.

The second approach to devising the structure of the LVI was conceptual. First, we reviewed the research on leadership behaviors; identified the ones that are similar to our forceful, enabling, strate-gic, and operational dimensions; and examined how these dimen-sions were defined both theoretically and behaviorally. Second, where possible, we examined empirical research relevant to the structure of these concepts. It is worth noting that most of what we found pertained to forceful and enabling leadership; there was very little theoretical and empirical work on the structure of strategic and operational leadership.

The first major structural division in the LVI is the distinction between *how* you lead and *what* you lead. This distinction is made in the spirit of a growing recognition among leadership scholars of the difference between the social aspects of leading and the func-tional/business aspects. Zaccaro (2001) contrasted the direct influ-ence that leaders have in social exchanges and interpersonal dynamics with the indirect influence leaders exert through deci-sions about direction, organizational structure, and objectives. Antonakis and House (2002) discussed the difference between *inspirational* leadership, which is an interpersonal matter, and *instru-mental* leadership, which concerns setting direction and facilitating the accomplishment of goals. In our view, how you lead, the social/interpersonal side of leadership, is represented by forceful and enabling. What you lead, the functional/business side of leadership, is represented by strategic and operational. Below is a summary of prior definitions and concepts that we used to guide our thinking in fleshing out the structure of the LVI.

Forceful and Enabling Leadership. Forceful and enabling leader-ship map onto the two major axes of interpersonal behaviors in lead-ership. In Bernard Bass's (1990, pp. 415–543) intellectual history and exhaustive review of the scientific study of leadership, he concluded that there are two overarching clusters of active leadership behaviors. One centers on both the "autocratic" use of power and a focus on task, while the other revolves around an "egalitarian" use of power and a concern for people. According to Bass, within each of these two distinct clusters are overlapping leadership behaviors characterized by the many dualities discussed over the years. These finer distinctions formed the basis for our three subdimensions within the forceful and enabling domains. Table A.2 lists prior conceptualizations of these two sides of the *how* of leadership and how they influenced our view of forceful and enabling leadership.

Strategic and Operational Leadership. The *what* of leadership concerns the business or organizational matters that leaders focus on to indirectly influence performance through goals, structures, and policies. We divide this space into the opposing dimensions of strategic and operational leadership. In our review, we found that these two dimensions are rarely contrasted or juxtaposed in the literature. One notable exception, however, is the distinction John Kotter (1990) made between leadership and management. Consistent with our view of strategic and operational leadership, these unique and complementary functions consist of leadership as inspiring with a vision of change and management as disciplined control. Table A.3 contains prior conceptualizations that informed our view of the subdimensions of the *what* of leadership, strategic and operational leadership.

Measurement Properties: Internal Characteristics

The following sections summarize statistical analyses of how well the LVI works as a measurement tool. The results are presented in terms of reliability and validity, first considering the instrument's internal properties and then reviewing external characteristics—how scores on the LVI are related to other variables (for example, alternative measures of similar concepts, leader effectiveness, follower job satisfaction). Some of the following material is

Table A.2. Conceptualizations of the *How* of Leadership

	Autocratic Focus on Work *Forceful Leadership*	*Egalitarian Concern for People* *Enabling Leadership*
	Locus of power: takes charge vs. empowers	
Stogdill & Coons (1957)	Initiation	Consideration
Likert (1967)	Influence skills	Interaction skills
Zaleznik (1974)	Power-oriented	Power-sharing
	Decision making: declares vs. listens	
Lewin & Lippit (1938)	Autocracy	Democracy
House (1971)	Directive	Participative
Vroom & Yetton (1973)	Directive and autonomous	Participative and inclusive
Bass & Valenzi (1974)	Directive/ persuasive	Consultative/ participative
	Orientation: pushes for performance vs. supports people	
Bales (1950)	Performance	Maintenance
Fleishman (1953)	Initiating Structure	Consideration
Blake & Mouton (1964)	Production emphasis	People emphasis
Fiedler (1967)	Task-oriented	People-oriented
Hersey & Blanchard (1969)	Direction	Support
House (1971)	Achievement focus	Supportive
Quinn (1988)	Producer and director roles	Mentor and facilitator roles

unavoidably technical. Although a familiarity with statistics and psychometric theory would be helpful, we have attempted to explain concepts in a way that is accessible to all readers. The major findings are also summarized in nontechnical terms in sidebars throughout this section.

The LVI has been developed and refined over several iterations. The current version of the instrument is the fourth and contains the fourth generation of forceful and enabling scales and the third generation of strategic and operational scales. At the time of this

Table A.3. Conceptualizations of the *What* of Leadership

	Forward-Looking Change *Strategic Leadership*	Present-Oriented Consistency *Operational Leadership*
	Timeline and activity: long-term direction vs. short-term execution	
Barnard (1938)	Provide direction	Manage day-to-day operations
Kotter (1990)	Establishing direction	Planning
Bennis & Nanus (1985)	Vision	
Conger & Kanungo (1994)	Vision	
Zaccaro (2001)	Setting direction	Implementation, tactics
Antonakis & House (2002)	Strategic leadership	Work facilitation
Bossidy & Charan (2002)		Execution
	Orientation: growth vs. efficiency	
Mintzberg (1975)	Entrepreneurial role	
Miles & Snow (1978)	Prospect new opportunities	Defend position
Porter (1996)	Growth	Operational efficiency
Neiman (2004)		Focus
Prince (2005)	Adding value	Reducing costs
	Climate: innovation vs. order	
Fayol (1949/1916)		Planning, organizing, controlling
Quinn (1988)	Innovator role	Coordinator and Monitor roles
Kotter (1990)	Creating change	Establishing control
Conger & Kanungo (1994)	Challenge the status quo	
Kouzes & Posner (1987)	Challenge the process	
Huy (2002)	Change	Continuity

writing, we have yet to collect data on these new scales; the research reported here was conducted on the earlier versions. Unless otherwise noted, the following analyses are based on seven distinct samples of 360-degree ratings for a total of 562 target managers from 5,334 coworkers. These samples are further described in Table A.4. All data were collected for the express purpose of developmental feedback and all raters were told their ratings would be anonymous, except for superiors, who were informed that their ratings would be identified as coming from them.

> The LVI has been studied and refined with seven independent samples of ratings from over 5,000 coworkers of over 550 middle managers and executives.

Reliability

Reliability has to do with the likelihood that repeated measurements will yield equivalent results. All measures are imperfect and

Table A.4. Description of Research Samples

Sample	# targets	Population	# raters	Date collected	Scale Versions Forc.-Enab.	Scale Versions Strat.-Op.
1	58	Executives	456	1994–1997	1	—
2	131	Executives	1230	1998–2001	2	1
3	54	Superintendents	568	2001	3	—
4	59	Executives	373	2002–2003	3	1
5	74	Middle managers	849	2003–2004	3	2
6	89	Middle managers	832	2003–2004	3	2
7	97	Executives	1026	2003–2004	3	2

Notes: For the forceful and enabling scales, the following numbers of item pairs were used in the research reported below: Version 1 = 9 pairs, Version 2 = 5 pairs, and Version 3 = 8 pairs. For the strategic and operational scales, these values were Version 1 = 5 pairs, Version 2 = 8 pairs.

contain some degree of error; reliability is an estimate of this property. We have examined issues of scale reliability on the LVI in two general ways. First, at the individual rater level of analysis, we calculated Cronbach's alpha as a measure of internal consistency. The average value for each scale across samples appears in Table A.5 on the next page. Nunally (1978) recommends .70 as the minimum acceptable value for alpha, but also indicates that .80 is preferred in practice.

The second way we considered reliability was in terms of convergence between multiple raters of the same target. Since 360-degree ratings involve data from multiple raters, we examined the degree of similarity among raters within the traditional three rating sources of superiors, peers, and subordinates. Following the recommended procedures of LeBreton, Burgess, Kaiser, Atchley, and James (2003), we considered both inter-rater reliability and inter-rater agreement. The first is a correlation-based technique and provides an index of the extent to which ratings of the same target made by different raters are consistent, following the same pattern of highs and lows. Inter-rater agreement is based on the absolute level of ratings and provides an index of the extent to which the ratings from different raters of the same target are of equal magnitude. The difference may seem subtle, but both considerations are necessary in addressing rating similarity.

> The reliability of the LVI has been studied from two perspectives: internal consistency and similarity across multiple raters. The analyses indicate that, overall, the reliabilities for the LVI scales meet accepted standards and are comparable to the reliabilities for leadership scales reported in the scientific literature. There is one exception: the operational scale is less internally consistent than desired.

Inter-rater reliability was calculated using the Intraclass Correlation Coefficient (ICC; Shrout & Fliese, 1976). First we calculated

Table A.5. Average Scale Reliabilities by Rating Source

| | | Superiors | | | | Peers | | | | Subordinates | | | |
| | | ICC(k) | | | | ICC(k) | | | | ICC(k) | | | |
Scale	α	ICC(1)	k = 2	k = 4	r$_{wg}$	ICC(1)	k = 4	k = 7	r$_{wg}$	ICC(1)	k = 4	k = 7	r$_{wg}$
Forceful	.82	.53	.69	.82	.89	.38	.71	.81	.85	.31	.64	.76	.85
Enabling	.81	.36	.53	.69	.91	.37	.70	.80	.88	.26	.58	.71	.89
Strategic	.79	.25	.40	.57	.92	.22	.53	.66	.89	.22	.53	.66	.89
Operational	.53	.36	.53	.69	.93	.23	.54	.68	.88	.20	.50	.64	.86
Average	.74	.38	.54	.69	.91	.30	.62	.74	.88	.25	.56	.69	.87

Notes: Reported data are based on the average values calculated across six independent samples (samples 2–7 in Table A4; rater-level data was not available to compute the statistics for sample 1).

the reliability for a single rater [ICC(1)]. Then we calculated the reliability of the average rating across multiple raters within each rating group [ICC(k), where k is the number of raters]. We used $k = 2$ and 4 for superiors and $k = 4$ and 7 for peers and subordinates to illustrate the importance of getting input from a sufficient number of raters (as the number of raters goes up, so does reliability). In organizational surveys, ICC(1) values typically range from .00 to .50 with an average of .12 (James, 1982); values of .05 are considered high enough to justify aggregation (Bliese, 2000). In the particular case of multi-source ratings of managers, reported ICC(1) values range from .2 to .45 and ICC(k) values range from .50 (for $k = 3$ raters) to .60 ($k = 5$ raters) (see Conway & Huffcut, 1997; Greguras & Robie, 1998; LeBreton, Burgess, Kaiser, Atchley, & James, 2003). The preferred cutoff for ICC(k) is .70, although values between .50 and .70 are usually deemed acceptable. Inter-rater reliability values increase with hierarchical relationship to the person being rated (subordinate ratings are least reliable, superiors' ratings are most reliable) and as the number of raters (k) increases.

Finally, inter-rater agreement was determined using the r_{wg} statistic. This index represents the extent to which different raters for the same target provide the same rating on each item. It is computed across all raters within a rating source for each rating target. Then the average r_{wg} is calculated within rating source across all targets. Mean r_{wg} values greater than .70 are generally regarded as acceptable with values closer to 1.00 indicating very high agreement (Bliese, 2000; James, Demaree, & Wolf, 1984).

Table A.5 shows the average reliability values for each scale and for each rating source in terms of internal consistency, inter-rater reliability [ICC(1) and ICC(k)], and inter-rater agreement (r_{wg}).

Overall, the various reliability statistics for the LVI are consistent with values commonly reported in research on 360-degree ratings and meet generally accepted standards. However, there are two qualifications to this supportive interpretation. First, four superiors, six peers, and seven subordinates are needed for their average ratings to meet the .70 standard for inter-rater reliability; at least this number of raters is encouraged in practice. Second, the operational leadership scale is notably less internally consistent than desirable. We have addressed this concern in the latest revision of the item content by redefining the three subdimensions to be more similar to one another.

Validity

Validity is often said to refer to "the extent to which a test measures what it purports to measure." One way to determine whether an assessment does this is by examining whether scores are related to each other and to other, non-test variables in a manner consistent with theory (Cronbach & Meehl, 1955).

There are two important validity considerations when it comes to evaluating the internal structure of the LVI. The first concerns the relationship between opposites, the correlations between forceful and enabling leadership and between strategic and operational leadership. The theory behind the LVI assumes that managers are often lopsided on these oppositions: they tend to overdo one side and underdo the other side. This suggests that there should be a negative correlation between pairs of opposites: more of one corresponds to less of the other. We refer to this as the "polarity effect" because the negative correlation is a way to statistically represent the tendency of managers to gravitate toward one side and away from the other side of an opposition.

Table A.6 provides a summary of the average correlation between forceful and enabling leadership and between strategic and operational leadership across the seven research samples. The ratings were first averaged across all raters in a given source; then the aggregated scale scores were correlated.

These results paint a mixed picture. On the one hand, the expected relationship was found for forceful and enabling leadership. The polarity effect was especially strong in the coworker rating groups with average correlations between −.56 and −.61.[3] On the other hand, we did not find evidence for a polarity effect for strategic and operational leadership overall. These correlations averaged around 0, essentially no relationship at all. Closer inspection of our data raised the possibility that this may be due to an artifact of our samples as well as a limitation to the instrument. Specifically, there was a very low incidence of overdoing strategic leadership (ratings of overdoing on forceful leadership, for instance, are about three times more likely than for strategic leadership). With this kind of restriction in the range of scores, it is very difficult to find a statistical relationship. We took this result very seriously in the latest revision of the LVI item content (for which we have no data yet to report).

A possible explanation for the restricted range of ratings for strategic leadership is that overdoing strategic leadership may be a relatively rare phenomenon in the population of managers. For instance, Lombardo and Eichinger (2000) reported that in their comprehensive assessments of over three thousand managers, the competencies in shortest supply were *Creativity, Dealing with Ambiguity, Managing Vision and Purpose, Planning,* and *Strategic Agility.* This is not to say that strategic leadership cannot be overdone; to the contrary, we find overdo ratings on the various strategic behaviors. They are just relatively infrequent.

The LVI is intended to measure lopsidedness on opposing dimensions of leadership. Thus, the correlations between forceful and enabling (and strategic and operational) should be negative: the higher the ratings on one side, the lower the ratings on the opposite side. And this is what we find for forceful and enabling leadership: the correlation between the two is negative and rather strong.

However, the correlation between strategic and operational leadership is not negative. Rather, there is no correlation between these two. This appears to be due to a low overall incidence of "too much" ratings on the strategic dimension. On the facets of strategic and operational leadership for which there is a higher incidence of overdoing the strategic behaviors, the correlations are indeed negative.

Table A.6. Average Correlation Between Opposites

Rater Source	Forceful-Enabling			Strategic-Operational		
	k	N	r	k	N	r
Self	7	529	−.26	5	443	.06
Superiors	7	487	−.61	5	420	.01
Peers	6	447	−.63	5	424	.06
Subordinates	6	464	−.56	5	432	.12

Notes: k = number of correlation coefficients, N indicates the total number of managers rated, and r values are the average correlation across the k studies. Peer and subordinate ratings were not separable in sample 1.

It is worth noting that we have found evidence for the inverse relationship between certain aspects of strategic and operational leadership. For instance, on the second-generation scales (samples 5, 6, and 7), we found a negative correlation ($r = -.17$) between the items, "Focused on long-term strategy" (strategic) and "Focused on short-term results" (operational). Moreover, we also found a negative correlation ($r = -.35$) between the subdimensions of Growth and Efficiency. Growth is the expansive aspect of strategic, whereas Efficiency is the more focused and restrictive aspect of operational. Negatively correlated items here include "Willing to make bold moves" and "Introduces change in small increments" ($r = -.24$), "Encourages out-of-the-box thinking" and "Stays with the tried and true" ($r = -.31$), and "Aggressive about growth" and "Respects limits" ($r = -.21$). As it happens, these strategic items are those on which we find a higher incidence of overdoing (more ratings of "too much"). This finding encouraged us to go to greater lengths to craft strategic leadership items on the revised scales that more readily admit of overdoing.

The fact that we did not find a positive correlation between strategic and operational leadership overall is a good sign. And if we had, it would cast doubt on our conceptualization of the two dimensions and how they are measured on the LVI.

The second consideration concerning the internal validity of the LVI involves how well the data fit the conceptual structure—the hierarchical model. Recall that the model specifies three subdimensions for each of the four dimensions, forceful, enabling, strategic, and operational leadership. We have previously reported factor analyses that demonstrate that forceful and enabling are two distinct, but correlated, general factors (Kaiser & Craig, 2001). Here we describe the validation of the hierarchical structure involving three subdimensions within each of the forceful and enabling dimensions. We do not report a similar structural analysis of the strategic and operational dimensions because the last version of those scales did not conform empirically to the model. This limitation was central to our revision of those scales.

We developed and tested the structure of the forceful and enabling scales in two stages. First, we used samples 3 and 4 described above to conduct item analyses and exploratory factor analyses to select items that fit the conceptual structure. Then we tested how well the combined data from samples 5, 6, and 7 fit this model using confirmatory factor analyses. Following the guidance of Hu and Bentler (1995), we used multiple statistical indices to arrive at an overall judgment of how well the data fit the conceptual model in each sample.

Underneath the distinction between forceful leadership and enabling leadership are three finer distinctions: between Takes Charge and Empowers, between Declares and Listens, and between Pushes and Supports. Another test of the internal validity of the LVI is: Does the data support these three distinctions? It does. So far, however, the data do not provide clear support for the three distinctions underneath strategic and operational leadership.

The results from the confirmatory factor analysis indicated that the seventeen items selected from the exploratory factor analyses to measure the three forceful subdimensions (Takes Charge, Declares, and Pushes) and three enabling subdimensions (Empowers, Listens, and Supports) provided an adequate measurement model.[4] Specific model fit statistics are provided in Table A.7. A visual representation of this structural model is presented in Figure A.2.

The seventeen items indicated in the preceding model formed the basis for the current revision of the forceful and enabling scales. Since the current model provides a good fit to the empirical data, we are hopeful that the next generation of items, being informed by this analyses and the product of accumulated experience with this new type of assessment, will make for an even more solid structural model. We have used a similar logic to reconstruct the strategic and operational scales and must await further data collection to test how well we did at building that model.

Measuring Versatility

Having created measures of the two major pairs of oppositions in leadership, forceful-enabling and strategic-operational, our next task was to derive a measure of versatility for each pair, a single number to quantitatively represent our conceptual definition of versatility as neither too much nor too little on both sides of a pair of

Table A.7. Fit Indices for Hierarchical Model of Forceful and Enabling Leadership

Population	N	χ^2	df	CFI[1]	GFI[2]	TLI[3]	RMSR[4]	RMSEA[5]
Executives and middle managers (samples 5, 6, & 7)	2,839	1962.55	109	.91	.92	.89	.08	.07

Notes: N = number of raters (selves, superiors, peers, and subordinates). Criteria for interpreting fit statistics are > .90 = good fit for [1]Comparative Fit Index, [2]Goodness of Fit Index, [3]Tucker-Lewis Index, and < .08 = good fit for [4]Root Mean Square Residual and [5]Root Mean Square Error of Approximation.

Figure A.2. Structural Model of Forceful and Enabling Leadership

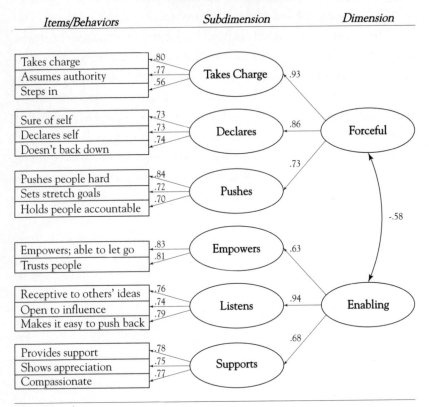

Note: Only the behavioral cores for each item are shown. Coefficients are standardized factor loadings at the latent level (i.e., corrected for measurement error).

opposites. We compute a versatility score for each duality by considering how close ratings are to 0 (the right amount) on both dimensions (for example, forceful and enabling). It represents the degree to which the individual is rated as moving freely in and out of opposing modes, that is, the extent to which he or she makes optimal use of both sides of the forceful and enabling duality (or the strategic and operational duality). Higher scores indicate greater versatility.

The versatility score is computed using geometry. Just as the Greek philosopher Aristotle defined virtue as the point between deficiency (underdo) and excess (overdo), we turned to Pythagoras, the Greek mathematician, to quantify versatility as a "double virtue." The versatility score is a mathematical representation of how close ratings are to 0 (*the right amount*) on both items in a pair, across all pairs in the duality. The versatility score can range from 0 (the most extreme possible scores of –4 and +4) to 100 (perfect scores of 0 and 0). Versatility scores are calculated using the Pythagorean theorem and the arithmetic shown in Figure A.3.

Using this method, a versatility score is computed for each pair of items that make up the forceful and enabling duality (or strategic and operational duality). This value is computed separately for each rater. Then the average of these values is computed across all item pairs, yielding the overall versatility score for that rater on that duality. Finally, the average versatility score across all raters in a given rating group is computed. Thus, the versatility score reflects how

Figure A.3. Calculation of the Versatility Score

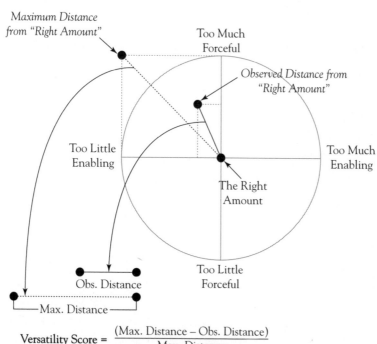

$$\text{Versatility Score} = \frac{(\text{Max. Distance} - \text{Obs. Distance})}{\text{Max. Distance}}$$

close the manager's ratings are to the "right amount" on both sides of the duality overall, across all raters and all pairs of items.

In Figure A.4 is an example of how the versatility score is computed for one item pair. In this example, the individual received a forceful score of +2.00 and an enabling score of –1.00.

As the computation in Figure A.4 shows, these hypothetical ratings yield a versatility score of 60.5 percent on this pair of items, meaning that the manager is rated as 60.5 percent of the way to using both behaviors to "the right amount." These values are computed separately for each pair of items on the forceful and enabling scales (or strategic and operational scales), and then the average across them is computed to represent overall versatility on that duality.

Versatility scores are highly reliable, which is expected because they are a function of the four reasonably reliable forceful, enabling, strategic, and operational scales. Table A.8 shows the average reliability values for the forceful-enabling and the strategic-operational

Figure A.4. Examples of Calculating the Versatility Score

Observed distance from optimal:

$$c^2 = a^2 + b^2$$
$$c^2 = (+2)^2 + (-1)^2$$
$$c = 2.236$$

Maximum distance from optimal

$$\underline{c}^2 = \underline{a}^2 + \underline{b}^2$$
$$\underline{c}^2 = (+4)^2 + (-4)^2$$
$$\underline{c} = 5.657$$

Versatility Score:

$$\frac{Max.\ Distance - Observed\ Distance}{Max.\ Distance}$$

$$= \frac{5.657 - 2.236}{5.657}$$

$$= .605$$

Versatility Score = 60.5%

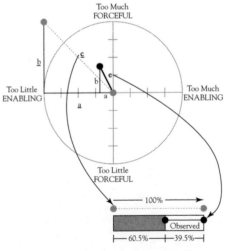
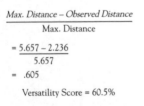

Table A.8. Reliabilities for Versatility Scores by Rating Source

Scale	α	Superiors				Peers				Subordinates			
			ICC(k)				ICC(k)				ICC(k)		
		ICC(1)	k = 2	k = 4	r_{wg}	ICC(1)	k = 4	k = 7	r_{wg}	ICC(1)	k = 4	k = 7	r_{wg}
Forceful-Enabling Versatility	.85	.45	.62	.76	.93	.39	.72	.82	.88	.33	.66	.78	.92
Strategic-Operational Versatility	.85	.37	.54	.70	.95	.28	.61	.73	.90	.24	.56	.69	.89
Average	.85	.41	.58	.73	.94	.34	.66	.77	.89	.29	.61	.73	.90

Note: Reported data are based on the average values calculated across seven samples.

versatility scores for each rating source in terms of internal consistency ($\propto$), inter-rater reliability [ICC(1) and ICC(k)], and inter-rater agreement (r_{wg}). These averages were computed across the seven samples described above.

An important question is how to interpret how "good" or "not-so-good" a versatility score is. Our research indicates that the average versatility score is around 80 percent, with values ranging from a low of 54 percent to a high of 98 percent. This distribution is strikingly similar to those used for grades in school, and we interpret versatility scores with that rule of thumb (90 to 100 percent, A; 80 to 89 percent, B; 70 to 79 percent, C; and so on.).

Measurement Properties: External Characteristics

The preceding section attests to the reliability and structural validity of the LVI and paints a picture supportive of the forceful and enabling scales while suggesting that the strategic and operational scales need further refinement. This conclusion was reached solely on the grounds of considerations internal to the LVI—examining the structural features of the instrument. We now turn to another important set of considerations, those that concern how scores on the LVI are related to external variables, those measured by means other than the LVI. What do ratings on the LVI predict? Do they converge with other measures of similar concepts? And how well do they predict outcomes compared to other measures?

Versatility and Effectiveness

In each of the seven research samples, we have studied the validity of versatility in predicting overall evaluations of leader effectiveness. The measure of overall effectiveness consisted of a single item: "Please give a rating of this person's overall effectiveness as a leader on a 10-point scale, where 10 is outstanding and 5 is adequate."

Our analyses suggest that this single-item rating is a reasonably reliable and valid measure of perceived overall effectiveness. Specifically, ICC(1) and ICC(k) meet standards for reliability [superiors, peers, and subordinates, respectively: ICC(1) = .46, .30. and .33; ICC(k) = .77 (k = 4), .75 (k = 7) and .78 (k = 7)]. Inter-rater agreement is also acceptable, with mean r_{wg} values of .84 (superiors), .79 (peers), and .82 (subordinates). And ratings from different coworker sources are moderately correlated with each other, providing convergent validity evidence (the average correlation between each source was superior-peer r =46; superior-subordinate r = .40, and peer-subordinate r = .43). Moreover, in one sample, the single-item rating was strongly correlated (r = .86) with a longer, five-item scale of overall effectiveness, offering even more evidence for convergent validity. We take this measure to represent the net-out overall evaluation observers make of a leader, the overall favorability of a leader's reputation.

We studied the relationship between versatility and overall effectiveness in three ways. First, we looked at correlations within the same rating source (for example, predicting average subordinate ratings of effectiveness with average subordinate ratings of versatility). Second, we looked at correlations between sources when each variable was measured by different sources (for example, using subordinate ratings of versatility to predict superior ratings of effectiveness). Finally, we looked at correlations within the same rating source, but used different raters for the two variables (for example, use the average of half of the subordinates' ratings on

> Forceful-enabling versatility is highly correlated with ratings of overall effectiveness, as is strategic-operational versatility. The correlations are very strong when versatility and effectiveness are rated by the same rater; but even when different raters are used to measure the two variables, the correlations are still significant.

versatility to predict the other half's average effectiveness rating). The latter two techniques remove the effects of having the same people rate both versatility and effectiveness. Within-rater correlations tell us about the relationship between versatility and effectiveness as it is in "the eye of the beholder." When ratings from one group of raters are used to predict ratings from another group, it tells us about relationships that exist outside that subjective realm.

Table A.9 presents the average correlations between forceful-enabling versatility and overall effectiveness both within and between rating sources. Correlations along the diagonal are within source (based on the average of all raters in the given rating source); the remaining correlations are between sources. Table A.10 contains an analogous table for the correlations between strategic-operational versatility and overall effectiveness.

Table A.11 presents the average within-source, split-sample correlations. These correlations are analogous to the correlations along the diagonal in Tables A.9 and A.10, with one important exception. They are calculated within rating source but using ratings from different individuals to measure versatility and effectiveness. To compute these values, we randomly split all subordinates, peers, and superiors in half in samples 5, 6, and 7. We then computed average versatility and effectiveness scores for the two halves.

Table A.9. Average Correlations Between Forceful-Enabling Versatility and Overall Effectiveness

Source for F-E Versatility	Source for Effectiveness			
	Self	Superiors	Peers	Subs.
Self	.28	.13	.12	.14
Superiors	.12	.60	.30	.37
Peers	.15	.29	.58	.23
Subordinates	.10	.29	.28	.68

Notes: Based on results across seven independent samples. All correlations are significant at $p < .01$. Within source correlations are in bold.

Table A.10. Correlations Between Strategic-Operational Versatility and Overall Effectiveness

Source for S-O Versatility	Self	Superiors	Peers	Subs.
		Source for Effectiveness		
Self	**.36**	.12	.11	-.01
Superiors	.13	**.64**	.25	.35
Peers	.17	.34	**.64**	.26
Subordinates	.16	.36	.35	**.68**

Notes: Based on results across five independent samples. All correlations significant at $p < .01$ (except for self-rated versatility and subordinate-rated effectiveness, *ns*). Within source correlations are in bold.

Table A.11. Average Within-Source, Split-Sample Correlations Between Versatility and Overall Effectiveness

Rating Source	F-E Versatility	S-O Versatility
Superiors	.43	.44
Peers	.29	.32
Subordinates	.34	.37

Notes: Only samples 5, 6, and 7 were included in this analysis. F-E = forceful-enabling; S-O = strategic-operational.

Next we correlated the first half's average rating of versatility with the average effectiveness rating from the second half. Then we correlated the average versatility rating from the second half with the average effectiveness rating from the first half. Finally, we computed the average of these two correlations to represent the "split-sample, within source" correlation. This was done separately for forceful-enabling versatility and strategic-operational versatility and separately for each rating source.

There are three things to note about the validity coefficients in these tables. First, there is substantial evidence that versatility on these two dualities is related to perceptions of overall effectiveness. Most of the correlations are sizable, especially for the coworker ratings. All of the average correlations based on superior, peer, and subordinate data are significant ($p < .001$), ranging from a low of .23 to several above .60, with an average of .42. Second, although self-ratings of versatility predict self-rating of effectiveness, these correlations are notably weaker than in the other rater groups. Also, self-ratings of versatility are barely related to coworker ratings of overall effectiveness (r's from $-.01$ to .14). It appears that self-ratings of versatility reflect something substantially different from coworker ratings, perhaps a function of the crooked thinking and emotionally charged biases in self-perception described in Chapter 4.

The third, and most important, point to note is that the relationship between versatility and effectiveness is moderate to strong, but the magnitude of the correlation varies as a function of who provided which ratings. The results are strongest for the within-source correlations, where the same raters were used to measure both versatility and effectiveness (across superiors, peers, and subordinates, the average forceful-

> Self-ratings of versatility are not related to coworker ratings of overall effectiveness. In other words, the extent to which managers view their own leadership as versatile has almost nothing to do with how their colleagues see their overall effectiveness. This emphasizes the importance of feedback: lopsided leaders don't see the link to ineffectiveness that is so apparent to those around them.

enabling versatility $r = .62$, strategic-operational versatility $r = .65$). The next highest correlations were for the split-sample, within-source method (average forceful-enabling versatility $r = .35$, strategic-operational versatility $r = .38$) followed closely by the between-source correlations (not including self-ratings; average forceful-enabling versatility $r = .29$, strategic-operational versatility $r = .32$). Thus, although the correlations are substantial when the relationships are examined within rating source using the same raters, when different raters are used to measure the two variables, the relationships remain practically significant and statistically significant.

We finally examined the validity of using both forceful-enabling versatility and strategic-operational versatility to predict overall effectiveness ratings. Given that each is significantly related to overall effectiveness, how well do the two types of versatility jointly predict effectiveness? To answer this, we conducted multiple regression analyses in the five samples that included both forceful-enabling and strategic-operational measures. To simplify the results, we used the average ratings of forceful-enabling versatility, strategic-operational versatility, and overall effectiveness calculated across all coworkers (superiors, peers, and subordinates combined). These results appear in Table A.12.

> Taken together, forceful-enabling versatility and strategic-operational versatility account for about 50 percent of the variance in the overall effectiveness of managers. Said in plain language, half of what separates the most effective from the least effective managers is captured by the LVI.

The results in Table A.12 point to three important conclusions. First, both types of versatility make a unique contribution to the prediction of overall effectiveness. The second conclusion is that

Table A.12. Results of Multiple Regression Analyses

			F-E Vers.	S-O Vers.	Model Statistics	
Sample	N	Population	β	β	R	F
2	131	Executives	.19	.58	.73	41.46***
4	59	Executives	.24	.65	.71	60.79***
5	74	Middle managers	.30	.34	.60	19.55***
6	89	Middle managers	.21	.51	.69	40.70***
7	97	Executives	.43	.45	.79	75.98***
		Average	.27	.51	.71	

Notes: All regression models significant at $p < .001$; all β weights significant at $p < .01$. F-E = forceful-enabling; S-O = strategic-operational. The average rating across all coworkers was used to measure the versatility and effectiveness variables.

versatility on the strategic-operational duality is a stronger predictor of overall effectiveness. Comparing the beta-weights β, which provides a rough estimate of relative contribution, indicates that strategic-operational versatility out-predicted forceful-enabling versatility in all five samples. Its average beta-weight (β = .51) is nearly twice as large as that for forceful-enabling (β = .27). The third conclusion is that versatility on these two dualities is highly related to perceptions of overall effectiveness; the average multiple correlation is R = .71, indicating that half of the variance in effectiveness ratings are a function of versatility on these two dualities (that is, R^2 = .71^2 = .50). In other words, half of what it means to be regarded as an effective leader is captured by forceful-enabling versatility and strategic-operational versatility. Whatever else contributes to one's reputation as a leader, and surely there are other important factors, it can't be more important than versatility. This isn't an opinion, it is a statistical fact: versatility accounts for half of what distinguishes leaders who are regarded as highly effective from those seen as less effective, leaving the remaining half to be accounted for by all the other factors combined.

Taken together, the results linking versatility to overall effectiveness paint a favorable picture of the LVI; the behaviors measured by the LVI are vital to how leaders are evaluated overall. This is particularly true within rating sources and also generalizes across rating sources: versatility as rated by one individual predicts effectiveness as rated by another individual. The only exception to this is self-ratings of versatility, which are unrelated to coworker ratings. Thus the LVI can be beneficial by providing managers with feedback about how their coworkers see them quite differently and that these differences are related to overall effectiveness.

Comparison to Similar Measures

A study by Lindberg and Kaiser (2004) compared three alternative methods for measuring managerial flexibility: versatility as measured by the LVI; a conceptually similar model of flexibility based on a different measurement procedure described by Quinn, Spreitzer, and Hart (1992); and a traditional scale measuring flexibility as a trait-like characteristic. The sample included ratings from 264 raters of twenty-nine middle managers who went through a leadership development program. The study, which the authors considered preliminary due to the small sample, was an examination of the convergent and discriminant validity of the three different measures and a comparison of their relative validity at predicting the single-item measure of overall effectiveness described above.

The trait-based measure of flexibility was a rating scale consisting of five items. It was based on a conceptualization that defines flexibility as a global construct along the lines of its dictionary meaning: the capability to adapt to new, different, or changing requirements. The range of specific behaviors is less important here than the generic tendency to change one's behavior in response to changing circumstances. For example, items in this scale include: "Varies his/her approach with the situation" and "Makes adjustments in his/her behavior." The items were rated using a 3-point evaluation scale (1 = Development Needed, 2 = Neither, and 3 = Strength). This type of flexibility measure is most common in practice.

> Versatility as measured by the LVI is related to other measures of managerial flexibility, suggesting that these alternative measures of this aspect of performance are indeed assessing a similar thing. However, of three distinct measures of flexibility that we studied, the LVI was the best predictor of overall effectiveness.

The second measure of flexibility was similar to the LVI model in that both look upon the concept as a higher-order skill reflecting the mastery of specific and opposing behaviors. Based on the work of Quinn, Spreitzer, and Hart (1992), these flexibility measures included "Tough Love," made up of the opposites of Task Accomplishment and Group Cohesion, and "Practical Vision," comprised of the opposites of Innovation and Stability. Also like the LVI model, the items on the component scales (Accomplishment and Cohesion or Innovation and Stability) are rated separately and then a statistical formula is used to combine the two scale scores into a single variable where high values indicate flexibility conceived as "integrative balance" between the opposites.[5] But unlike the LVI, the behaviors are rated on a typical Likert-type response scale (a 3-point evaluation scale where 1 = Development Needed, 2 = Neither, and 3 = Strength).

Lindberg and Kaiser (2004) noted another similarity between the LVI versatility measures and the two measures based on Quinn, Spreitzer, and Hart (1992): the two dualities in each model represent the *how* versus *what* distinction. The social/interpersonal *how* is represented by forceful-enabling versatility and "tough love," while the functional/business *what* of leadership is represented by strategic-operational versatility and "practical vision."

Thus, there were three distinct methods and five different measures of flexibility: the trait-based flexibility scale was one method, forceful-enabling versatility and strategic-operational versatility from the LVI represented one mastery-of-opposites method, and tough love and practical vision based on Quinn, Spreitzer, and Hart (1992) represented a second mastery-of-opposites method. The correlations among these variables and the rating of overall effectiveness are presented in Table A.13.

Concerning convergent validity, some support is provided by the fact that all five measures of flexibility were significantly and positively related. This suggests that they may be measuring a common underlying construct. However, most of the correlations are only of moderate magnitude. Closer inspection reveals that the most convergent validity is apparent for the two mastery-of-opposites methods, the LVI versatility measures and the tough love and practical vision measures. In fact, both convergent and discriminant validity is evident in that tough love is most related to forceful-enabling versatility ($r = .43$) and practical vision is most related to strategic-operational versatility ($r = .50$). This provides construct validity evidence for both the *how* versus *what* distinction and the mastery-of-opposites approach to flexibility more broadly.

Table A.13. Correlations Among Flexibility Measures and Overall Effectiveness Ratings

Measure	1.	2.	3.	4.	5.
1. Trait-Based Flexibility	(.74)				
2. Tough Love	.39	(.78)			
3. Practical Vision	.32	.33	(.72)		
4. Forceful-Enabling Versatility	.30	.43	.35	(.73)	
5. Strategic-Operational Versatility	.26	.29	.50	.51	(.79)
6. Overall Effectiveness	.28	.37	.49	.52	.61

Notes: $N = 264$. All correlations are significant ($p < .001$). Reliability estimates appear along the diagonal.

Based on J.T. Lindberg and R.B. Kaiser (2004). *Assessing the behavioral flexibility of managers: A comparison of methods.* Presented at the 19th Annual Conference of the Society for Industrial and Organizational Psychology, Chicago, Illinois.

The next consideration was the validity of each method in predicting ratings of overall effectiveness. As shown in the bottom row of correlations in Table A.13, the trait-based measure was least correlated with effectiveness ($r = .28$). Next were tough love ($r = .37$) and practical vision ($r = .49$). The strongest correlations were for the two LVI versatility measures, forceful-enabling ($r = .52$) and strategic-operational ($r = .61$). Thus, the LVI appears to be the most valid of the three methods for measuring managerial flexibility.

A final consideration was *incremental* validity: How much above and beyond the other two methods does each method add to the prediction of overall effectiveness? Since all three methods are correlated, Lindberg and Kaiser (2004) wanted to determine the unique contribution each could make in predicting effectiveness. To test this, they examined three hierarchical regression models, first entering the terms for the first two methods, then testing the additional variance accounted for by the focal method. Their results indicated that the trait-based flexibility measure added no incremental validity over the two mastery-of-opposites approaches. In other words, the LVI and Quinn, Spreitzer, and Hart measures contained all of the criterion-related variance of the trait measure. The Quinn method represented by tough love and practical vision enhanced the prediction of overall effectiveness by a significant 4.2 percent beyond the 42.5 percent accounted for by the trait-based and versatility methods. Finally, the versatility method accounted for an additional 17.4 percent of the variance in effectiveness beyond the 29.4 percent attributable to the combination of the trait-based and Quinn methods. Thus, although the two mastery-of-opposites methods demonstrated appreciable convergence, the duality-based method contains about four times more unique variance related to overall effectiveness (that is, $17.4/4.2 = 4.14$).

Lindberg and Kaiser (2004) drew three conclusions from this study. First, the way flexibility is typically assessed in organizations—as a trait-like characteristic using a traditional rating scale with items describing general tendencies—is severely deficient. It was the least valid method. Second, the mastery-of-opposites approach showed promise as a higher-order conceptualization: the LVI measures of versatility and the Quinn measures of tough love and practical vision showed construct validity evidence in the pattern of convergent and divergent correlations. Furthermore, they were substantially more related to overall effectiveness than the trait-based measure. Finally, the LVI measures of versatility were the most valid at predicting overall effectiveness. They showed higher validity coefficients and contained about four times as much unique variance related to overall effectiveness than did the Quinn measures. The authors concluded by speculating that this difference may be due to the unique rating scale on the LVI that separates overkill from deficiency as two distinct types of performance problems.

Versatility, Job Satisfaction, and Commitment

The final study of the LVI concerns predicting additional organizational outcomes other than perceived effectiveness. In a doctoral dissertation, Coberly (2004) studied the relationship between leadership and organizational commitment in collaborative Industry-University Research Centers. These institutions are funded by federal programs such as the National Science Foundation and fees paid by private companies to sponsor university faculty to conduct applied research on topics of interest. The research centers are housed in various universities but are supervised by managers from industry. They are responsible for research and development of new products and processes for use in industry. Faculty participation is voluntary, and the success of these research centers is thought to hinge on the recruitment and retention of top-notch faculty. Thus, Coberly (2004) examined the factors that contribute to a faculty member's satisfaction with and commitment to a research center.

Coberly (2004) developed a theoretical model including funding, reward factors (that is, intrinsic rewards like feelings of accomplishment and extrinsic rewards such as recognition and prestige), and leadership (a shortened version of the forceful-enabling versatility scale) as predictors of faculty members' levels of job satisfaction. In turn, job satisfaction was expected to predict commitment to the research center and retention cognitions (thoughts about staying or leaving). Data were collected via an Internet survey from 198 faculty members from thirty-six different Industry-University Research Centers around the United States.

> Forceful-enabling versatility is related to employee job satisfaction, commitment, and turnover. Versatile managers have subordinates who are more satisfied and committed. Subordinates of lopsided leaders, however, are less satisfied with their jobs, feel less committed to the organization, and are more distracted by thoughts about seeking a new employer.

The results from Coberly's (2004) Path Analysis (a statistical test of structural relationships) supported the theoretical model. Specifically, she found that forceful-enabling versatility predicted job satisfaction, which in turn was a strong predictor of commitment to the research center and a moderate predictor of retention cognition (thoughts about staying versus leaving the research center). These results are presented in Figure A.5.

Figure A.5. How Leadership Versatility Affects Subordinate Commitment and Retention

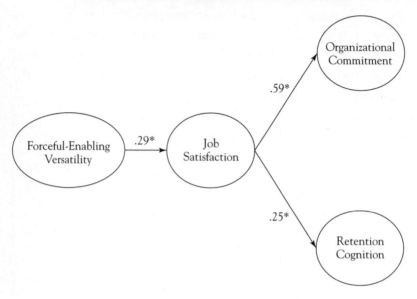

Note: Coefficients are standardized path loadings. * = $p < .05$

From B.M. Coberly (2004). *Faculty Satisfaction and Organizational Commitment with Industry-University Research Centers.* Ann Arbor, MI: Dissertation Information Service, University Microfilms International.

Coberly (2004) also found that the reward and funding variables also predicted job satisfaction, allowing for a relative comparison to the magnitude of the relationship for forceful-enabling versatility. Specifically, intrinsic rewards was the strongest predictor of job satisfaction (path coefficient = .38), followed by extrinsic rewards (.29) and the supervisor's leadership versatility (.29), and, finally, level of funding (.15). Thus, when it comes to predicting faculty commitment and desire to remain affiliated with a research center, the central variable is job satisfaction. And job satisfaction is largely a function of intrinsic rewards (challenging work, accomplishing personally meaningful goals), extrinsic rewards (recognition), and the versatility of one's manager in terms of forceful and enabling leadership. This indicates that the LVI provides data linking leaders to how satisfied employees feel and, in turn, how likely they are to voluntarily leave the organization versus remain fully committed to it.

Summary

The conceptual foundation of the Leadership Versatility Index is grounded in our firm's leadership-consulting practice and in the research literature on leadership. And the instrument itself is an innovation in performance assessment with a new type of rating scale that separates overkill and deficiency as two distinct types of performance problems.

Concerning the LVI's internal properties, the statistical analyses are generally supportive. First, the scales have adequate internal consistency (except for operational leadership), and inter-rater reliability and inter-rater agreement is acceptable. Second, the strong negative correlation between forceful and enabling leadership and the negative correlation between certain aspects of strategic and operational leadership are consistent with the underlying theory of versatility. Third, data collected for middle managers and executives fit the complex conceptual structure of the forceful and enabling scales—that is, the three pairs of subdimensions, Takes Charge and Empowers, Declares and Listens, Pushes and Supports. The LVI's primary limitations at this stage of its evolution are the low internal consistency for the operational scale, the lack of a negative correlation between the overall strategic and operational dimensions, and a lack of empirical support for the conceptual structure of the strategic-operational duality. We take some comfort in knowing that the LVI's empirical limitations reside in the scales we began developing later and concern aspects of leadership that have received less scholarly attention.

Concerning the LVI's external validity, its ability to predict other important variables, the statistical results are again supportive. Both forceful-enabling versatility and strategic-operational versatility are good predictors of perceptions of overall effectiveness. Further, about half of the variance in overall effectiveness can be accounted for by versatility on both dualities. Clearly, the LVI taps a great deal of what it means to be considered an effective leader. It is worth noting that despite the weaker support for its internal structure, the strategic-operational duality was nonetheless a solid predictor of overall effectiveness.

There is also evidence for the LVI's convergent and discriminant validity. The LVI correlates with other, independent measures of managerial flexibility. Furthermore, the LVI's distinction between forceful-enabling versatility and strategic-operational versatility, representing the *how* and *what* of leadership, holds up empirically. And according to one study of alternative measures of managerial flexibility, the LVI appears to be one of the more robust measures of this characteristic in terms of predicting effectiveness. Of course, further research is needed to replicate these findings.

The LVI has also been linked to more specific processes having to do with leader effectiveness. One study showed how a manager's degree of forceful-enabling versatility is linked to employee job satisfaction, which then predicts organizational commitment and thoughts about staying or leaving the organization. Versatile leaders had more satisfied subordinates, who were more committed to the organization. Lopsided leaders, on the other hand, had less satisfied subordinates, who identified less with the organization and were more concerned with finding a new employer.

Taken together, the data indicate that the LVI is a reliable and valid measure of aspects of leadership that are of central importance to how well leaders are regarded overall and to the engagement and commitment of their teams. Thus, it is fair to say that feedback on the LVI has the potential to boost individual and organizational performance.

Notes

1. We are grateful for the skillful assistance of the following researchers, our colleagues at North Carolina State University, who have helped with various analyses summarized and referenced in this appendix: S. Bart Craig, Jennifer T. Lindberg,

Phillip Braddy, Eric G. Kail, Jacqui McLaughlin, and Beth Coberly.

2. We have provided a full description of our research and development efforts to validate this new response scale in two sources. One is a brief article for human resources and training professionals (Kaiser & Kaplan, 2005a) and the other is a book chapter focused on a comparison between alternative rating scales and a lengthy discussion of the new one (Kaiser & Kaplan, 2005b).

3. It is worth noting that measures of similar leadership dimensions based on traditional 1-to-5 Likert-type scales do not show such a negative correlation. Rather, supposedly opposing dimensions routinely correlate in the neighborhood of $r = +.50$ (see Kaiser & Kaplan, 2005b; Lindberg & Kaiser, 2004).

4. The higher-order factor model was evaluated with confirmatory factor analysis (CFA) using the CALIS procedure of the SAS System 9.1 (SAS Institute, 2005). This model specified that each of the seventeen items loaded only on its own subdimension, that the three forceful subdimensions in turn loaded on a second-order forceful factor, and the three enabling subdimensions loaded on a second-order enabling factor. The two second-order factors (forceful and enabling) were specified to correlate. All item and subdimension cross-loadings were constrained to be 0. Covariances among residual (error) terms were also initially constrained to be 0. Although several model fit indices indicated an adequate fit to the data for this initial model, some indices fell outside the generally accepted ranges for adequate fit. Inspection of the Lagrange modification indices suggested that fit could be improved by allowing certain error terms to covary. This was somewhat anticipated in that correlated error terms between opposing subdimensions could arise if raters tend to think naturally of forceful and enabling pairs as truly bi-polar—a single continuum ranging from forceful to enabling. This was the case empirically, with the largest correlated error terms resulting for the forceful (*Takes Charge*) and enabling (*Empowers*) subdimensions. The model was revised

slightly to include the covariance between these two error terms. This revised model resulted in a model of acceptable fit (see Table A.7 for fit indices).

Modification of a factor model on the basis of CFA and subsequent retesting of the model with the same data risks over-optimizing the model for a specific sample and can result in a model that does not generalize (Hatcher, 1994). However, we believe this risk is minimal in this case for several reasons. First, simulation studies have found that the risk of creating a non-generalizable model decreases as sample size increases (MacCallum, Roznowski, & Necowitz, 1992). Our sample size (N = 2,839) would be considered quite large in the context of CFA, suggesting that it is unlikely that these data would be unrepresentative of the population. Second, only a single modification was made to our original model. MacCallum, Roznowski, and Necowitz showed that the risk of over-optimizing for the sample increases as the number of modifications increases. Third, and most important, our modification was not without theoretical rationale. Specifically, if most raters think of forceful and enabling leadership as opposing ends of a single continuum, then it would make sense that errors in rating forceful behaviors would be related to errors in ratings of opposing enabling behaviors. Therefore we expect that the factor model proposed for the LVI will indeed provide an acceptable fit to data collected in the future.

5. Quinn, Spreitzer, and Hart (1992) described how to derive an overall measure of flexibility from scores on two distinct but oppositional rating scales. Specifically, they recommended a formula developed by psychometricians for integrating bi-polar constructs. The formula was provided as a way to construct a single continuous variable to represent the integrative balance of conceptually opposing constructs (for example, androgyny as balance on the two separate dimensions of masculinity and femininity). In the present application, high scores indicate managers who are rated high but relatively equal on contrasting concepts. Lower

scores reflect high on one, low on the other. Thus, this procedure reflects what Quinn, Spreitzer, and Hart (1992) call "interpenetration," an integrative balance representing relatively equal standing on both sides in a given pair of opposites.

References

Antonakis, J., & House, R.J. (2002). An analysis of the full-range leadership theory: The way forward. In B.J. Avolio & F.J. Yammarino (Eds.), *Transformational and charismatic leadership: The road ahead* (pp. 3–33). Greenwich, CT: Elsevier Science/JAI Press.

Barnard, C.I. (1938). *The functions of the executive*. Cambridge, MA: Harvard University Press.

Bass, B.M. (1990). *Bass and Stogdill's handbook of leadership: Theory, research, and managerial applications* (3rd ed.). New York: The Free Press.

Bass. B.M., & Valenzi, E.R. (1974). Contingent aspects of effective management styles. In J.G. Hunt & L.L. Larson (Eds.), *Contingency approaches to leadership*. Carbondale, IL: Southern Illinois University Press.

Bales, R.F. (1950). *Interaction process analysis*. Reading, MA: Addison-Wesley.

Bennis, W.G., & Nanus, B. (1985). *Leaders: The strategies for taking charge*. New York: Harper & Row.

Blake, R.R., & Mouton, J.S. (1964). *The managerial grid*. Houston, TX: Gulf.

Bliese, P.D. (2000). Within-group agreement, non-independence, and reliability: Implications for aggregation and analysis. In S.W.J. Kozlowski & K.J. Klein (Eds.), *Multilevel theory, research, and methods in organizations*: 349–381. San Francisco: Jossey-Bass.

Bossidy, L., & Charan, R. (2002). *Execution: The discipline of getting things done*. New York: Crown Business.

Coberly, B.M. (2004). *Faculty satisfaction and organizational commitment with industry-university research centers*. Ann Arbor, MI: Dissertation Information Service, University Microfilms International.

Conger, J.A., & Kanungo, R.N. (1994). Charismatic leadership in organizations: Perceived behavioral attributes and their measurement. *Journal of Organizational Behavior, 15*, 439–452.

Conway, J.M., & Huffcut, A.I. (1997). Psychometric properties of multisource performance ratings: A meta-analysis of supervisor, peer, subordinate, and self-ratings. *Human Performance, 19*, 331–360.

Cronbach, L.S., & Meehl, P. (1955). Construct validity in psychological tests. *Psychological Bulletin, 52*, 281–302.

Fayol, H. (1949). *General and industrial management* (C. Storrs, Trans.). London: Sir Isaac Pitman & Sons Ltd. (Original work published in 1916).

Fiedler, F.E. (1967). *A theory of leadership effectiveness*. New York: McGraw-Hill.

Flanagan, J.C. (1954). The critical incident technique. *Psychological Bulletin, 51*, 327–358.

Fleishman, E.A. (1953). The description of supervisory behavior. *Journal of Applied Psychology, 37*, 1–6.

Greguras, G.J., & Robie, C. (1998). A new look at within-source interrater reliability of 360-degree feedback ratings. *Journal of Applied Psychology, 83*, 960–968.

Hatcher, L. (1994). *A step-by-step guide to using the SAS system for factor analysis and structural equation modeling*. Cary, NC: SAS Institute.

Hersey, P., & Blanchard, K.H. (1969). Life cycle theory of leadership. *Training & Development Journal, 23*, 26–34.

House, R.J. (1971). A path-goal theory of leader effectiveness. *Administrative Science Quarterly, 16*, 321–338.

Hu, L., & Bentler, P.M. (1995). Evaluating model fit. In R.H. Hoyle (Ed.), *Structural equation modeling: Concepts, issues, and applications* (pp. 76–99). Thousand Oaks, CA: Sage.

Huy, Q.N. (2002). Emotional balancing of organizational continuity and radical change: The contribution of middle managers. *Administrative Science Quarterly, 47*, 31–69.

James, L.R. (1982). Aggregation bias in estimates of perceptual agreement. *Journal of Applied Psychology, 67*, 219–229.

James, L.R., Demaree, R.G., & Wolf, G. (1984). Estimating within-group interrater reliability with and without response bias. *Journal of Applied Psychology, 69*, 85–98.

Kaiser, R.B., & Craig, S.B. (2001). *Leadership Versatility Index technical report: Item selection and validation*. Greensboro, NC: Kaplan DeVries Inc.

Kaiser, R.B., & Kaplan, R.E. (2005a). Overlooking overkill? Beyond the 1-to-5 rating scale. *Human Resources Planning, 28(3)*, 7-11.

Kaiser, R.B., & Kaplan, R.E. (2005b). On the folly of linear rating scales for a non-linear world. In S. Reddy (Ed.), *Performance appraisals: A critical view* (Ch. 12, pp. 170-197). Nagarjuna Hills, Hyderabad, India: ICFAI University Press.

Kotter, J.P. (1990). *A force for change: How leadership differs from management*. New York: The Free Press.

Kouzes, J.M., & Posner, B.Z (1987). *The leadership challenge: How to get extraordinary things done in organizations*. San Francisco: Jossey-Bass.

LeBreton, J.M., Burgess, J.R.D., Kaiser, R.B., Atchley, E.K., & James, L.R. (2003). The restriction of variance hypothesis and inter-rater reliability and agreement: Are ratings from multiple sources really dissimilar? *Organizational Research Methods, 6*, 78–126.

Lewin, K., & Lippitt, R. (1938). An experimental approach to the study of autocracy and democracy: A preliminary note. *Sociometry, 1*, 292–300.

Likert, R. (1967). *The human organization.* New York: McGraw-Hill.

Lindberg, J.T., & Kaiser, R.B. (2004, April). *Assessing the behavioral flexibility of managers: A comparison of methods.* Presented at the 19th Annual Conference of the Society for Industrial and Organizational Psychology, Chicago, Illinois.

Lombardo, M.M., & Eichinger, R.W. (2000). *The leadership machine.* Minneapolis, MN: Lominger Limited, Inc.

MacCallum, R.C., Roznowski, M., & Necowitz, L.B. (1992). Model modifications in covariance structure analysis: The problem of capitalization on chance. *Psychological Bulletin, 111*, 490–504.

Miles, R.E., & Snow, C.C. (1978). *Organizational strategy, structure, and process.* New York: McGraw-Hill.

Mintzberg, H. (1975). The manager's job: Folklore and fact. *Harvard Business Review, 53*(4), 100–110.

Neiman, R.A. (2004). *Execution plain and simple.* New York: McGraw-Hill.

Nunnally, J.C. (1978). *Psychometric theory.* New York: McGraw-Hill.

Porter, M.E. (1996). What is strategy? *Harvard Business Review, 74*(6), 61–78.

Prince, E.T. (2005). *The three financial styles of very successful leaders.* New York: McGraw-Hill.

Quinn, R.E. (1988). *Beyond rational management.* San Francisco: Jossey-Bass.

Quinn, R.E., Spreitzer, G.M., & Hart, S.L. (1992). Integrating the extremes: Crucial skills for managerial effectiveness. In S. Srivastva and R.E. Fry (Eds.), *Executive and organizational continuity* (pp. 222–252). San Francisco: Jossey-Bass.

SAS (2005). *SAS/STAT user's guide* (Vol. 4). Carey, NC: SAS Institute.

Schwartz, N. (1999). Self-reports: How the questions shape the answers. *American Psychologist, 54*, 93–105.

Shrout, P., & Fleiss, J. (1979). Intraclass correlations: Uses in assessing rater reliability. *Psychological Bulletin, 86*, 420–428.

Stogdill, R.M., & Coons, A.E. (1957). *Leader behavior: Its description and measurement.* Columbus, OH: Bureau of Business Research, Ohio State University.

Vroom, V.H., & Yetton, P.W. (1973). *Leadership and decision making.* New York: John Wiley & Sons.

Zaccaro, S.J. (2001). *The nature of executive leadership: A conceptual and empirical analysis of success.* Washington, DC: American Psychological Association.

Zaleznik, A. (1974). Charismatic and consensual leaders: A psychological comparison. *Bulletin of the Menninger Clinic, 38*, 222–238.

Notes

Preface

1. *New York Times*, May 3, 2004, B3 Metro, p.2.

Chapter 1

1. Even after Rob Kaiser and I had published an article pointing out this oversight, we continued to use the conventional headings "Strengths" and "Weaknesses/Limitations." Only recently have we have gone over to "Strengths" and "Weaknesses and Strengths Overused."
2. Kennedy, P. (1987). *The rise and fall of the great powers: Economic change and military conflict from 1500 to 2000.* New York: Random House.
3. Emerson, R.W. (1968). Napoleon: Man of the world. In *Selected writings of Ralph Waldo Emerson.* Atkinson, B. (Ed.). New York: Modern Library, 1968.
4. Aristotle (undated). *Nicomachean ethics.* Translated by H. Rackham (1982). Cambridge, MA: Harvard University Press.
5. Is it not remarkable that the leadership field has not made a place for overdoing it in its conception of performance problems or its apparatus for measuring leadership performance? Perhaps the oversight is due to a societal mind-set that takes liabilities to be gaps to be filled. Perhaps it reflects an unconscious collective assumption that more is better. And one can only wonder what effect this institutionalized bias has had over the several decades that assessment tools have been in use. Could it have fed into the already expansive tendencies of the managerial class in America? Hard to know. What we can say is that the absence of a measure of overkill has not acted as a governor on those tendencies. In any case, there's been a considerable collective blind spot.
6. Kaplan, R.E., & Kaiser, R.B. (2003). Developing versatile leadership. *MIT Sloan Management Review, 44*(4), 19–26.

7. The idea that excesses constitute just as important a class of performance issues as deficiencies is a staple of modern thought on leadership development (McCall & Lombardo, 1983; McCall, 1988). But it is rarely reflected in the design of standard assessment tools; even when the idea is taken into account, it tends to be treated as an afterthought or as a supplemental feature rather than integral to the design of the measure.

For instance, there are a few instruments that have respondents rate how often the manager engages in a number of specific behaviors and then, at the end, ask respondents to indicate whether the manager should do more, less, or the same amount of not each specific behavior, but of the handful of larger categories those several behaviors comprise. And there are instruments that render prescriptions for development by comparing ratings of, on the one hand, "how often" the manager does a particular thing to, on the other hand, an "ideal amount" that is estimated using a statistical formula. Even this, however, is rare—a recent review of prominent 360-degree tools found only three instruments that employ this retro-fitted statistical solution. (For specific examples of these methods, see the review of 360-degree instruments in the Center for Creative Leadership's book, *Feedback to Managers* [Leslie & Fleenor, 1998]).

Overdoing it can also be found implicit in an approach to assessment developed by our colleagues, Mike Lombardo and Bob Eichinger. In addition to measuring competencies, their instrument, *Voices*, also sizes up managers on another class of characteristics they call derailers, career stallers, and stoppers. These lists contain performance problems, some of which we would describe as overdoing it (e.g., "Overly Ambitious," "Overmanaging"; Lombardo & Eichinger, 2000). Lombardo and Eichinger have also recently added an innovation to the assessment of competencies that was inspired by our research and development. When a rater selects the highest two options on the typical Likert-type rating scale of their online survey, another screen appears and asks whether the person overuses the particular skill (M. Lombardo, personal communication to Rob Kaiser, December 2, 2004).

Although we acknowledge these few and notable exceptions, they indeed are exceptions to the rule that the feedback tools commonly used in organizations today overlook overkill.

Leslie, J.B., & Fleenor, J.W. (1998). *Feedback to managers: A review and comparison of multi-rater instruments for management development*. Greensboro, NC: Center for Creative Leadership.
Lombardo, M.M., & Eichinger, R.W. (2000). *The leadership machine*. Minneapolis, MN: Lominger Limited, Inc.
McCall, M.W. (1998). *High flyers: Developing the next generation of leaders*. Boston, MA: Harvard Business School Press.
McCall, M.W., & Lombardo, M.M. (1983). *Off the track: Why and how successful executives get derailed*. Greensboro, NC: Center for Creative Leadership.

8. It is hard to say why modern assessment tools have not been equipped to detect excess. The answer may lie in the historical development of rating scales. The basic format in use today was originally developed by Rensis Likert (1932) as a solution to the problem of measuring attitudes. Likert presented respondents with a series of statements and asked them to indicate how much they agreed with each on a 5-point, disagree/agree response scale. In applying this method to performance measurement, it appears that it was assumed to be equally appropriate to evaluating the behavior of others as to describing one's own attitudes. Whether or not this assumption is tenable is debatable (Kaiser & Kaplan, 2005a; 2005b). One thing is certain: providing a way for raters to indicate "too much" was clearly neglected in adapting Likert's method for performance appraisal.

Kaiser, R.B., & Kaplan, R.E. (2005a). Overlooking overkill? Beyond the 1-to-5 rating scale. *Human Resources Planning*, 28(3), 7-11.
Kaiser, R.B., & Kaplan, R.E. (2005b). On the folly of linear rating scales for a non-linear world. In S. Reddy (Ed.), *Performance*

appraisals: A critical view (Ch. 12, pp. 170-197). Nagarjuna Hills, Hyderabad, India: ICFAI University Press.

Likert, R. (1932). A technique for the measurement of attitudes. *Archives of Psychology, 140,* 5–53.

9. I too fell prey to this oversight. The first leadership questionnaire I designed, SKILLscope for Managers®, employed a conventional scale that suffered from the same limitation. It didn't capture excess. Like the rest of the leadership questionnaires, it didn't catch that fish because it wasn't designed to catch it.

10. McLean, B., & Elkind, P. (2005). *The smartest guys in the room.* New York: Penguin.

11. Ibid, pp. 27, 39, 71–76, 78, 84–90.

Chapter 2

1. This was one of the key findings from my original research on what makes executive development unique (Kaplan, 1984): senior leaders were the least informed about how others saw their performance. Upward feedback was quite rare, especially at the top of organizations.

   Kaplan, R.E., Drath, W.H., & Kofodimos, J. (1984). High hurdles: The challenges of executive self-development. *Academy of Management Executive, 1,* 195–205.

2. We have determined, through analyses of large databases for several commercial and proprietary 360-degree instruments that employ both traditional frequency and effectiveness rating scales, that about 70 to 75 percent of ratings are either a 3 or 4 on a 5-point scale. When you compute scale scores by taking the average item ratings across multiple raters, about 85 percent of scale scores fall between 3.25 and 4.25 (Kaiser & Kaplan, 2005; see also LeBreton, Burgess, Kaiser, Atchley, & James, 2003). With the scores clumped together at the high end of the scale, it is no mean feat for the naked eye to detect peaks and valleys worthy of note. In other words, relative strengths and developmental needs are hard to discern.

Kaiser, R.B., & Kaplan, R.E. (2005). On the folly of linear rating scales for a non-linear world. In S. Reddy (Ed.), *Performance appraisals: A critical view* (Ch. 12, pp. 170-197). Nagarjuna Hills, Hyderabad, India: ICFAI University Press.

LeBreton, J.M., Burgess, J.R.D., Kaiser, R.B., Atchley, E.K., & James, L.R. (2003). The restriction of variance hypothesis and interrater reliability and agreement: Are ratings from multiple sources really dissimilar? *Organizational Research Methods, 6,* 78–126.

3. For example, with our involvement, Motorola adopted a response scale that gave raters the option of indicating "do more" or "do less." This scale was used in conjunction with an effectiveness scale (Kaiser, Craig, Kaplan, & McArthur, 2002). Incidentally, the do-more/do-less scale added significantly to the survey's predictive validity (Kaiser & Kaplan, 2005).

Kaiser, R.B., Craig, S.B., Kaplan, R.E., & McArthur (2002, April). Practical science and the development of Motorola's leadership standards. In K.B. Brookhouse (Chair), *Transforming leadership at Motorola.* Practitioner Forum presented at the 17th annual Conference of the Society for Industrial and Organizational Psychology, Toronto, Ontario.

Kaiser, R.B., & Kaplan, R.E. (2005). Overlooking overkill? Beyond the 1-to-5 rating scale. *Human Resources Planning, 28*(3), 7-11.

4. These are the average ratings for 107 senior managers from a total of 507 subordinates.

5. Of course, this may not be the only way to pick up strengths overused in an assessment. For instance, interviewing coworkers or providing them a way to write in comments will often bring out instances where a manager does something too often or too intensely (Kaplan & Palus, 1994). But ratings from coworkers are so commonplace it seems that the paradigm needs to be modified to make room for detecting excesses too.

Kaplan, R.E., & Palus, C.J. (1994). *Enhancing 360-degree feedback for senior executives: How to maximize the benefits and minimize the risks*. Greensboro, NC: Center for Creative Leadership.

6. Although I came up with the idea of measuring overkill and assessing for lopsidedness with an instrument called the Inventory of Executive Roles™ in the early 1990s, I have worked closely with Rob Kaiser since 1997 to refine the tool into its present form as the Leadership Versatility Index©.

7. To simplify this case example, I have cherry-picked a subset of Ella's results that capture the essence of her leadership. The full assessment included a total of sixty-four rating items from the Leadership Versatility Index© and several pages of open-ended comments provided by her coworkers in their own words.

8. Arthur Freedman (1998; 2005) has described the psychology behind the difficulty many managers have making upward transitions. In his pathways-and-crossroads model, a promotion to a bigger job requires that managers add on skills and perspectives that were previously irrelevant, let go of what worked before but is now anachronistic, and preserve those things that continue to be useful. But the tendency to fall back on what made you effective in the previous job is powerful, in part because the success it brought can create a "behavioral addiction" that is hard to kick. A similar phenomenon is described in *The Leadership Pipeline* (Charan, Drotter, & Noel, 2001), the recent best-seller describing how the role of management changes with each big step up the hierarchy.

Our own research found that the success formula is different at middle levels from upper levels (Kaiser & Craig, 2004, 2005). For middle managers, effectiveness depended on a decisive, action orientation and very little of an empowering, participative style. But the reverse was true for executives: effectiveness at the top depended on a participative approach, whereas an action orientation diminished effectiveness. This crossover in what makes a manager effective poses a challenge for freshly minted executives.

Charan, R., Drotter, S., & Noel, J. (2001). *The leadership pipeline*. San Francisco: Jossey-Bass.

Freedman, A. (1998). Pathways and crossroads to institutional leadership. *Consulting Psychology Journal: Practice and Research*, 50, 131–151.

Freedman, A. (2005). Swimming upstream: The challenge of managerial promotions. In R.B. Kaiser (Ed.), *Filling the leadership pipeline* (Ch. 2, pp. 25-44). Greensboro, NC: Center for Creative Leadership.

Kaiser, R.B., & Craig, S.B. (2004, April). What gets you there won't keep you there: Managerial behaviors related to effectiveness at the bottom, middle, and top. In R.B. Kaiser and S.B. Craig (Co-chairs) *Filling the pipe I: Studying management development across the hierarchy*. Symposium presented at the 18th Annual Conference of the Society for Industrial and Organizational Psychology, Chicago, Illinois.

Kaiser, R.B., & Craig, S.B. (2005, October). How is executive success different? Presented at *Leadership at the Top*, Fall Consortium sponsored by the Society for Industrial and Organizational Psychology, St. Louis, Missouri.

9. For more on how to distill the essence of feedback data by creating hub-and-spoke maps that lead naturally to results-oriented action planning, see my chapter in the book *Individual Assessment* (Kaplan, 1998).

Kaplan, R.E. (1998). Getting at character: The simplicity on the other side of complexity. In R. Jeanneret & R. Silzer (Eds.), *Individual assessment: The art and science of personal psychological evaluation in an organizational setting*. San Francisco, CA: Jossey-Bass.

10. Diane Ducat, personal communication, July 12, 2005.

Chapter 3

1. The larger movement here has been dubbed "Positive Psychology" by former American Psychological Association president Martin Seligman. He and his colleagues have inspired a growing cadre of psychologists who are intent on moving

beyond remedies for pathology to focus on promoting lives of fulfillment—helping individuals experience deep satisfaction and
well-being, identify and engage their talent, and establish a sense
of meaning and purpose in their lives (Seligman & Csikszentmihalyi, 2000; Seligman, 2002). In the field of organizational
development, David Cooperrider of Case Western Reserve University has originated a similar theory and methodology called
appreciative inquiry. According to Cooperrider (1995), appreciative inquiry is about focusing on the value, strength, and
potential of individuals to overcome the limits that people
impose, often unconsciously, upon themselves.

Cooperrider, D.L. (1995). Introduction to appreciative inquiry.
In W. French & C. Bell (Eds.), *Organization development* (5th
ed.). Englewood Cliffs, NJ: Prentice Hall.
Seligman, M.E.P. (2002). *Authentic happiness: Using the new pos-
itive psychology to realize your potential for lasting fulfillment*. New
York: Free Press/Simon & Schuster.
Seligman, M.E.P., & Csikszentmihalyi, M. (2000). Positive psy-
chology: An introduction. *American Psychologist, 55*, 5–14.

2. I am referring to the StrengthsFinder instrument, promoted by
The Gallup Organization and made available through the book
Now, Discover Your Strengths (Buckingham & Clifton, 2001).
Designed much like a personality test, respondents indicate
their agreement with a series of statements, each of which refers
to one of thirty-four areas in which one might excel (such as
Achiever, Relator, Analytical, and Self-Assured). For those
who take the test through the book, the feedback consists of a
list of their top five strength themes, along with a description of
that strength and how it can be applied. The rationale is that
most people don't know their strengths and that, if only they
knew them, they could use them more. It overlooks the important points that (1) many people overuse their strengths and (2)
they can have considerable difficulty being objective about
their strengths and truly internalizing them.

Buckingham, M., & Clifton, D.O. (2001). *Now, discover your strengths*. New York: Simon & Schuster.

3. Although from the verbal input managers can sense how pleased or frustrated their coworkers are with their performance, and although from quantitative 360-degree ratings managers can infer what shape they are in, they can't tell what overall grade all that nets out to. So if you can, include in the assessment an overall measure of effectiveness, another way to know where you stand.

4. At first, it may seem odd that underestimating oneself could lead to either of such opposite reactions, underdoing or overdoing. But which road it goes down depends on your strategy for coping with the threat that comes from feeling inadequate. For instance, the social psychologist Carol Dweck (1986) has described two different types of motivation involved in learning: those who are oriented toward mastering the subject and those who are worried about how their performance will be judged. The worried group can be further divided into those who go all out to prove their ability and those who try to avoid looking foolish. Interestingly, these two opposing motivations both link to a low opinion of one's own competence and to fear of failure (Eliot & Church, 1997). Further, E. Tory Higgins (1997) has described two very different ways that people cope with strong emotions like those activated by a fear of failure. Individuals who take a "promotion orientation" focus on what they can do to advance their interests and prevail, whereas those taking a "prevention orientation" focus on minimizing risk and staying out of trouble. These opposing reactions appear to be fundamental and rooted in the innate fight-or-flight reflex (Kaiser & Kaplan, in press).

Dweck, C. (1986). Motivational processes affecting learning. *American Psychologist, 41*, 1040–1048.

Elliot, A., & Church, M. (1997). A hierarchical model of approach and avoidance achievement motivation. *Journal of Personality and Social Psychology, 72*, 218–232.

Higgins, E.T. (1997). Beyond pleasure and pain. *American Psychologist, 52*, 1280–1300.

Kaiser, R.B., & Kaplan, R.E. (in press). Outgrowing sensitivities: The deeper work of executive development. *Academy of Management Learning and Education*.

5. Recent research by Bob Eichinger and Mike Lombardo (2003) has underscored the problems that come with an inflated view of oneself. Looking at patterns of self-ratings compared to ratings from coworkers across thousands of managers receiving 360-degree feedback, they found that managers who rated themselves higher than their coworkers rated them tended to be the weakest performers. More interestingly, the over-raters were over 50 percent more likely to be terminated within the following two years. Another study of derailment found that a group of middle managers who were showing early signs of slipping off-track had inflated self-views and were more likely to actually derail. Those who managed to turn it around and get back on track, however, had self-ratings that were much more similar to the ratings they received from their coworkers (Shipper & Dillard, 2000).

Eichinger, R.W., & Lombardo, M.M. (2003). 360-degree assessment. *Human Resource Planning, 26*(4), 34–44.

Shipper, F., & Dillard, J. F. (2000). A study of impending derailment and recovery of middle managers across career stages. *Human Resource Management Journal, 39*, 331–345.

6. This appears to be a fairly common phenomenon. For instance, two psychologists recently published a widely read study entitled, "Unskilled and Unaware." The finding that grabbed attention was that those individuals who were least skilled in a given social or intellectual area, for instance, humor, grammar, or logic, were the ones most likely to overestimate their competence. Like the children of Garrison Keilor's Lake Wobegone, they all saw themselves as "above average." But what we find even more compelling is that those individuals who were the funniest, the best writers, or the most logical, as reflected in

their actual performance, described themselves as just "average." In a series of four studies, the researchers demonstrated that these highly competent individuals assumed that everyone else was just as skilled as they were and didn't see the extent of their unique strengths (Kruger & Dunning, 1999).

Kruger, J., & Dunning, D. (1999). Unskilled and unaware of it: How difficulties in recognizing one's own incompetence lead to inflated self-assessments. *Journal of Personality and Social Psychology, 77,* 1121–1134.

7. Ella may in part have been contending with "the modesty effect," which Morrison, White, and Van Velsor (1987) found in women executives.

Morrison, A.M., White, R.P., & Van Velsor, E. (1987). *Breaking the glass ceiling.* Reading, MA: Addison-Wesley.

8. For more on how to bombard an individual with compelling feedback on his or her strengths, see my report published by the Center for Creative Leadership (Kaplan, 1999).

Kaplan, R.E. (1999). *Internalizing strengths: An overlooked way of overcoming weaknesses in managers.* Greensboro, NC: Center for Creative Leadership.

9. The social psychologist Bill Swann conducted research for twenty years that helps to explain why people don't so readily accept praise. At least since Freud, psychologists and lay people alike have assumed that a primary motive is the pleasure principle: to seek out opportunities for positive, reinforcing, and self-enhancing experiences and avoid negative, painful experiences. Evidently, as Swann's research has illustrated (Swann, 1997; Swann, Griffin, Predmore, & Gaines, 1987; Swann, Pelham, & Krull, 1989), our need to maintain a consistent view of ourselves is at least as strong as our need to feel good about ourselves. This helps to explain why it takes a powerful intervention—in this case, a heavy dose of positive feedback—to influence upward a manager's depressed view of his or her strengths.

Swann, W.B. (1997). The trouble with change: Self-verification and allegiance to the self. *Psychological Science, 8,* 177–180.

Swann, W.B., Griffin, J.J., Predmore, S., & Gaines, B. (1987). The cognitive-affective crossfire: When self-consistency confronts self-enhancement. *Journal of Personality and Social Psychology, 52,* 881–889.

Swann, W.B., Pelham, B.W., & Krull, D.S. (1989). Agreeable fancy or disagreeable truth? Reconciling self-enhancement and self-verification. *Journal of Personality and Social Psychology, 57,* 782–791.

10. See Chapter 5 in *Beyond Ambition* (Kaplan, 1991).

Kaplan, R.E. (with W.H. Drath & J.R. Kofodimos). (1991). *Beyond ambition: How driven managers can lead better and live better.* San Francisco, CA: Jossey-Bass.

Chapter 4

1. Dorfman, H., & Kuehl, K. (1995). *The mental game of baseball: A guide to peak performance.* South Bend, IN: Diamond Communications.

2. It is curious how the field of management development has kept a safe distance from the idea that developing as a leader can usefully include growing personally (Kaplan, 1991). For instance, the most common forms of management training are based on behavior modeling (Burke & Day, 1986; Wexley & Latham, 1991), which as the term suggests, emphasizes the outer work of development and generally bypasses the inner work (Kaiser & Kaplan, in press).

Burke, M.J., & Day, R.R. (1986). A cumulative study of the effectiveness of managerial training. *Journal of Applied Psychology, 71,* 232–246.

Kaiser, R.B., & Kaplan, R.E. (in press). Outgrowing sensitivities: The deeper work of executive development. *Academy of Management Learning and Education.*

Kaplan, R.E. (with W.H. Drath & J.R. Kofodimos). (1991). *Beyond ambition: How driven managers can lead better and live better*. San Francisco: Jossey-Bass.

Wexley, K.N., & Latham, G.P. (1991). *Developing and training human resources in organizations* (2nd ed.). New York: HarperCollins.

3. Estimates vary on how long it takes to get oriented to and take charge in a senior leadership role (Gabbarro, 1987; Watkins, 2003). Recent pipeline models (Charan, Drotter, & Noel, 2001) or pathways-and-crossroads models of career transitions (Freedman, 1998; 2005) have described the radical change in moving from supervisor to functional head to middle management to an executive role.

Charan, R., Drotter, S., & Noel, J. (2001). *The leadership pipeline: How to build the leadership-powered company*. San Francisco: Jossey-Bass.

Freedman, A. (1998). Pathways and crossroads to institutional leadership. *Consulting Psychology Journal, 50*, 131–151.

Freedman, A. (2005). Swimming upstream: The challenge of managerial promotions. In R. Kaiser (Ed.), *Filling the leadership pipeline* (Ch. 2, pp. 25-44), Greensboro, NC: Center for Creative Leadership.

Gabarro, J.J. (1987). *The dynamics of taking charge*. Boston, MA: Harvard Business School Press.

Watkins, M. (2003). *The first 90 days*. Boston, MA: Harvard Business School Press.

4. Bob Kegan, a developmental psychologist at Harvard, sees this as the essence of what it means for adults to grow. He describes the "basic grammar" of adult development as the shift from being utterly subject to something to being able to take it as object (Kegan, 1982, 1994). Being subject means being unaware of it, taking it for granted, lacking objectivity about it. Being able to take that something as object refers to being consciously aware of it and being aware of it in the moment. When we are subject to a belief, an assumption, a fear, we are under its

control. It has us. When, however, we become objective about it, we gain a measure of control over it.

Kegan, R. (1982). *The evolving self: Problem and process in human development*. Cambridge, MA: Harvard University Press.
Kegan, R. (1994). *In over our heads: The mental demands of modern life*. Cambridge, MA: Harvard University Press.

5. Several different researchers have found that it is not high standards alone that make for perfectionism. It is the presence of an excessive concern about making mistakes or the fear of being harshly judged for one's mistakes that accounts for the personal turmoil that perfectionists experience (Blatt, 1995; Frost, Marten, Lahart, & Rosenblate, 1990).

Blatt, S.J. (1995). The destructiveness of perfectionism: Implications for the treatment of depression. *American Psychologist, 50,* 1003–1020.
Frost, R.O., Marten, P., Lahart, C., & Rosenblate, R. (1990). The dimensions of perfectionism. *Cognitive Therapy and Research, 14,* 449–468.

6. Role playing is another technique for making behavior change with plenty of documented research evidence attesting to its effectiveness (Goldstein & Sorcher, 1974). The key appears to be the opportunity to practice and rehearse a new or altered behavior in a relatively safe environment, where the individual isn't overwhelmed by performance anxiety or fearful expectations. When combined with reflection and deep processing, like a conversation with your role-play partner about the various levels of performance, role playing goes beyond a purely behavioral technique to also change your mental model. In this example, you can also see how it afforded the manager a chance to recalibrate his sense of the intensity of each level of the behavior he was demonstrating.

Goldstein, A.P., & Sorcher, M. (1974). *Changing supervisor behavior*. New York: Pergamon.

7. For more on how sensitivities affect performance, and how leaders can manage and grow past them, see Kaplan and Kaiser (2003) and Kaiser and Kaplan (in press).

Kaiser, R.B., & Kaplan, R.E. (in press). Outgrowing sensitivities: The deeper work of executive development. *Academy of Management Learning and Education*.
Kaplan, R.E., & Kaiser, R.B. (2003). The turbulence within: How sensitivities throw off performance in executives. In R.J. Burke & C.L. Cooper (Eds.), *Leading in turbulent times* (Ch. 2, pp. 31–53). Oxford: Blackwell.

8. The psychotherapist and scholar Sydney Blatt calls this defensive avoidance. In his model of adult growth, it is not just that you identify strongly with one line of human development; it is that you also actively avoid the complementary line of development (Blatt & Shichman, 1983).

Blatt, S.J., & Shichman, S. (1983). Two primary configurations of psychopathology. *Psychoanalysis and Contemporary Thought*, 6, 187–254.

9. For more on how cultures as well as managers and individuals show a clear bias in favor of one side and a distinct prejudice against the other side of common dualities, see the work of Charles Hampton-Turner (1981).

Hampton-Turner, C. (1981). *Maps of the mind*. New York: Collier Books.

Chapter 5

1. The distinction I make between forceful and enabling leadership takes its place in a longstanding tradition. Writing about the Gallic Wars, Julius Caesar described his leadership style in terms of these two different approaches (Bass, 1990, p. 11). Modern scholarly work on leadership has also been dominated by various "two factor" theories (Yukl, 1989), beginning with

Kurt Lewin's seminal research on small group process, in which he studied two very different uses of power, autocracy versus democracy (Lewin & Lippit, 1938). Since that time, these themes have been contrasted over and over in one form or another. They formed the twin pillars of the "leader behavior" paradigm, the first major movement in the modern study of leadership. They also played a central role in the second major paradigm, "contingency theory."

Bernard Bass (1990, pp. 415–543) provided a detailed intellectual history of the distinction between these two sides of leadership. In an exhaustive review of over fifty years of research, Bass concluded that there are two overarching clusters of active leadership behaviors. One cluster centers on the "autocratic" use of power and a focus on the work to be done, while the other cluster revolves around an "egalitarian" use of power and a concern for people. Clearly, what we call forceful leadership belongs in Bass' "autocratic" cluster, while enabling leadership fits snugly in his "egalitarian" cluster.

Bass, B.M. (1990). *Bass and Stogdill's handbook of leadership: Theory, research, and managerial applications* (3rd ed.). New York: The Free Press.

Lewin, K., & Lippit, R. (1938). An experimental approach to the study of autocracy and democracy: A preliminary note. *Sociometry, 1*, 292–300.

Yukl, G. (1998). *Leadership in organizations* (4th ed.). Upper Saddle River, NJ: Prentice Hall.

2. Blake and Mouton (1964) were among the first to take this position. In their influential book, *The Managerial Grid*, they described different combinations of high and low standing on two dimensions, concern for production and concern for people. They argued that a leadership style high in both concern for production and people would be optimal. A great deal of statistical research since then has supported their position: the findings link both sides of leadership positively to a variety of

measures of leader effectiveness (e.g., see a quantitative review in Judge, Piccolo, & Ilies, 2004).

Perhaps the most interesting of the studies was conducted at International Harvester (Fleishman & Harris, 1962). It demonstrated the importance of both sides in finding that task-oriented, directive leadership was associated with positive employee attitudes and performance, but only when the manager was also supportive and considerate. Directive managers who were not also considerate actually had a negative impact on their employees.

Blake, R.R., & Mouton, J.S. (1964). *The managerial grid.* Houston, TX: Gulf.

Fleishman, E.A., & Harris, E.F. (1962). Patterns of leadership behavior related to employee grievances and turnover. *Personnel Psychology, 15,* 43–56.

Judge, T.A., Piccolo, R.F., & Ilies, R. (2004). The forgotten ones? The validity of consideration and initiating structure in leadership research. *Journal of Applied Psychology, 89,* 36–51.

3. McGregor (1960) made this point in *The Human Side of Enterprise,* a widely read book that helped usher in the participative management movement.

McGregor, D. (1960). *The human side of enterprise.* New York: McGraw-Hill.

4. See page 237 in *The Managerial Mystique* (Zaleznik, 1989).

Zaleznik, A., (1989). *The managerial mystique: Restoring leadership in business.* New York: Basic Books.

5. See the Appendix for more details on the research findings reported here.

6. For the data cited here and for a discussion of the problems with traditional rating scales and the potential benefits of our rating scale, see "Overlooking Overkill" (Kaiser & Kaplan, 2005).

Kaiser, R.B., & Kaplan, R.E. (2005). Overlooking overkill? Beyond the 1-to-5 rating scale. *Human Resources Planning, 28(3),* 7-11.

7. Tim Judge and colleagues at the University of Florida reviewed 130 studies that examined the classic distinction made by Ohio State researchers in the middle of the 20th century, consideration and initiating structure (Judge, Piccolo, & Illies, 2004). Their results indicated that, of the several measures of these leader behaviors, the Leader Behavior Description Questionnaire-Form XII (LBDQ-XII; Stogdill, 1963) was the most valid: its scales had the highest correlations with indices of leader effectiveness such as employee satisfaction, motivation, and job performance, as well as unit performance. Moreover, the average correlation between the LBDQ-XII consideration and initiating structure scales (corrected for unreliability) was +.46.

Judge, T.A., Piccolo, R.F., & Ilies, R. (2004). The forgotten ones? The validity of consideration and initiating structure in leadership research. *Journal of Applied Psychology, 89*, 36–51.
Stogdill, R.M. (1963). *Manual for the Leader Behavior Description Questionnaire Form XII*. Columbus, OH: Bureau of Business Research, Ohio State University.

8. In his narrative review, Bass (1990) emphasized the much-researched distinction between consideration and initiating structure, noting that, "Theoretically . . . initiation and consideration should be independent, but such is not the case" (p. 515). He further noted that "the positive association routinely found between [the two]" (p. 518) is troublesome and likely the result of a general evaluative bias factor called "halo error." Gary Yukl (1998) has made a similar observation in his textbook on leadership, as did Shriesheim and Stogdill (1975) in an earlier measurement study.

Bass, B.M. (1990). *Bass and Stogdill's handbook of leadership: Theory, research, and managerial applications* (3rd ed.). New York: The Free Press.
Shriesheim, C.A., & Stogdill, R.M. (1975). Differences in factor structure across three versions of the Ohio State leadership scales. *Personnel Psychology, 28*, 189–206.
Yukl, G. (1998). *Leadership in organizations* (4th ed.). Upper Saddle River, NJ: Prentice Hall.

9. Although Kurt Lewin established autocratic and democratic as two sides of leadership (Lewin & Lippit, 1938), he also identified a third pattern called laissez-faire or "non-leadership." The distinction Lewin made was that the first two are active forms of leadership while laissez-faire is passive.

Lewin, K., & Lippit, R. (1938). An experimental approach to the study of autocracy and democracy: A preliminary note. *Sociometry, 1*, 292–300.

10. Although the two higher-order categories of autocratic and egalitarian leadership are useful (see the work of Bass [1990] described in Note 1 of this chapter), there is also a need for finer distinctions within each. Consulting the various conceptualizations of these two sides of leadership in the literature, we think that they can be divided into three finer distinctions. This conceptualization, including where prior views of these two sides of leadership fit in, is presented in the Appendix.

Bass, B.M. (1990). *Bass and Stogdill's handbook of leadership: Theory, research, and managerial applications* (3rd ed.). New York: The Free Press.

Chapter 6

1. Whereas the distinction between forceful and enabling leadership takes its place in a long tradition in the behavioral sciences, there has been far less scholarly study of more functional, business-oriented dimensions like strategic and operational leadership. Jerry Hunt, former editor of the journal, *Leadership Quarterly*, has estimated that 90 percent of leadership research has been concerned with some form of interpersonal influence, most involving the two factors described in the previous chapter (Hunt, 1991). It appears, however, that researchers are beginning to realize this oversight. For instance, Steve Zaccaro (2001) recently contrasted the direct influence leaders have in social exchanges and interpersonal dynamics with the indirect influence leaders exert through decisions about direction,

organizational structure, and objectives. And John Antonakis and Bob House (2002) have also recently called attention to the difference between inspirational leadership, which is an interpersonal matter, and instrumental leadership, which concerns setting strategy and facilitating the accomplishment of goals.

Antonakis, J., & House, R.J. (2002). An analysis of the full-range leadership theory: The way forward. In B.J. Avolio & F.J. Yammarino (Eds.), *Transformational and charismatic leadership: The road ahead* (pp. 3–33). Greenwich, CT: Elsevier Science/JAI Press.
Hunt, J.G. (1991). *Leadership: A new synthesis.* Newbury Park, CA: Sage.
Zaccaro, S.J. (2001). *The nature of executive leadership: A conceptual and empirical analysis of success.* Washington, DC: American Psychological Association.

2. Much has been made of the distinction between leadership and management. John Kotter (1990) delineated it in his book *A Force for Change* and went to great lengths to emphasize that both roles are vital to organizational effectiveness.

Kotter, J.P. (1990). *A force for change: How leadership differs from management.* New York: The Free Press.

3. Across five samples totaling 450 managers (287 executives and 163 middle managers), we found the average correlation between versatility on the strategic-operational pair and overall effectiveness to be .65. (See the Appendix for more detail on these research findings.)

4. Rob Kaiser and I have not found the same degree of inverse relationship between strategic and operational leadership as we have for forceful and enabling leadership. A likely explanation is that it is unusual for managers to be rated too much on strategy, at least on the strategy items as we have so far written them. For a correlation to be inverse, there must be a healthy incidence of overdoing it on both sides of a duality. We got a later start on strategic and operational leadership, and our operationalization of it lags behind the other duality. Perhaps we haven't written strategy items that are amenable to overdoing.

It is also possible that the incidence of overdoing strategic leadership in the managerial population is low. For more on our research concerning this point, see the Appendix.

5. The study was conducted by two Central Michigan University researchers at Dow Chemical to understand better how to create new business opportunities (Janovics & Christiansen, 2003). The authors found that, on the front end of new business development, unconstrained thinking and facility with abstract possibilities is vital to coming up with fresh ideas. But downstream, practicality and hard-nosed realism make all the difference in bringing the new idea to life. Moreover, those characteristics that were conducive to new ideas were the very same characteristics that inhibited disciplined execution, and vice-versa, a good example of an inverse relationship between a strategic function and an operational function.

Janovics, J.E., & Christiansen, N.D. (2003). Profiling new business development: Personality correlates of ideation and implementation. *Social Behavior and Personality, 31,* 71–80.

6. In five samples with a total of 450 managers, Rob Kaiser and I found that it is much more common for managers to receive too-little scores on strategic leadership than on forceful, enabling, or operational leadership. This is true for senior managers as well as lower-level managers. Only a handful of managers were rated as too strategic. The strategic behaviors most frequently rated as excessive are "Aggressive about growth" and "Open to new strategic possibilities."

Lombardo and Eichinger (2000) reached a similar conclusion based on their analyses of comprehensive competency assessments of over three thousand individuals from more than 130 different companies. They found that the least developed competencies among managers of all stripes—from supervisors to executives—were Creativity, Dealing with ambiguity, Managing vision and purpose, Planning, and Strategic agility.

Lombardo, M.M., & Eichinger, R.W. (2000). *The leadership machine.* Minneapolis, MN: Lominger Limited, Inc.

7. As with Forceful and Enabling leadership, our view of Strategic and Operational leadership and their three subdimensions is informed by similar ideas offered by other leadership theorists. How our conception squares with these other views is presented in the Appendix.

8. Circa 650 B.C., Pythagoras assembled a Table of Opposites that included ten pairs of contrary qualities—Unlimited and Limited, Odd and Even, One and Plurality, Right and Left, Male and Female, At rest and Moving, Straight and Crooked, Light and Darkness, Good and Bad, Square and Oblong—all thought to represent the structure of the cosmos. For Pythagoras, beauty was the result of structural balance and harmony among such oppositions.

Pythagoras (undated). *The Pythagorean sourcebook and library.* Translated by K.S. Guthrie, edited by David Fideler (1987). Grand Rapids, MI: Phanes Press.

9. Manfred Kets de Vries, a psychoanalytically oriented student of leadership, has reported that narcissistic leaders are given to grandiose ideas which, though compelling at first, in the end cause much waste and distress because they are not founded in reality and defy successful implementation (Kets de Vries & Miller, 1985).

Kets de Vries, M.F.R., & Miller, D. (1985). Narcissism and leadership: An object relations perspective. *Human Relations, 38,* 583–601.

10. Emerson, R.W. (1968). Napolean: Man of the world. In B Atkinson (Ed.), *Selected writings of Ralph Waldo Emerson.* New York: Modern Library.

11. There is a fair bit of research linking functional experience to how managers run their units. For instance, managers with a background in marketing or R&D tend to take a "prospector" approach (Miles & Snow, 1978) that emphasizes innovation, risk taking, and the seeking of new opportunities, whereas those with a background in finance or production tend to prefer a "defender" approach that emphasizes stability, efficiency, and a

reputation with customers for reliability for quality (Gupta & Govindarajan, 1984). The former corresponds to strategic leadership, the latter to operational leadership.

Gupta, A.K., & Govindarajan, V. (1984). Business unit strategy, managerial characteristics, and business unit effectiveness at strategy implementation. *Academy of Management Journal*, *27*, 25–41.
Miles, R.E., & Snow, C.C. (1978). *Organizational strategy, structure, and process*. New York: McGraw-Hill.

12. See Myers and McCaulley (1985) for more on the wildly popular but scientifically suspect Myers-Briggs Type Indicator (MBTI), an application of Jung's theory of personality. See Kirton (1994) for more on the distinction between the two problem-solving styles, adaptors and innovators.

Kirton, M.J. (1994). *Adapters and innovators: Styles of creativity and problem solving* (2nd ed.). London: Routledge.
Myers, I.B., & McCaulley, M.H. (1985). *Manual: A guide to the development and use of the Myers-Briggs type indicator*. Palo Alto, CA: Consulting Psychologists Press.

13. Perhaps the single best treatment of how personality shapes our career choices and how those choices in turn reinforce and further refine our personality is the seminal work of John Holland (1966).

Holland, J.L. (1966). *The psychology of vocational choice: A theory of personality types and model environments*. Waltham, MA: Blaisdell.

14. Research by Mike Lombardo and Bob Eichinger has demonstrated that the career paths of the most successful executives are "zig-zag"; that is, they involve quite a few lateral moves, plenty of new and unfamiliar assignments, and many different functional areas. In contrast, the career path of less successful managers, including many "derailers," is characterized as "straight up the fast track," spending less time in each job and with many jobs involving similar roles and responsibilities (Lombardo & Eichinger, 2000). These differences in career histories are likely the reason that the

former group of managers develops a wide repertoire of skills, while the latter group is more limited and is characterized by overdeveloped skills in some areas and a lack of skills in other areas.

Lombardo, M.M., & Eichinger, R.W. (2000). *The leadership machine*. Minneapolis, MN: Lominger Limited, Inc.

Chapter 7

1. Again, the notable exception to my suggestion that the field of leadership has paid very little attention to the excesses of overkill is the original "derailment" research done at the Center for Creative Leadership by Morgan McCall and Mike Lombardo (1983) and the work they have continued to do (Lombardo & Eichinger, 2000; McCall, 1998).

    Lombardo, M.M., & Eichinger, R.W. (2000). *The leadership machine*. Minneapolis, MN: Lominger Limited, Inc.
    McCall, M.W. (1998). *High flyers: Developing the next generation of leaders*. Boston, MA: Harvard Business School Press.
    McCall, M.W., & Lombardo, M.M. (1983). *Off the track: Why and how successful executives get derailed*. Greensboro, NC: Center for Creative Leadership.
2. This reference is to the intuitive, rapid cognition described by the best-selling popularizer of psychological research, Malcom Gladwell, in his recent book, *Blink* (Gladwell, 2005).

    Gladwell, M. (2005). *Blink: The power of thinking without thinking*. Boston: Little, Brown.
3. Several methods for managing tension and nervous energy fall under the heading of "relaxation techniques" and range from simple regimens like deep breathing exercises, guided imagery, applied relaxation (Ost, 1987), and progressive muscle relaxation (Jacobson, 1938), to more elaborate and intensive methods like autogenics (Schultz & Luthe, 1969) and transcendental meditation (Benson, 1975). An excellent aid for beginners is the cassette tape, "Learning to Relax," available from the non-profit Institute for Rational-Emotive Therapy (www.rebt.org).

Benson, H. (1975). *The relaxation response*. New York: Avon.

Jacobson, E. (1938). *Progressive relaxation*. Chicago: University of Chicago Press.

Ost, L. (1987). Applied relaxation: Description of a coping technique and review of controlled studies. *Behavior Research and Therapy, 25*, 397–409.

Schultz, J.H., & Luthe, W. (1959). *Autogenic training: A psychophysiologic approach in psychotherapy*. New York: Grune and Stratton.

4. Years of research have consistently identified ongoing feedback as a key ingredient to achieving goals (Locke & Latham, 1990). Because so much of excessive behavior is routine and habitual, feedback helps the person to recognize it as it happens. In addition, it keeps him or her focused on the developmental goal and puts coworkers who provide the feedback on the lookout for changes in behavior.

Locke, E.A., & Latham, G.P. (1990). *A theory of goal setting and task performance*. Englewood Cliffs, NJ: Prentice Hall.

5. One of the great findings from the study of social psychology is the power of public commitments. Once individuals share a goal with other people, their odds of achieving the goal are dramatically increased because of an enhanced personal commitment to those goals and increased effort in their pursuit (Cialdini, 2001).

Cialdini, R.B. (2001). *Influence: Science and practice* (4th ed.). Boston: Allyn and Bacon.

6. See a recent article by Bob Hogan and Rodney Warrenfeltz (2003) on the two distinct, yet intimately related and ultimately interdependent ways of learning, the Gestaltist construction of mental models and the behaviorist acquisition of skills. The point is that these are two sides of an integrated learning cycle; any effective learning strategy must consider both the outer and the inner aspects.

Hogan, R., & Warrenfeltz, R. (2003). Educating the modern manager. *Academy of Management Learning and Education, 2*, 74–84.

7. Phil Simms is quoted here from a 1996 *New York Times* article (Anderson, 1996).

Anderson, D. (1996, September 29). Required reading for Brown and O'Donnell. *The New York Times*, pp. D1, D3.

8. This story of Sandy Koufax was originally reported in a 1940 *Sports Illustrated* article that was reprinted some fifty years later (Olsen, 1994).

Olsen, J. (1994, April 25). The very best act in town. *Sports Illustrated*, pp. 38–44.

9. The scholarly study of leadership flexibility has touched on both the outer and inner aspects of this complex matter. On the inside is the cognitive task of sizing up a situation and determining how best to respond. On the outside is behavioral skill at acting on those insights and decisions. For example, the research of Steven Zaccaro of George Mason University showed how leader adaptability is a function of both social perceptiveness and behavioral flexibility (Zaccaro, Gilbert, Thor, & Mumford, 1991).

Zaccaro, S.J., Gilbert, J.A., Thor, K.K., & Mumford, M.D. (1991). Leadership and social intelligence: Linking social perceptiveness and behavioral flexibility to leader effectiveness. *Leadership Quarterly, 2,* 317–342.

10. I thank Sandy Danzinger and Rebecca Henson for bringing this point about "more-than" to my attention.

11. The psychoanalyst Karen Horney (1950) wrote of the "tyranny of the shoulds." Many people have internalized impossibly high standards and expectations, against which they judge themselves and come away with an excessively critical self-appraisal and the accompanying negative emotions.

Horney, K. (1950). *Neurosis and human growth*. New York: Norton.

12. This interpretation of Vince Foster's suicide comes from an article by the Yale psychotherapist and theorist, Sidney Blatt.

Blatt, S.J. (1995). The destructiveness of perfectionism: Implications for the treatment of depression. *American Psychologist, 50,* 1003–1020.

13. The Drucker quote comes from the jacket to the book, *Now, discover your strengths* (Buckingham & Clifton, 2001).
    Buckingham, M., & Clifton, D.O. (2001). *Now, discover your strengths*. New York: Simon & Schuster.
14. This account of Stalin's unchecked autocracy is drawn from Simon Montefiore's biography (2004).

    Montefiore, S. (2004). *Stalin: The court of the red tsar*. New York: Knopf.
15. Ibid, p. 527.

Chapter 8

1. Carnegie relays this anecdote in his best-seller, *How to Stop Worrying and Start Living* (Carnegie, 1975).

    Carnegie, D. (1975) *How to stop worrying and start living*. New York: Simon & Schuster.
2. Sigmund Freud wrote about the powerful, if subtle, effects of repression. As he put it: "The essence of repression lies simply in turning something away, and keeping it at a distance, from the conscious" (1915, p. 147). Defining the mechanism of repression and how it functions has proved to be one of his most enduring contributions to psychology.

    Freud, S. (1915). Repression. In J. Strachey (Ed. & trans.), *The standard edition of the complete psychological works of Sigmund Freud* (Vol. 14, pp. 143–158). London: Hogarth Press.
3. Systematic desensitization is a technique developed by Joseph Wolpe (1958) for curing phobias and anxiety, originally in cats that were traumatized in lab experiments! It was subsequently modified and successfully applied to people (see, for example, A. Lazarus, 1971). Desensitization is aimed at reducing a person's sensitivity to, say, flying on airplanes, riding on subways, or encountering a snake or spiders. Most researchers agree that the critical factor is exposing the person gradually to the feared situation and demonstrating that the expected catastrophe doesn't occur. An important part of the technique is to have individuals

calm themselves first using a relaxation technique. Over time and with increasing exposure, the anxiety diminishes. The technique has proven remarkably robust in treating anxiety and phobias, sometimes after only one practice trial. The greatest benefits accrue through repeated practice. Moreover, it can be self-administered. To learn more about the research basis and to find out how to use this method yourself, see Martin Seligman's (1993) book, *What You Can Change and What You Can't*.

Lazarus, A.A. (1971). *Behavior therapy and beyond*. New York: McGraw-Hill.
Seligman, M. (1993). *What you can change and what you can't*. New York: Knopf
Wolpe, J. (1958). *Psychotherapy by reciprocal inhibition*. Palo Alto, CA: Stanford University Press.

4. The organizational psychologist Karl Weick has pointed out that most change efforts are doomed to fail because they begin with an impossibly ambitious goal. He recommends, instead, the psychology of "small wins." The idea is to start small and, in increments, build mental momentum to scale up to the larger goal (Weick, 1984).

Weick, K.E. (1984). Small wins: Redefining the scale of social problems. *American Psychologist, 39*, 40–49.

5. Years of research on goal setting has proved it to be one of the most effective techniques known for enhancing performance. However, merely setting a goal is not enough, especially if it is a complex or difficult task like changing a longstanding habit of avoiding something. Feedback is also crucial. Without feedback on progress toward goals and on the effectiveness of performance-improvement strategies, the benefit of setting goals drops to nearly nil (Locke & Latham, 1990).

Locke, E.A., & Latham, G.P. (1990). *A theory of goal setting and task performance*. Englewood Cliffs, NJ: Prentice Hall.

6. E. Tory Higgins (1997), a psychologist at Columbia University, distinguished between a prevention strategy and a promotion strategy, two different ways in which individuals regulate their

behavior as they pursue goals. A prevention focus leads to inhibition because the goal is to not provoke an undesired outcome, whereas a promotion focus leads to a compulsive urge because the concern is with doing all one can to secure a desired result.

Higgins, E.T. (1997). Beyond pleasure and pain. *American Psychologist, 52*, 1280–1300.

7. There is a long history to the idea that the language we use reflects the way we think and what we think about. For the history of the idea and a theoretical model that explains how our use of language is an indication of psychological maturity, see Susanne Cook-Greuter's (1999) doctoral dissertation, done at the Harvard Graduate School of Education.

Cook-Greuter, S.R. (1999). *Postautonomous ego development: A study of its nature and measurement.* Thesis presented to the Faculty of the Graduate School of Education of Harvard University.

8. This is another example of what the psychoanalyst Karen Horney (1950) calls the "tyranny of the shoulds," described in Note 11 of Chapter 7.

Horney, K. (1950). *Neurosis and human growth.* New York: Norton.

9. Known as "the column exercise," Kegan describes this technique for self-discovery with his colleague, Kim Lahey, in their very readable book, *How the Way We Talk Can Change the Way We Work* (Kegan & Lahey, 2001a), and in their *Harvard Business Review* article, which is geared toward helping managers use it with employees (Kegan & Lahey, 2001b).
Kegan, R., & Lahey, L.L. (2001a). *How the way we talk can change the way we work: Seven languages for transformation.* San Francisco: Jossey-Bass.

Kegan, R., & Lahey, L.L. (2001b). The real reason people won't change. *Harvard Business Review, 79*(5), 85–92.

10. I have previously described this kind of development as a "character shift" (Kaplan, 1990; Kaplan, 1991). While not a revolution in who a person is, such a shift does amount to a significant inner change. In a dissertation entitled "Freer to Be Me," my

colleague Denise Lyons describes how several men and women at mid-life found a comprehensive feedback and assessment process to be liberating, much like Rick Freed in this example. What is striking is that the managers across these different studies all report a greater comfort with being themselves. For an abbreviated article based on Denise's research, see Lyons (2002).

Kaplan, R.E. (1990). Character change in executives as "reform" in the pursuit of self-worth. *Journal of Applied Behavioral Science, 26,* 461–481.

Kaplan, R.E. (with W.H. Drath & J.R. Kofodimos). (1991). *Beyond ambition: How driven managers can lead better and live better.* San Francisco: Jossey-Bass.

Lyons, D. (2002). Freer to be me: The development of executives at mid-life. *Consulting Psychology Journal: Practice and Research, 54,* 15–27.

Chapter 9

1. According to one model of human development, progress is an upward spiral in which the individual alternates between an orientation to self and an orientation to others (Blatt, 1990; Kegan, 1982). A common step up is the shift that many adults make from an interpersonal stage, in which one's sense of self is derived from relationships, to an autonomous stage, in which the individual becomes author and judge of his or her own identity as something distinct and apart from relationships.

Blatt, S.J. (1990). Interpersonal relatedness and self-definition: Two personality configurations and their implications for psychopathology and psychotherapy. In J. L. Singer (Ed.), *Repression and dissociation: Implications for personality theory, psychopathology and health* (pp. 299–335). Chicago: University of Chicago Press.

Kegan, R. (1982). *The evolving self: Problems and process in human development.* Cambridge, MA: Harvard University Press.

2. Two models of personality put a focus on the extent to which an individual's use of power is "socialized." David McClelland

(1985) distinguished between a "personalized" versus a "social-ized" need for power. Highly personalized power is egocentric and is associated with little inhibition or self control; highly socialized power is directed at serving others and at sharing influence and authority and can verge over into disabling inhi-bition. Jack Block (Block & Block, 1980), in a discussion of ego control, described under-control as the result of improper social-ization and over-control as the product of excessive suppression of one's needs. [See also the work of E.T. Higgins (1999), previ-ously described in Note 4 of Chapter 3.]

Block, J.H., & Block, J. (1980). The role of ego-control and ego-resiliency in the organization of behavior. In W. A. Collins (Ed.), *The Minnesota Symposia on Child Psychology, 13*, 39–101. Hillsdale, NJ: Lawrence Erlbaum.
McClelland, D.C. (1975). *Power: The inner experience*. New York: Irvington.

3. Chapter 4's section on trigger points discusses the part played by the fight-or-flight response.
4. John Lahr. Commencement address, Riverdale Country School, June 2004.
5. This is an example of a "stretch assignment" (McCauley, Eastman, & Ohlott, 1995), but in this case the manager rather than a higher-up makes the choice.

McCauley, C.D., Eastman, L.J., & Ohlott, P.J. (1995). Linking management selection and development through stretch assignments. *Human Resource Management, 34*(1). 93–115.

6. Recent breakthroughs in neuroscience have identified the phys-ical locations in the brain responsible for most of its functions. Most emotional functioning, especially having to do with fear, appears to be located in the limbic system in a part of the brain called the amygdala, a small, almond-shaped organ that sits atop the brain stem and is a part of all the nervous systems shared by all vertebrates (Damacio, 1994).

Damasio, A. (1994). *Descartes' error*. New York: Grossett-Putnam.

7. Amery, J. (1980). *At the mind's limits: Contemplations by a survivor on Auschwitz and its realities* (translated by S. Rosenfeld & S. Rosenfeld). Bloomington, IN: Indiana University Press.
8. In two overlapping articles, Rob Kaiser and I (2003; Kaiser & Kaplan, in press) discuss how managers can outgrow sensitivities.

Kaplan, R.E., & Kaiser, R.B. (2003). The turbulence within: How sensitivities throw off performance in executives. In R.J. Burke and C.L. Cooper (Eds.), *Leading in turbulent times* (Chapter 2, pp. 31–53). Oxford: Blackwell.
Kaiser, R.B., & Kaplan, R.E. (in press). Outgrowing sensitivities: The deeper work of executive development. *Academy of Management Learning and Education*.

Chapter 10

1. What I call "read and respond" correspond, respectively, to what leadership scholar Robert Hooijberg (1996) calls "behavioral differentiation" and "behavioral repertoire" and what Steve Zacarro has identified as social perceptiveness and behavioral flexibility (Zaccaro, Gilbert, Thor, & Mumford, 1991).

Hooijiberg, R. (1996). A multi-directional approach toward leadership: An extension of the concept of behavioral flexibility. *Human Relations, 49*, 917–946.
Zaccaro, S.J., Gilbert, J.A., Thor, K.K., & Mumford, M.D. (1991). Leadership and social intelligence: Linking social perceptiveness and behavioral flexibility to leader effectiveness. *Leadership Quarterly, 2*, 317–342.
2. Circumplex models go back at least to the interpersonal theorist Harry Stack Sullivan (1953). They have proven remarkably effective at both mapping the structure of interpersonal relationships and guiding corrective or remedial action in troubled relationships (Leary, 1957; Wiggins, 1982).

Leary, T. (1957). *The interpersonal diagnosis of personality*. New York: Ronald.

Sullivan, H.S. (1953). *The interpersonal theory of psychiatry*. New York: Norton.

Wiggins, J.S. (1982). Circumplex models of interpersonal behavior in clinical psychology. In P.C. Kendall & J.N. Butcher (Eds.), *Handbook of research methods in clinical psychology* (pp. 183–221). New York: John Wiley & Sons.

3. Recent research on the personality characteristic of "neuroticism" or "emotional instability" is perfectly consistent, down to the actual language, of this vignette. Specifically, researchers have determined that the inconsistency in the performance of individuals plagued by self-doubt, volatile mood swings, and chronic worry (that is, neuroticism) is the result of "mental noise," inner voices creating a chorus of second-guessing, criticism, and catastrophic images that directs attention away from the situation and the regulation of one's responses. It appears to be this "mental noise" that accounts for the fact that, relative to emotionally stable people, those high in neuroticism try just as hard but are more variable in their performance, less effective in their performance, and less effective at coping with stress (Robinson & Tamir, 2005).

   Robinson, M.D., & Tamir, M. (2005). Neuroticism as mental noise: A relation between neuroticism and reaction time standard deviations. *Journal of Personality and Social Psychology, 89,* 107–114.

4. This point, that emotions are vital in leadership, hasn't always been a prevailing view. But much more attention is being given to the role of emotions thanks to a movement in academic research concerned with how leaders transform followers and the rising popularity of "emotional intelligence" in the workplace.

5. Lucretius (undated), *De Rerum Natura*. Translated by C.D.N. Costa (1984). Oxford: Oxford University Press.

6. This passage is from Csikszentmihalyi's (1990, p. 36) book on peak performance, *Flow*.

   Csikszentmihalyi, M. (1990). *Flow: The psychology of optimal experience*. New York: Harper & Row.

7. Joe Morgan tells this story in Chapter 4 of his autobiography (Morgan & Falkner, 1993).

Morgan, J., & Falkner, D. (1993). *Joe Morgan: A life in baseball*. New York: W.W. Norton.

8. The neurologist Oliver Sacks (2004) recently described how people's inner experience of time can slow down dramatically, allowing them to "take in more" of what is happening around them. Although it isn't clear yet just how this feat is accomplished, the evidence suggests that it is not just a figment of imagination but a very real phenomenon. Harvard scholar and leadership expert Ron Heifeitz (1994) is referring to a similar kind of thing in his concept of "getting on the balcony" so as to watch the "dance" unfold from an objective perspective.

Heifetz, R.A. (1994). *Leadership without easy answers*. Cambridge, MA: Belknap Press.

Sacks, O. (2004, August 23). Speed. *The New Yorker*, pp. 60–69.

9. Although the idea of the "troubled artist" is a popular conception, there is little empirical evidence to support such a conclusion (Rothenberg, 1990). It appears that the notable exceptions like Sylvia Plath, Vincent Van Gogh, and Jackson Pollack give us an exaggerated sense that great artists must necessarily be disturbed.

Rothenberg, A. (1990). *Creativity and madness: New findings and old stereotypes*. Baltimore, MD: Johns Hopkins University Press.

10. This portrayal of General George Marshall is based on his biography, *General of the Army* (Cray, 1990).

Cray, E. (1990). *General of the army: George C. Marshall, soldier and statesman*. New York: W.W. Norton.

11. The inspiration for this idea comes from a biography of Charles Darwin (Browne, 1995).

Browne, J. (1995). *Charles Darwin: Voyaging*. Princeton, NJ: Knopf.

Index

About the Authors

Bob Kaplan is a partner with Kaplan DeVries Inc., a leadership consulting firm and R&D shop founded in 1992. In the previous twelve years he worked at the Center for Creative Leadership, where he remains an honorary senior fellow. He has a B.A. and a Ph.D. from Yale University and lives in New York City with his wife, Becky, and their three children, Josh, Emily, and Andrew. Bob's email address is bobkaplan@kaplandevries.com.

Rob Kaiser is a partner with Kaplan DeVries Inc. He began his career at the Center for Creative Leadership studying how executives are hired. He joined Kaplan DeVries in 1997 to expand the firm's research and development capabilities. Rob has sixty publications and presentations on leadership, assessment, personality, and executive development. He also has an active consulting practice, with an emphasis on preparing high-potentials for senior roles. Rob offers a unique type of contract research aimed at helping companies frame, study, and solve vexing leadership issues.

Rob earned a B.S. in psychology and sociology and an M.S. in industrial-organizational psychology from Illinois State University. He lives in Greensboro, North Carolina, with his wife, Molly, and their children, Claire and Ben. Rob's email address is robkaiser@kaplandevries.com.

Kaplan DeVries Inc.
Our firm, in its fifteenth year at the time of this book's publication in 2006, specializes in consulting to senior managers on leadership. We work with management teams, including CEO-COO pairs, and we also do for individuals what has come to be called executive coaching. We also offer leadership development programs built around our own theory, techniques and tools.

Our firm also has a research-and-development function. We do original research on leadership and leadership development, and we conduct contract research on leadership for organizations. In addition, we devise our own assessment tools, and we create customized leadership models and 360-degree surveys for organizations.

To learn more about the firm, visit our website: www. kaplandevries.com

About the (patented) Leadership Versatility Index®*

There is a reason why the **Leadership Versatility Index**® is patented. No other 360-degree tool does what it does. The **Leadership Versatility Index**® (LVI) is the only 360-degree survey that assesses managers for lopsidedness, perhaps the most common development need among managers. No other tool directly captures this pervasive tendency in managers to do too much of one essential function and too little of the opposing and complementary function. Too focused on short-term results and not strategic enough, too decisive and not participative enough, too sensitive to people's feelings and not direct enough: the list is endless.

The **LVI**® is, in fact, cutting-edge. It is the next generation of coworker-feedback tool.

The **LVI**® and this book go hand in hand. The book elaborates a framework for leadership assessment and development and the **LVI**® is the tool for applying the framework.

The **LVI**® feedback report is brief—only 55 items—yet is valid and reliable. It covers both the what of leading (the strategic-operational duality) and the how of leading (the forceful-enabling duality).

The **LVI**® works beautifully as a stand-alone assessment in coaching, training, and development. And because of its validity, brevity, and focus, along with its ability to detect the overuse of strengths, the **LVI**® can also supplement an organization's own 360-degree survey.

To learn more about the **Leadership Versatility Index**® or to take an abbreviated self-rating version, visit our website: www.versatileleader.com.

CERTIFICATION

Feedback on the **LVI**® is only as good as the professional delivering it, whether that person is an external consultant or an internal HR manager, a development specialist or the boss. To protect quality of service, all persons who wish to deliver feedback with the **LVI**® must be certified.

*Patent Pending

COACHING SERVICES & TRAINING PROGRAMS

The **LVI**® is a highly effective vehicle for coaching individual managers. It sets up coaching not just by bringing to light a leader's strengths, strengths over-used, and deficiencies but also by pinpointing where he or she is lopsided and where he or she is versatile.

The **LVI**®, together with the framework laid out in this book, also forms a strong basis for leadership development programs. It's a fresh, practical way for managers to think about leadership and to take stock of their own way of leading.

References available on request.

To learn more about certification workshops as well as coaching services and training programs based on the **LVI**®, call Kaplan DeVries Inc at 336.288.9018 or visit our website: www.versatileleader.com

Pfeiffer Publications Guide

This guide is designed to familiarize you with the various types of Pfeiffer publications. The formats section describes the various types of products that we publish; the methodologies section describes the many different ways that content might be provided within a product. We also provide a list of the topic areas in which we publish.

FORMATS

In addition to its extensive book-publishing program, Pfeiffer offers content in an array of formats, from fieldbooks for the practitioner to complete, ready-to-use training packages that support group learning.

FIELDBOOK Designed to provide information and guidance to practitioners in the midst of action. Most fieldbooks are companions to another, sometimes earlier, work, from which its ideas are derived; the fieldbook makes practical what was theoretical in the original text. Fieldbooks can certainly be read from cover to cover. More likely, though, you'll find yourself bouncing around following a particular theme, or dipping in as the mood, and the situation, dictate.

HANDBOOK A contributed volume of work on a single topic, comprising an eclectic mix of ideas, case studies, and best practices sourced by practitioners and experts in the field.

An editor or team of editors usually is appointed to seek out contributors and to evaluate content for relevance to the topic. Think of a handbook not as a ready-to-eat meal, but as a cookbook of ingredients that enables you to create the most fitting experience for the occasion.

RESOURCE Materials designed to support group learning. They come in many forms: a complete, ready-to-use exercise (such as a game); a comprehensive resource on one topic (such as conflict management) containing a variety of methods and approaches; or a collection of like-minded activities (such as icebreakers) on multiple subjects and situations.

TRAINING PACKAGE An entire, ready-to-use learning program that focuses on a particular topic or skill. All packages comprise a guide for the facilitator/trainer and a workbook for the participants. Some packages are supported with additional media—such as video—or learning aids, instruments, or other devices to help participants understand concepts or practice and develop skills.

- *Facilitator/trainer's guide* Contains an introduction to the program, advice on how to organize and facilitate the learning event, and step-by-step instructor notes. The guide also contains copies of presentation materials—handouts, presentations, and overhead designs, for example—used in the program.

- *Participant's workbook* Contains exercises and reading materials that support the learning goal and serves as a valuable reference and support guide for participants in the weeks and months that follow the learning event. Typically, each participant will require his or her own workbook.

ELECTRONIC CD-ROMs and web-based products transform static Pfeiffer content into dynamic, interactive experiences. Designed to take advantage of the searchability, automation, and ease-of-use that technology provides, our e-products bring convenience and immediate accessibility to your workspace.

METHODOLOGIES

CASE STUDY A presentation, in narrative form, of an actual event that has occurred inside an organization. Case studies are not prescriptive, nor are they used to prove a point; they are designed to develop critical analysis and decision-making skills. A case study has a specific time frame, specifies a sequence of events, is narrative in structure, and contains a plot structure—an issue (what should be/have been done?). Use case studies when the goal is to enable participants to apply previously learned theories to the circumstances in the case, decide what is pertinent, identify the real issues, decide what should have been done, and develop a plan of action.

ENERGIZER A short activity that develops readiness for the next session or learning event. Energizers are most commonly used after a break or lunch to stimulate or refocus the group. Many involve some form of physical activity, so they are a useful way to counter post-lunch lethargy. Other uses include transitioning from one topic to another, where "mental" distancing is important.

EXPERIENTIAL LEARNING ACTIVITY (ELA) A facilitator-led intervention that moves participants through the learning cycle from experience to application (also known as a Structured Experience). ELAs are carefully thought-out designs in which there is a definite learning purpose and intended outcome. Each step—everything that participants do during the activity—facilitates the accomplishment of the stated goal. Each ELA includes complete instructions for facilitating the intervention and a clear statement of goals, suggested group size and timing, materials required, an explanation of the process, and, where appropriate, possible variations to the activity. (For more detail on Experiential Learning Activities, see the Introduction to the *Reference Guide to Handbooks and Annuals*, 1999 edition, Pfeiffer, San Francisco.)

GAME A group activity that has the purpose of fostering team spirit and togetherness in addition to the achievement of a pre-stated goal. Usually contrived—undertaking a desert expedition, for example—this type of learning method offers an engaging means for participants to demonstrate and practice business and interpersonal skills. Games are effective for team building and personal development mainly because the goal is subordinate to the process—the means through which participants reach decisions, collaborate, communicate, and generate trust and understanding. Games often engage teams in "friendly" competition.

ICEBREAKER A (usually) short activity designed to help participants overcome initial anxiety in a training session and/or to acquaint the participants with one another. An icebreaker can be a fun activity or can be tied to specific topics or training goals. While a useful tool in itself, the icebreaker comes into its own in situations where tension or resistance exists within a group.

INSTRUMENT A device used to assess, appraise, evaluate, describe, classify, and summarize various aspects of human behavior. The term used to describe an instrument depends primarily on its format and purpose. These terms include survey, questionnaire, inventory, diagnostic, survey, and poll. Some uses of instruments include providing instrumental feedback to group members, studying here-and-now processes or functioning within a group, manipulating group composition, and evaluating outcomes of training and other interventions.

Instruments are popular in the training and HR field because, in general, more growth can occur if an individual is provided with a method for focusing specifically on his or her own behavior. Instruments also are used to obtain information that will serve as a basis for change and to assist in workforce planning efforts.

Paper-and-pencil tests still dominate the instrument landscape with a typical package comprising a facilitator's guide, which offers advice on administering the instrument and interpreting the collected data, and an initial set of instruments. Additional instruments are available separately. Pfeiffer, though, is investing heavily in e-instruments. Electronic instrumentation provides effortless distribution and, for larger groups particularly, offers advantages over paper-and-pencil tests in the time it takes to analyze data and provide feedback.

LECTURETTE A short talk that provides an explanation of a principle, model, or process that is pertinent to the participants' current learning needs. A lecturette is intended to establish a common language bond between the trainer and the participants by providing a mutual frame of reference. Use a lecturette as an introduction to a group activity or event, as an interjection during an event, or as a handout.

MODEL A graphic depiction of a system or process and the relationship among its elements. Models provide a frame of reference and something more tangible, and more easily remembered, than a verbal explanation. They also give participants something to "go on," enabling them to track their own progress as they experience the dynamics, processes, and relationships being depicted in the model.

ROLE PLAY A technique in which people assume a role in a situation/ scenario: a customer service rep in an angry-customer exchange, for example. The way in which the role is approached is then discussed and feedback is offered. The role play is often repeated using a different approach and/or incorporating changes made based on feedback received. In other words, role playing is a spontaneous interaction involving realistic behavior under artificial (and safe) conditions.

SIMULATION A methodology for understanding the interrelationships among components of a system or process. Simulations differ from games in that they test or use a model that depicts or mirrors some aspect of reality in form, if not necessarily in content. Learning occurs by studying the effects of change on one or more factors of the model. Simulations are commonly used to test hypotheses about what happens in a system—often referred to as "what if?" analysis—or to examine best-case/worst-case scenarios.

THEORY A presentation of an idea from a conjectural perspective. Theories are useful because they encourage us to examine behavior and phenomena through a different lens.

TOPICS

The twin goals of providing effective and practical solutions for workforce training and organization development and meeting the educational needs of training and human resource professionals shape Pfeiffer's publishing program. Core topics include the following:

Leadership & Management

Communication & Presentation

Coaching & Mentoring

Training & Development

e-Learning

Teams & Collaboration

OD & Strategic Planning

Human Resources

Consulting

What will you find on pfeiffer.com?

- The best in workplace performance solutions for training and HR professionals

- Downloadable training tools, exercises, and content

- Web-exclusive offers

- Training tips, articles, and news

- Seamless on-line ordering

- Author guidelines, information on becoming a Pfeiffer Affiliate, and much more

Discover more at www.pfeiffer.com